ASTROLOGY AND THE SEVEN RAYS

Interpreting the Rays through the Natal Chart

Bruno and Louise Huber

HopeWell
Knutsford, England

A transcript of a 1998 seminar by the Hubers with the same title
was first published in booklet form by API(UK) in 1999

This revised and updated version published by HopeWell 2006

HopeWell,
PO Box 118, Knutsford
Cheshire WA16 8TG, U.K.

Includes translation of new information that was added to
the German translation of the above booklet
Astrologie und die Sieben Strahlen, API-Verlag 2006

Transcribed by API(UK)
Additional material translated by Heather Ross
Edited by Barry Hopewell

Jacket design by Michael Huber

ISBN 0-9547680-6-X

Contents

Editor's Preface   *vii*
Foreword by Louise Huber   *ix*

1. Introduction   1
Our Esoteric Background   2
Esotericism and Astrology   3
What is Esotericism?   4
The Four Subtle Human Bodies   7

2. What does Esoteric Mean?   11
Esoteric Thinking   12
Why? The Esoteric Question   12
Motivations, Energies and Principles   13
Crosses and Temperaments   14
Separation of Layers   15
Consciousness and Will   15
The Seven Rays   16
Rays of Crosses and Temperaments   16
Astrology and Esoteric Thinking   17
Psychosynthesis and Astrology   18
The Seven Planes   20
Physical Plane   20
Physical/Etheric Levels   21
Emotional Plane   21
Mental Plane   22
Higher Mental – Uranus   22
Buddhic Plane – Neptune   24
Atmic Plane – Pluto   25
Questions   27

3. The Entity of the Seven Cosmic Rays   29
The Entity - a Living Being   30
Universal and Analogical Thinking   31
The Solar System and the Seven Lords   32
Etheric Level and the Planetary Logos   34
The Seven Rays   35
The Rays of Crosses, Temperaments and Planets   35
First Ray: Will and Power   36
Second Ray: Love and Wisdom   37
Third Ray: Active Intelligence   37
Fourth Ray: Harmony through Conflict   38

Fifth Ray: Concrete Knowledge 39
Sixth Ray: Devotion and Idealism 40
Seventh Ray: Ceremonial Magic, Ritual and Order 40
Global Transformations **42**
Agni Yoga/ Violet Flame 42
Soul Kingdom 42
Initiation of Planetary Logos 44
Third Initiation for Disciples 45
Holistic Approaches 45
Pluto in Sagittarius 46
Year 2000 at MC 46
Questions **47**

4. Finding the Rays in your Chart **49**
Personality Rays **51**
Personality Ray 51
Example - Bruno Huber 52
Rays of the Three Bodies 54
Combinations of Rays 55
Questions 56
Example – Albert Einstein 62
The Moon Nodes and the Rays 65
Questions 66
The Soul Ray **69**
Soul Consciousness 69
Soul Ray 69
The Causal Body 70
Primary Rules – Major Ray 71
Secondary Rule 73
Questions 74
Summarising the Rays 77
Discovery of the Method of Finding the Rays 78

5. The Effect of the Rays on the Personality **79**
Psychosynthesis Typology **80**
Psychosynthesis Typology and the Seven Rays 80
Assagioli's Background 81
Psychology of the New Age 82
Experiencing the Rays in Daily Life 82
The Threefold Personality **83**
Rays of the Physical Body 84
Rays of the Emotional Body 90
Rays of the Mental Body 96
Rays of the Personality 99
Rays of Famous People 106

6. Transformations   107

The New Age and the Seventh Ray   108
Heart and Mind   108
Synthesis – The Highest and The Lowest Meet   108
Transformation of Consciousness   110
Invocation and Evocation   111
The Constitution of Man   112
Gap in Consciousness   114
Soul Consciousness   114
Building the Antahkarana   115
Initiation   117
The Soul Ray and the Personality Ray   119
Transformations of the Seven Rays   119
The Rays of the Masters   122
Ray Words of Power   124
Shamballa, the Plan, and the Hierarchy   126
Cosmic Evolution   126
Living the Soul's Purpose   127
Sacred Planets   128
The Monad   129
Closing Thoughts   130
Monadic Meditation   131

7. The Law of the Triangles in the Signs   133

The Law of the Triangles in the Signs   135
Aries, Leo, Capricorn: Ray 1   135
Libra: Ray 3   136
Transformation Crisis   136
Cancer: Rays 3,7   137
Aquarius: Ray 5   137
Sagittarius: Rays 4,5,6   138
Scorpio and Taurus : Ray 4   139
Pisces and Virgo: Rays 2, 6   140
Gemini: Ray 2   141
Colour and the Rays   142
Rays and Personality Types   144

8. The Spiritual Planets and Spiritual Growth   147

Relevance of Past Esoteric Schools   148
The Spiritual Planets   150
Paranormal Functions   152
Time and Cosmic Order   154
Material Values   154
Uncultivated Spiritual Planets   155

Uranus   155
Neptune   158
Pluto   160
Motivation and Function   163
Questions   164

9. Questions   **173**
Questions   **174**
Astrological Psychology   **189**

Notes and References   **193**

Index   **199**

Contacts and Resources   **204**

Symbols of the Planets

Sun	☉	♂	Mars
Moon	☽	♃	Jupiter
Saturn	♄	♅	Uranus
Mercury	☿	♆	Neptune
Venus	♀	♇	Pluto
ascending Moon Node	☊		

Symbols of the Signs

Aries	♈	♎	Libra
Taurus	♉	♏	Scorpio
Gemini	♊	♐	Sagittarius
Cancer	♋	♑	Capricorn
Leo	♌	♒	Aquarius
Virgo	♍	♓	Pisces

Abbreviations

AC	=	Ascendant	HC	=	House Cusp
IC	=	Imum Coeli	LP	=	Low Point
DC	=	Descendant	BP	=	Balance Point
MC	=	Medium Coeli	GM	=	Golden Mean

Aspects

Green	Semi-sextile	Angle of 30°	⩛
	Quincunx	Angle of 150°	⩚
Blue	Sextile	Angle of 60°	✶
	Trine	Angle of 120°	△
Red	Square	Angle of 90°	□
	Opposition	Angle of 180°	☍
Orange	Conjunction	Angle of 0°	☌

Editor's Preface

The workshop *Astrology and the Seven Rays* was held at the Beacon Centre, near Exeter from 30th August to 2nd September 1998. This was to be the last workshop given together by Bruno and Louise Huber in England due to the untimely death of Bruno in 1999.

The Hubers' teaching on *Astrology and the Seven Rays* provides a unique and valuable synthesis in bringing together and marrying astrology with psychosynthesis and their common esoteric roots. We therefore felt it important to make available this teaching, which is not otherwise available in English.

This book contains an edited version of the original transcript of the talks given by Bruno and Louise at the workshop, first published as an internally available booklet by API(UK). It is only thanks to the many hours of effort by the original transcription team of Joyce Hopewell, Barry Hopewell, Richard Llewellyn, David Kerr, and Jane Kerr that this work can be made available.

The original booklet was eventually translated into German and published as *Astrologie und die Sieben Strahlen* by API-Verlag in 2006. This version included improved diagrams and some additional material by Louise Huber, which filled in gaps where there had not been time to cover material during the seminar.

These additions have now been translated back into English and incorporated in this new version of the English text, revised to improve fluency and clarity, but aiming to retain some sense of the conversational style of the Hubers.

Thanks are due to Louise Huber and to API(UK) for their permission to publish this material in book form.

We would like to dedicate this work to the memory of Bruno Huber, a true server of mankind, who brought light where there was darkness, and helped many along the way.

Barry Hopewell, Editor, November 2006

x

Foreword

Louise Huber

I would like to thank the API(UK) preparation team for the many hours that they spent working on the transcript of the tape recording of the seminar *Astrology and the Seven Rays*, first published in English in a booklet by API(UK). The content of the seminar was presented in such a graphic and lively way that we had the lectures translated from English into German and published in book form.

That German version included supplementary material added by myself. These additions have now been translated back into English and are included in this new revised English edition, published in book form for the first time.

The individual lectures give a clear insight into a new and practical approach to the theory of the seven rays, combined with astrology. It is now possible to determine your own individual ray combination and also those of your friends and family. This is a valuable supplement to the theory of Alice A. Bailey and makes new age esoteric psychology more accessible.

From a spiritual point of view, the study of the seven rays is a search for the original source, the "return to the father's house", which is called the "path of initiation" in esoteric literature. A contribution of esoteric astrology is to use the three spiritual planets to determine the stages, the conversion processes and the expansions of consciousness that must be passed through. The theory of the rays brings an added dimension to this; it taps our spiritual potential and gives us a new sense of identity that enables us to align our lives with the cosmos.

May you gain much new insight from your studies.

Louise Huber, November 2006

Louise and Bruno Huber
giving the seminar *Astrology and the Seven Rays* in 1998

1

Introduction

Bruno and Louise Huber

Our Esoteric Background

Esotericism and Astrology

What is Esotericism?

• The Ethereal World and the Seven Rays •
• The Meaning of the Seven Rays •
• What is Light? •
• Ether and Science •

The Four Subtle Human Bodies

• Etheric Body (Physical) •
• Astral Body (Emotional) •
• Mental Body (Thought) •
• Causal Body •
• The Seven Centres or Chakras •

Our Esoteric Background

Our esoteric background was with Alice Bailey[1]. When we were very young we were asked to build up the Arcane School[2] centre in Geneva. We worked hard there for three years. When they built up the school they did not have any money and depended on sponsors. We worked for three years there for very little money. It was hard work! Our idealism was very much needed.

Then we went to work for a further three years with Roberto Assagioli[3] in Florence, Italy, helping to bring out his first manual on techniques of psychosynthesis[4]. We were able to use Assagioli's extensive client records to undertake our astrological researches, which eventually led to our 'system' of astrological psychology, the Huber Method.

We then established our Huber School (API)[5] in Switzerland where we have since continued to teach, counsel and perform further research with a group of tutors and collaborators. 1998 was our 30th anniversary year! We have a very stable school, the biggest in Switzerland, with a good reputation.

All our diploma holders have to sign the international astrologers' oath, reflecting their accepted responsibility to use astrological psychology in the right way, ethically.

Esotericism and Astrology

We have heavy material ahead of us – it's all esoteric! It is of course our main interest not to speak of the esoteric and nothing else – we want absolutely to link it up to astrology. Our astrology is pure esotericism, clearly based on the esoteric sources and on the ever-true values of esotericism in all the cultures, going way back to the early human cultures.

There are basics, and we will explain them of course, that are also the basics of astrology. We use astrology from there. So that's what we are up to in this book, to see how astrology is based on very deep and very simple basic principles.

Of course, esotericism cannot be dealt with in a short book to the last extent, in all depth, with all the great consequences that come from it. The idea is that we put forward the essentials, because in our time and present culture there is clearly the tendency to live on symptoms, as we call it from an esoteric point of view. You know the ins and outs, the formal things that make your life – the better you handle them the better you are off, right?

The danger of the times is that the underpinning roots are not known, so that people don't know why they do things the way they do. That's always the idea of our astrology – to lead back to the cause, to know why you do so-and-so. That's basic, essential in our teaching – and that's basically the idea of esotericism.

To go back to the roots, and to understand why those many manifestations of the cosmos, or of the human being, or of the human being's world, come about. Then you can take life in a different way, if you look from there. And then again that makes things meaningful – makes it meaningful that you do astrology for instance, and then probably go on and use astrology to tell people about themselves, and make their life more meaningful. That is, I think, the idea.

Our astrology is pure esotericism.

What is Esotericism?

According to Alice A. Bailey, the theory of the Seven Rays lays the foundation for the psychology of the New Age[6]. It is an esoteric science, also known as esoteric psychology. I would like to start by defining what we mean by esotericism. If you look the word up in a dictionary, you see that "esotericism" is derived from the Greek "esoterikos", which quite simply means "inner" or "hidden". Esotericism therefore means that which lies behind external appearances; invisible energies, which evoke different outward forms  and bodies and also the effects they produce. It concerns the subtle world of energies and forces, the intrinsic, the self or the soul that lies hidden behind all external forms. This applies to a person, a planet or any kind of being. It can be the organism of an atom, a plant, an animal or a person. In any case, the esoteric factor is the qualitative, vital principle from which every living organism draws its energy.

Esotericism also deals with the nature of life itself, which penetrates all forms and sustains life, from the tiniest atom to the most gigantic entities that we call planets or solar systems. That is why it is important to start by realizing that each person is just a tiny part of an immeasurable and all-encompassing whole; that the energies that drive each of us and life as a whole are the energies "of a life in which we go about our daily business". To understand esotericism, we must understand that any semblance of apartness, of separation from the whole is just an illusion. If we assume that all life is one, everything that exists originates from a single source.

The study of the seven rays is also therefore the search for the original source, for the "return to the father's house", which is called the "path to initiation" in the esoteric literature. This is what esoteric astrology deals with, where the three spiritual planets and the three horoscopes: moon node, natal and house horoscope help us to determine the stages, conversion processes and expansions of consciousness that must be passed through.

The Ethereal World and the Seven Rays

The life principle that makes all forms of life possible is also referred to as ether in the esoteric literature and prana in Indian philosophy. Ether penetrates all levels, takes on their form and colour and is thus constantly finding new ways for life to express itself. It exists on all seven cosmic planes. The mystic knows that behind the world of appearances lies a hidden ethereal, i.e. spiritual world, which is actually the guiding and stimulating force in every living thing. The ether, or the light of space, is the area in which and through which the energy that comes from many sources is active. The theory of the seven rays is based on this fact. The ethereal body of the whole universe, our planet and every single person resembles a golden network of energy fluxes that is in continual, inexorable motion – an eternal medium for the exchange and transmission of energies and information.

The Meaning of the Seven Rays

This approach also enables the effect of the seven rays to be understood. The seven cosmic rays are seven types or manifestations of light, based on the special substance of each plane i.e. a different colour quality appears on each of the seven levels, when the light falls on the matter or substance on these levels. The colours of the spectrum are an example of this. We are familiar with the rays of light that fall on matter and produce colour. Different colours are formed when light reflects on matter, depending on what the matter is made of. For example, when a ray of light is reflected in smooth glass or in a drop of water, the whole of the spectrum is visible. This is a good way to represent the effect of the seven cosmic rays. They are all-pervasive; they bring life to everything and are the source of our existence. This is why they transcend normal astrology. They are primal energies that condition our lives, they are forms of energy that generate and sustain creativity.

What is Light?

Light is the centralizing life principle; it is the ether, the moving and generating life energy; light is divine. Seen in a different way, the seven cosmic energies or rays are the embodiments of seven types of force, which represent the seven divine qualities. These seven qualities again influence the matter and form in the universe in seven different ways, and they also have seven types of relationship with each other. There is a fantastic interplay and interpenetration of light in the universe, the extent of which is hard to comprehend. It is easiest to understand it by analogy.

This explains why we understand this all-connecting network of light by taking the view that there is an ethereal world, which has always been known in esotericism as "Mysterium Magicum", from which everything living is born and to which everything returns. In other words, light and ether are the same thing, they are the light of the soul, the Fohat of the Monad or the universal soul, which is considered to be the matrix of the universe.

It is interesting to note that, in its manifestation on the astral plane, the ether is also known as the Akashic Records. The ether is that primal substance in which everything that has ever lived is preserved. In old esoteric books, the ethereal dimension was also compared to a desert in which the traces of all the ages remain, including those of every human life. The Moon Node horoscope includes these traces in the sand.

Ether and Science

Modern science is also researching the ethereal world as the world of energies. Physicians and astronomers know that space is permeated by constantly moving electro-magnetic currents and fields that are constantly communicating "information". Biologists and doctors are investigating the key role of electro-magnetic phenomena in the animal kingdom, and in human nerve stimulus transmission and brain activity. Apparently inanimate objects only truly reveal their internally pulsating forces and their structures under the electron microscope.

Experiments have shown the microscopic world of atomic physics to be a rich source of insight. Meanwhile, researchers into quantum theory and the hypothetical elementary particles have investigated still deeper into the subtle structures of the world that are hidden from the human eye. Connections are increasingly suggested between energy and matter, and between order and "chaos". Modern scientists are increasingly approaching the "ancient" knowledge of mystics and philosophers. The holistic view of the world is increasingly being recognized as accurate.

The development of modern science is a good example of the fact that scientific knowledge has enabled us to learn more and more about the nature of our existence. It has made what used to be hidden, arcane and esoteric and incomprehensible by mere mortals more accessible. Today we learn many arcane facts and associations in such a purely scientific, matter-of-fact way, that we often no longer notice that they deal with ancient mysteries that are now becoming common knowledge and thereby losing their mystical and esoteric aspect.

Another aspect of this topic is the esoteric concept of the structure of man, which allows the seven rays to find their rightful place in the evolutionary process.

The Four Subtle Human Bodies

Figure 1.1 shows the esoteric structure of man. The different shades show the etheric body located directly around the physical body, the emotional or astral body in the middle layer, then the mental body, and on the outside the causal body.

Etheric Body (Physical)

Esoteric theory states that man derives the life forces for his physical body from the subtle, etheric field. The purely physical is dead matter without ether; a corpse. During the death process, the etheric, or vital, body separates from the physical body and returns to the planetary ether from whence it came, and the physical body returns to the earth. The etheric body is somewhat larger than the physical body and provides its organs with a life-long, fluid supply of vitality. In astrology, the etheric body is ruled by Saturn. As we shall see later on, the physical ray is determined by the position of Saturn in the horoscope.

Aura, Chakras and the Seven Rays

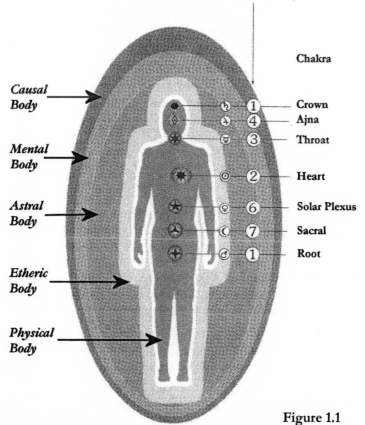

Chakra

Causal Body

Crown
Ajna
Throat

Mental Body

Heart

Astral Body

Solar Plexus
Sacral
Root

Etheric Body

Physical Body

Figure 1.1

Astral Body (Emotional)

The etheric body draws its energy from the astral or emotional body, the source of all emotions from anger to self-sacrificing love. The astral body corresponds to the Moon plane and the Moon Node horoscope reflects the contents of this body. It is dominated by polarities and opposites. Love and hate, ebb and flow, good and evil are constantly alternating like the pulse of life itself. In astrology, the emotional body corresponds to the Moon. The emotional ray is determined by the position of the Moon in the horoscope.

Mental Body (Thought)

The mental body is located beyond the astral body, and is even subtler and pervades everything coarser. Thought processes take place here and thought streams are received and emitted through it. Knowledge is collected here and it is here that we can liberate ourselves from the duality and delusional tendencies of the astral body. Thinking enables us to develop the necessary intelligence to learn to think without prejudice by using sophisticated discriminating abilities, and to understand more and more the laws of life in cosmic connections, in the light of developmental thought. The intellectual and reasoning power of the mental body corresponds to the Sun. The ray of the mental body is determined by the position of the Sun in the horoscope.

Causal Body

Beyond these three human bodies lies the unchanging and immortal self (in the horoscope this is symbolized by the empty centre circle). All our earthly emotional and mental experiences are sorted here and are stored as essence, life quality or life motivation. It is the causal body, which is constantly exchanging information with the Akashic Records and where clairvoyants can read when they want to see into a person's past or future. Every life that a person lives is processed on the causal plane; the essence is extracted and stored there as experience.

The content of the causal body can be represented at the end of the life by a certain geometric figure. We know that aspect connections in the horoscope form symbolic lines that represent the geometry and structure of the pattern of individual consciousness. This approach enables us to say that the aspect pattern reflects the causal body and gives an indication as to the ray of the person's soul. We will hear more about this later.

The Seven Centres or Chakras

Around the edge of Figure 1.1, in addition to the seven centres or chakras, we also see a list of the corresponding planets and rays. The control of form by seven kinds of energy or by seven centres is a constant rule for the understanding of man's inner structure. Five of these centres or lotus flowers are located along the spine, the other two centres are in the head.

1. The Crown chakra is ruled by the first ray, Pluto and Vulcan. It corresponds to the pineal gland (epiphysis) and only functions in spiritually awakened individuals. It is specifically the organ of spiritual willpower. The pineal gland is ruled exoterically by Saturn.

2. The Ajna chakra is located between the eyebrows and is ruled by the fourth ray and Venus. It is the chakra of the integrated personality and corresponds in terms of location and function to the pituitary gland, which is ruled by Jupiter.

3. The Throat chakra (thyroid and parathyroid glands) corresponds to the third ray and is ruled by the Earth and Saturn. The thyroid is the organ of intelligent creativity and is ruled by Mercury.

4. The Heart chakra corresponds to the thymus gland. It is ruled by the Sun and esoterically by Jupiter. It conveys the energy of the second ray of love and wisdom.

5. The Solar Plexus is the chakra of personal emotions and feelings. It is ruled by the sixth ray of Devotion, Mars and Neptune. It corresponds to the pancreas, which is also ruled by Venus.

6. The Sacral chakra is ruled by the seventh ray and the planet Uranus. It corresponds to the gonads or the ovaries, which are ruled by the Moon.

7. The Root chakra is the organ of the life force, in which a very special force lies latent, called kundalini. It is ruled by the first ray of will and power, and by Pluto. It corresponds to the adrenal gland, which is ruled by Mars.

The attributions to the chakras are mainly true for the average person. In another context, Alice A. Bailey attributes the Ajna chakra to the fifth ray and the Root chakra to the fourth ray[7], because in this case there is a special developmental stage involved.

Research tells us that we can measure the vibration of the chakras by the energy they radiate and find out which healing forces can be used. For example, we can purify our own centres and recharge them with energy by means of chakra meditation. We will also discover that we can work on the chakras with vibrations or colours in order to revitalise or heal them. According to Alice A. Bailey, many illnesses can be attributed to the congestion and atrophy of an etheric centre. You can read more on this subject in her books[8].

2

What does Esoteric Mean?

Bruno Huber

Esoteric Thinking

• Why? The Esoteric Question •
• Motivations, Energies and Principles •
• Crosses and Temperaments •
• Separation of Layers •
• Consciousness and Will •

The Seven Rays

• Rays, Crosses and Temperaments •
• Astrology and Esoteric Thinking •
• Psychosynthesis and Astrology •

The Seven Planes

• Physical Plane •
• Physical/Etheric Levels •
• Emotional Plane •
• Mental Plane •
• Higher Mental – Uranus •
• Buddhic Plane – Neptune •
• Atmic Plane – Pluto •
• Conclusion •

Questions

Esoteric Thinking

Now we settle down to esotericism. I first put a question: what does esoteric mean? I think we have to somewhat define it, because, looking around, it is modern to speak of esotericism, or 'this is esoteric', etc. By going deeper we find a lot of these people have no notion of what it is, or they mean completely different things. Now esoteric has nothing to do with eating no meat; this is your personal decision if you do that! This is a level that esotericism is not really concerned with – it is body stuff.

Why? The Esoteric Question

So what is esoteric? Esoteric thinking means that you look behind the surface of things. You don't look at forms or the symptoms that appear on the surface of your life. You ask "why is it that way?" – it could be this way or that way etc. You want to know why. That's basically the idea behind it. The question 'why?' is essential to esotericism. That's not explaining it yet of course, but it's very important.

Esoteric thinking means that you first of all start thinking of the energies behind the scenes that move those symptoms, those forms that you encounter in your practical life. There are energies behind, energies that direct symptoms and physical phenomena. They create forms, so to speak – these forms we live with.

This room is made of mineral stuff, wood etc. It has certain forms we can see – that's our world. A face looks like this, and another face looks different and we can discriminate them. Yes, but we can also more than just discriminate – to this face belongs this name, and to this other face belongs this other name. That would be just factual acceptance that you have there those different faces and that is how it is. And we may know that this face behaves like this, that face behaves like that, I might like the one more than the other, etc. But that's remaining on the surface – dealing with the facts, the figures, the forms.

But I might ask why is this face built that way. Esotericism says that faces are not just happenings, accidents, or something like that; faces are expressions of something behind them, of a character, an individual, a human potential. This potential, the human personality, has a destiny.

But again destiny is something that we can see on the surface. He broke his leg on the 25th October – that's a factual thing you can see. Of course that's part of the destiny of that person. But we don't know why that person has broken the leg.

There must be something behind; it's not just an accident. Certain people break legs and other parts of their body, others never. Why? Why? The esoteric question. What's behind? Why do certain people

Why? Why? The esoteric question

attract certain sicknesses. Why? Others don't; they select other illnesses that are typical for them.

That's the way esoteric thinking starts. That's not the last answer, but it's the beginning of questioning esoterically. You want to know what's standing behind, what the moving forces are, or the moving conditions, or the moving motivations (that's even deeper).

Motivations, Energies and Principles

For instance, people have motivations. Some of them know their motivations; others tell us some but often don't know what's really behind; and even more people have no notion that they have motivations.

There are things like 'life motivations'. We know them from the horoscope. That central part, the aspect structure, is a motivational structure. There is the secret of that life in it. That person wants to encounter certain conditions in order to solve certain problems, to attack certain problems that exist, probably even beyond their personal concerns, simply as human problems etc.

They want to learn certain things that they need to learn to get further in their own development. That creates a motivational structure that then leads their life. It's not the accidents you have – the accidents are explained by that, right? That's the other way of thinking. So esotericism has always dealt with moving forces or motivational forces.

But that's still not the deepest level, because energies is the next plane after the plane of forms. I have explained the 'forms' – the things which you see, which you perceive, which you deal with, which you take into your hand, which you think about etc. The next deeper plane is the plane of energy – those moving energies; they move things on the upper plane, the plane of forms, but there's more behind it.

There are principles. Scientists would say there are laws of nature. It's another way of saying the same thing. Principles make for certain possibilities of creation. Natural laws do the same; they give a frame within which you can move, within which you can be creative. They also say certain things are impossible; they do not belong to this cosmos, so to speak.

The aspect structure is a motivational structure.
There is the secret of that life in it.

Principles have a potential, not the potential of energy, but the potential of mind, of thinking, of knowing. They are potentials of consciousness. They move by knowing, not by energy. They state 'this must be'. Then the energies go about working them out and creating forms. That's the way it goes.

Crosses and Temperaments

Then, within that layer of principles you even have sub-layers. There we meet with astrology. In our teaching the zodiac, for instance, is made of three crosses and four temperaments, plus then the planets of course, but that's not the zodiac itself.

So we have the number three and the number four. Some specialists love to speak of those numbers, and they work with the numbers. Kabala for instance has developed quite an old esoteric structure, but it is very hard to enter this business and to understand it – it's very complex.

Anyway, we have the number three, as we have three crosses (See Figure 2.1). Every cross contains all four elements, or temperaments. We discriminate that the crosses are a motivation or purpose.

Crosses say why and what for. Temperaments are the next layer, they tell us how and when and where. That's the difference isn't it? First you have to know why and what for, that is you have to have an aim; otherwise your doing is useless. And then the temperaments you have at hand tell you how to go about it, to make that happen.

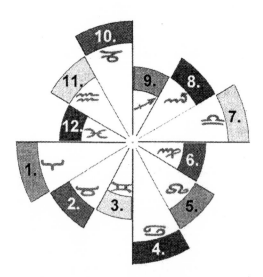

Figure 2. 1 The Three Crosses

> Crosses say why and what for.
> Temperaments tell us how and when and where.

Separation of Layers

Separation of layers is very important in esoteric thinking – to always keep the layers or planes cleanly discriminated. Don't mix terms from one layer with the terms from another, because you get 'off the beam'. You will never find out why.

This is one of the main characteristics of present-day astrology. They mix the terms from different levels and try arguments to prove something. Of course it must go wrong; it can't come out clear-cut and straight. So this is very important – keep the levels clear. Know of what level you speak, and don't mix up the terms of the different levels. Link them up – that's different – showing that one term of one level produces these terms on the other plane. That is valid because it shows the relationship. All planes are related to each other.

Consciousness and Will

But somewhere it begins and then develops, and then at the end it's our world, the forms of our real livable world. So what esotericism does is go back layer by layer to the original source, which is always consciousness that wants to create.

So we have three basic principles of purpose or motivation – the three crosses have that important position of being originators of a conscious will, of three types. We don't speak of God, because that would be 'one'. All the big religions speak of a trinity of God, because you can never name and never define God – that one thing, that original will. But the first manifestations of God, in all main religions, are the three basic principles, those wills of three orders. And then each will has the four temperaments or elements at hand to go to work. They are conditions of functioning.

> Esotericism goes back layer by layer
> to the original source, which is always
> consciousness that wants to create.

The Seven Rays

I now come to the rays. These are related to the crosses and temperaments in the following table – the crosses to rays 1,2,3, and the temperaments to rays 4,5,6,7 – the holy number seven.

```
┌─────────────────────────────┐
│ Crosses                     │
│       1 – Cardinal          │
│       2 – Mutable           │
│       3 – Fixed             │
│ Temperaments                │
│       4 – Water             │
│       5 – Air               │
│       6 – Fire              │
│       7 – Earth             │
└─────────────────────────────┘
```

Rays of Crosses and Temperaments

Astrologers keep asking me why the age point goes by six years rather than seven – they're all fixed on seven! Seven is the number of living form, a form that we can live with, and a form that we can create. It is here in the rays, for instance the ray of definite form creation. It creates the last, then remaining and living-on form, that pesists, that's for keeps, that keeps going for a long time, that is strong, that can be used and lived, etc.

So seven is a different number from six. Seven, in the esoteric idea, is a combination of three and four. But the three is not on the same order as four. The four is serving the three – this is very important. The four temperaments serve the three crosses; that's why they exist in all three crosses. It's the same four principles of action, of doing, of performing, but each cross handles them differently, because it is of a different purpose.

We discriminate between **major rays** (the three) and **minor rays** (the four).

Now the number seven does have importance – as we see 3+4=7 – no way of getting out of that! But it's not even equal numbers – they don't have the same value – three has a different value from four. We should never put them on the same level – that would be wrong, because then the system does not work any more. But in total it is seven, and in seven we have the completed creation.

Six is a number that is still striving towards that state of completion. It comes before seven and is idealistically wanting to achieve it.

Astrology and Esoteric Thinking

As you learn from this book, you'll find how astrology is constantly linked up with basic esoteric structures. Astrology is an expression, and I would say the foremost expression, of esoteric thinking. There is no other discipline that comes near to that complete usage of esoteric thinking that astrology does. And I know a lot of disciplines, having gone through most of them in my younger years. None of them is in a similar way absolutely pervaded with spiritual principles.

No wonder, because in the beginning of culture, in the early cultures, the two went together. There were temples with initiates and their novices learning the esoteric truth and there were those who created astrology, back in Sumeria. They started around 4000BC or earlier, and by 2500BC they had the whole thing finished already! That's 4500 years ago – the whole of astrology complete, and since then just refinement. We are recently rediscovering where it was really founded, and I don't mean that historically but that astrology is basically founded in esotericism and is a direct expression of esoteric thinking.

The great thing is that it is directly applicable to human existence, to human character, to human destiny, to understand people, very personally, absolutely individually. Don't look for another discipline that can do all this – there is none! They are all specialised – certain aspects of life, certain aspects of people, etc.

So we're involved in a great thing that strictly has to do with the culturing mind of the human being since it started – the self culturing of the human mind. Because the human mind is built that way – it cultivates itself day by day – some unconsciously (they have a slower pace), some consciously (they have a faster pace), some very consciously (they have a huge pace). It thrusts forward in its widening of consciousness, and understanding of the universe. And we have the guiding lines in astrology, or in esoteric thinking, whichever name you want to give it – basically it's the same!

So we are faced with a fantastic thing! I have to lead you into more complicated things now.

**Astrology is the foremost expression
of esoteric thinking.**

Psychosynthesis and Astrology

You have probably heard of Roberto Assagioli's egg model[1] (Figure 2.2). There he puts down these basic principles in purely psychological terms, in terms of psychosynthesis, not in terms of psychoanalysis. In the egg three layers are easily discernible. Assagioli says that the human consciousness lives in that egg. That's the human personality, with all its parts, conscious, unconscious, super-conscious etc.

There are three layers. You can understand them as, for instance, consciousness, feeling and body – or everyday consciousness, unconscious and collective unconscious, or etc. You can make different kinds of discriminations and label them in different ways. If you remain in the frame of words then you always have the three principles.

From encountering and working with Assagioli[2] I tried to put the egg of psychosynthesis together with astrology, but it did not work. So I worked my own scheme, which became the Huber amphora or bottle in Figure 2.3.

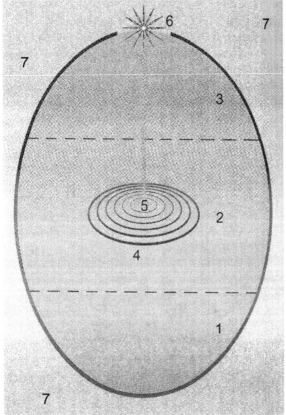

1. Lower unconscious
2. Middle unconscious
3. Superconscious
4. Field of consciousness
5. Personal self or "I"
6. Transpersonal self
7. Collective unconscious

Figure 2.2 Assagioli's Egg

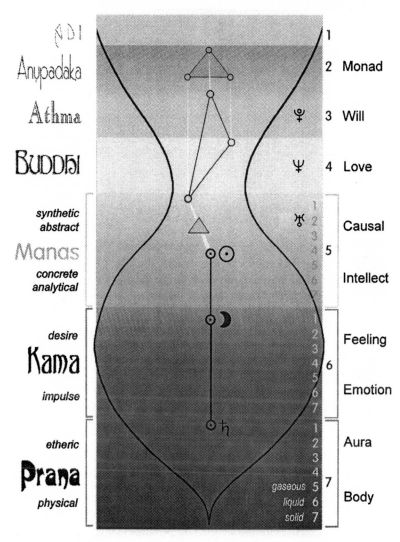

Figure 2.3 Amphora

Every human being is a bottle! In German, a bottle is someone who knows nothing! The Huber bottle still contains Assagioli's egg, but it has a neck, above which it widens and opens out.

The levels are shaded, illustrating planes of energy qualities of different orders. This is esoteric thinking in the terms of Blavatsky and Alice Bailey. As you see I added other points like the planets. You can even put the houses or signs in if you want.

The idea is to show where the human being lives in the cosmos. No one lives on the upper levels. Normal people have no notion that something exists up there. They are told, for instance in church, that there is somebody up there, a God – that's it! There might be a Christ also, one storey lower. But it remains rather vague. Esoteric thinking of the last centuries and way back thinks of a very differentiated scheme of planes.

The shading in Figure 2.3 also illustrates the application of colour. Certain colours go with certain planes of energy, of substance, of quality. But I don't want to go into these colours and their ins and outs here.

The Seven Planes

What is important in the discrimination of esoteric planes is that there are seven major planes, which we describe in chapter 6 (Figure 6.1 on page 113). Each of these planes is subdivided into sub-levels of seven sub-planes. This again has to do with creation – seven always has to do with creation.

On these seven planes respective forms can manifest by way of creation. Most human beings are creating up to the concrete thinking level – not normally higher. Some artists, some searchers of a scientific or other order, may go upward and create on higher levels, but they are the rare exception in general. Most people live not higher than the level of concrete thinking. That's the frame of normal personality consciousness. You have a physical body, an emotional and feeling nature, and a mind and thinking apparatus of sorts.

These lower levels are basically concerned with the physical world, getting through there and having a good living if possible. No need to go upstairs! In order to have a good living you can stay there and it works. That's the human world. You can even be creative in that whole of three possible layers – the physical, the emotional and the mental level.

Physical Plane

There are discriminations. As you see from the amphora the physical plane (matter) is composed of two parts. One is the physical plane in the sense of dense physical bodies or forms, not only the physical body of the human being but all that exists in nature and all that human beings build from there, like houses and cars – all that is physical, dense matter. That's the lowest part.

The three discriminations within that sub-part of the whole physical level is dense, liquid, gaseous, and we have a fourth level – plasmatic.

There you have the four elements again! Dense is earth; liquid is water; gaseous is air; and plasmatic is fire. That's the four physical conditions we know of the universe. Astronomers have 99.9999% to do with plasma, because very little matter in the universe is either dense or liquid or gaseous.

Physical/ Etheric Levels

Then there is a higher order of the physical plane – the etheric world, where all kinds of phenomena are busying people who start into esotericism – like telepathy, precognition, etc. They are phenomena of the etheric level. The etheric level, according to Bailey and Blavatsky, contains a living double of the physical body of the human being, or other living things – so a plant has a living double on the etheric level.

The etheric level is really causative. If the etheric double is taken away the physical form dies. That is of interest in the question of dying. For instance, normally people are only buried three days after death. Why? Because the etheric has to completely dissolve from the physically dense body. If you start too early – burn the person one day after – you may harm the etheric double. This may be bad because it is being reinstituted to higher levels, and the effects of it are used in the next incarnation. So it's important that you don't do wrong. Funnily enough, people who bury people today don't know that, but they still wait for three days!

That's just the physical level. There are actually seven sub-levels. Three levels are etheric and contain the causative body of the physical appearance of the human being, and four levels are then the manifestations of the raw physical existence.

Emotional Plane

In a similar way the emotional body has two main layers. The upper one is the feelings. Feelings we know – we have feelings, we like things, we love people, we hate this and that. We are pretty conscious of them. Very often we stand behind them and say they're good feelings – or we don't like some feelings but still have them, so we hate ourselves for them. But we are conscious of them. That's what I call feeling.

Emotion is unconscious and compulsive. Because it's unconscious, but wants to be lived, it is compulsive. I do it reacting to an emotional impulse. I need no reason for that. Surely I will give some reason – this person looked at me badly so I hit them! But that's probably not

---

**Feelings we know... we are conscious of.
Emotion is unconscious, and is compulsive.**

the real reason – it's some emotional structure in me that does that – probably waited for something to hit. So emotion is unconscious and therefore compulsive. Of course a lot of that stuff happens to us and we don't really know why.

Again in the upper conscious area of feelings there are patterns that serve us to explain the emotions. Just as we have an etheric double that makes the physical body live, so we have conscious feelings that are so-to-speak the philosophy you need to justly have emotions.

Mental Plane

On the mental level we have a similar thing again. At the lower mental level we normally function with our thinking, with our brains – we think about the facts of life, about physical existence, about people as physical living beings, how they behave, what they do etc.

We learn a lot of knowledge that has nothing to do with persons we know, or anything that needs to interest us for our survival. What we learned in schools for instance is all lower intellect – knowledge we need or may need – but not all we need. Young schoolboys and schoolgirls often say today "what should I learn this for – I don't need it". It's something very stupid – they may need it, but they don't know or understand then, therefore they say "I don't want to learn it".

You can know a lot about this world; you can learn lifelong lower-mentally and you will not know all about this world that can be knowable in that sense. It is that which we can scientifically know and scientifically explain. But it is not the sort of thinking that is able to find out new things which we hadn't known before. That is important.

Higher Mental – Uranus

On the edge of the higher mental level, which is abstract thinking, I have positioned Uranus. The German symbol[3] for Uranus ⛢ contains the Sun symbol, which means that's my consciousness which has learned everything it could learn in this world – it knows. The sphere of consciousness has the I-point in the middle – my location in the middle of my consciousness space. That's the sun symbol. And then you have the arrow going up vertically, not at an angle like Mars. Also, Mars has no point in the centre of the circle, so Mars is not an I-conscious being like the Sun and Uranus.

Uranus knows so much, but then it wonders what's beyond, and beyond can only be of a higher order, because I don't yet know about it. I must go upwards in order to find a higher reason for that which I don't understand within my current frame of knowledge. That's the push upward and the sense of growth of consciousness. For instance, it's the push that a scientific researcher follows, or you yourself in learning astrology. In astrology you go beyond what you learn in school and books. You find out reasons that you cannot know from any other source that you can learn from.

So rightly many astrologers say that astrology's planet is Uranus. It is in that sense. You may take Neptune for another good reason, but anyway...

The higher mental is the realm of abstract thinking. It doesn't need the concern of the 'I' to give meaning to things that happen, and to which I have to react in order to survive, or to have a good living. It is knowledge that I try to find because I want to know it, because I want to understand – not myself but for the order of things – to be able to understand certain phenomena of the normal realm of human functioning. Nobody can explain all the phenomena that exist in the human world, so there is always ample reason to go further in order to find out why certain phenomena appear constantly again and again. And we can't do anything because we don't know where they come from, so to speak, or why they come. So there I go searching. That's the drive of Uranus.

When I superimpose Assagioli's Egg onto the Amphora, Uranus is positioned at the round ridge on top of the egg. I call it the egg-breaker. It breaks through the egg layer and looks further up, at what's up there, in order to explain things that I don't understand.

Uranus – I call it the egg-breaker.

This is a very important function, always used only by a minority of human beings, but always moving human history on. Because the search with Uranus is not primarily of personal interest, but is driven by the need to understand phenomena that disturb human beings, and that need be explained in order to get control of them.

That's another urge of human beings – to gain control, and we do that by understanding. That's the only way. If we only know what's there and never ask why, we never get full control. This basic thinking is very important – the 'why?' question makes us move to understand. If we don't ask 'why?' we can never get full control, because some phenomena happen without our understanding and therefore are out of control.

This is the urge manifest in Uranus. Uranus is therefore very important. Uranus is the higher order of establishing security, therefore a higher order of Saturn. Saturn is happy with what he knows, making large walls around himself for protection. Only after a very long time does Saturn understand "I can't make it – they break through my walls again and again; there must be something outside that does that", and then Uranus can go and look for the reasons. This is a very important mechanism in the development of human consciousness.

With Uranus you can get a lot of understanding of why the world functions this way, that way, or the other way, and how many variations can possibly appear. Then you get into a condition described in Goethe's *Faust*. The prologue begins with the basic idea that "I know all about the world but I don't understand it any more". That is the end of lower mental development – thinking in terms of cause and effect. This can get pretty far, but it ends where the world of phenomena ends, where it goes into the dimension of principle. There this logical thinking no longer has purchase.

That's the end of that line of mental development. You can go on and on, and you get what they call eggheads in America – those extremely intelligent people who walk two metres above the ground. They have no link, not even to their families any more. Their families say "yes he's a very intelligent person; we never see him". Not down on the ground! Everything is absolutely logical up there, but they are hardly actually able to exist. That's why they're mostly part of a system, the academic world and its function. Then they are safe; they have a family for their good name, because a man without a family is no man. Anyway they live up there.

In our time there are a lot of people from that layer who follow very 'funny' deeply emotional gurus. They jump out of their scientific world and follow gurus, who lead them to a deep emotional experience, which in some cases ended with death, in full conviction. That kind of order is going round very much. It is often very intelligent people who follow such gurus, not the poor and the dumb. But the texts that come from those gurus are dumb – it hurts you!

So that's where Faust goes, in his hopelessness, in his state of being mentally stranded. They go there, because something suddenly fills up their body, their feeling nature. That all seemingly has meaning because there's no meaning any more in their world. They are at the narrowest point of the bottle. This can be completely blocked – blocked with too much knowledge which has no more meaning. It's like a cork, but in the middle of the bottle, so it's difficult to get out.

Buddhic Plane – Neptune

There is only one way – to go on to the next level, and that means love. That is the quality of the next plane, Buddhi, where Neptune is at home. This is identification with being, being self, being others, no limits. Being means 'I am here', 'I encounter' and 'I am there' too.

It's a quality that astrologers should need. If they work, as most astrologers think, only by Uranus it's a hard business – hard for the ones 'done with' because they get logically analysed with Uranus. In the end you know all about yourself and understand less than you ever understood before of yourself!

Go round and look at astrologers – they do it! Not all of them, and the number that don't do it that way is growing, such as this group! Still, there are too many who do it that wrong way, that purely Uranic way. They know all about astrology, the ins and outs, all the quotations from all the books. They can deal it out and shatter existences in the worst of cases.

It needs Neptune, it needs that understanding that comes from the identification with being, whatever being I'm encountering. I even encounter me, myself. Being to understand being, to understand the quality and the special combination of qualities that make that being. It's not a question of logic, it's a question of experiencing that Neptune. If you reach that quality you get through that court, that is the court dissolves and up you grow – to the next level.

Astrology needs Neptune, that understanding that comes from the identification with being

---

Atmic Plane – Pluto

It gets a bit more difficult with the names. We've had Manas and Buddhi, now Atma. These are Sanscrit terms. Atma means will. Normal astrology would say 'will – look at Mars'. Mars and will – 'to be willed' is more appropriate – 'set the motor and say go' and they do it and do it and do it – that's Mars.

We have seen that there is a boundary at the mental level where Uranus the egg-breaker needed to break through to grow. That is the boundary to transpersonal living, transpersonal functioning of consciousness. That needs different ways of living, different ways of functioning, different ways of communicating, etc. There is no longer the interest of 'me' surviving and living well, but the interest of human beings living, for instance, and hopefully we can make it better than before. So there's a transpersonal interest, or spiritual interest, or superconscious motivation.

You have then to grow first through the Neptune state in order to really be permeated by that experience of commonality with all existing beings on all the different planes or layers, in order to come to an understanding of this world or this cosmos.

You can conceive of this world (I don't mean the humanly created world – say our earth or in a larger frame the solar system or the whole cosmos) that it has been created to be meaningless. Even the scientists say for instance that astronomers are looking for explanations of how the cosmos came about, with big bang cosmology etc, trying to explain something a bit like the bible but a bit more complicated! Once it was created – bang!

Even those people who are seemingly in that pre-Uranic state, or the middle/ higher order of the Uranic state, try to understand how it came about. They keep changing it, because it constantly doesn't really function – they have to add this and postulate that etc, but it doesn't really fit – as is typical for extreme Uranic functioning.

But the urge is there, to understand how this world was built originally, what is the meaning behind it, etc. Again the question is 'why?', but now in a quite immense dimension. You cannot put any border, any limit, to the thinking of Pluto on the world plane. Borders are borders of your thinking, and you won't have to do with Pluto if you think that way.

Pluto thinking, or real world consciousness, can go to any dimension at ease, because there's no question of dimensions in that sense – but an understanding of how things should work towards what, or an understanding of why this world is there now at this stage, and where the next stages will go. These are frames of thinking, for that round.

It's necessary to have gone through the other stages before. One can get hunches from the lower levels beforehand, even in the lower mental level, and that may set you off to go all the way up until you are in the spiritual levels. Very often this is the beginning – these hunches, sudden insights of greatness that you can't know how they came about in your consciousness, can make you go for driving at spiritual development or development of consciousness.

> **Very often this is the beginning –
> these hunches can make you go for spiritual
> development or development of consciousness**

Conclusion

That was a little trip through the scales. I think a bit of knowledge of that sort is needed to have the esoteric stepping stones.

Keep coming back to the very simple discrimination. There are three principles that have four modes of action. That makes the number seven, and seven is the number of manifestation.

> **There are three principles that have four modes
> of action. That makes the number seven, and
> seven is the number of manifestation.**

Questions

Audience: You said that principles were laid down between 4000BC and 2500BC, and they are being rediscovered now. Why now?

Bruno Huber: In the last six or seven years specialists of old languages have been able to decipher the Sumerian language. It couldn't be read before; therefore little was known of the Sumerians. Now they have started deciphering the tablets – in the British Museum lie 30,000 of them not yet deciphered. It will take many years to discover the whole culture of the Sumerians.

However the development of astrology is already pretty clear. By 2350BC, the end of the first pure Sumerian kingdom, they had created the astrology that we know.

The pure Sumerians were not semitic, they were indo-germanic, coming from the north. They intruded into the area and controlled everything with their more intelligent and more cultured way of thinking, living and functioning – controlling Babylonians, Chaldeans and others around.

The Sumerian culture also developed writing, they invented the wheel, all kinds of things that have earlier been attributed to other cultures. An amazing people!

Why does this come out now? I think because we live in a time that has completely lost orientation, because it thinks too much only in symptoms, in superficial values, in material values. And therefore has lost orientation.

Go to any public place and ask people 'why?'. They say 'uh' or 'stupid' or something. They don't give you an answer, because they have never asked such stupid questions like 'why?'! "Why do you stare into that window like that?" "I want to have it!" Nobody asks that – either you have the money and buy it, or you don't have the money and you go home.

Audience: Another possible answer comes from Alice Bailey, who said that the explosion of the atom bomb is a reflection of the sudden push through of the soul to the personality. If you notice from the 1940's there was a huge surge in spiritual knowledge which is much more soul-orientated than personality-orientated.

Bruno Huber: Again I would be careful of that. Alice Bailey should know, but this is just an instance in a special area, of how spiritual development in this century is gigantic compared with earlier times. We are on a breakthrough for sure. That we see such a lot of bad things has to do with the masses of people who still resist the question 'why?'. From the teaching they get nowadays they should be able to think about it, but they don't do it. They are happy to be moved by fewer people who do it. These fewer are getting more and more in this century, and that is just one phenomenon that shows it. You can see in all ways of life that it happens.

The number of thinking people who go after the 'why?' is growing constantly. Of course these people have always existed in history as a small minority, but they were never noisy people, never appeared in public. In our time we would say they never appeared on TV! They're working their way through, and then they're writing it down or telling others, and then it slowly takes over and goes into the masses, takes decades or whatever. Earlier it needed centuries or millennia; nowadays it's probably in decades that the world is changed through the thinking of the few, who are getting more and more.

3

The Entity of the Seven Cosmic Rays

Louise Huber

The Entity - a Living Being

• Universal and Analogical Thinking •
• The Solar System and the Seven Lords •
• Etheric Level and the Planetary Logos •

The Seven Rays

• The Rays, Crosses, Temperaments and Planets •
• First Ray: Will and Power •
• Second Ray: Love and Wisdom •
• Third Ray: Active Intelligence •
• Fourth Ray: Harmony through Conflict •
• Fifth Ray: Concrete Knowledge •
• Sixth Ray: Devotion and Idealism •
• Seventh Ray: Ceremonial Magic, Ritual and Order •

Global Transformations

• Agni Yoga/ Violet Flame • Soul Kingdom •
• Initiation of Planetary Logos • Third Initiation for Disciples •
• Holistic approaches • Pluto in Sagittarius • Year 2000 at MC •

Questions

The Entity – a Living Being

You may be surprised by our title: 'the entity of the seven cosmic rays'. You know what entity means – it is a living being, and the seven cosmic rays are living beings.

Light

This is a different approach to the seven rays. As we said before, we are dealing with principles, with the meaning of life, with the inner approach towards the rays. In a different way I want to put forward that the *Treatise on the Seven Rays[1]* is a very deep approach towards life.

It is nothing other than that it deals with light. We need light for our life, and light comes from the sun, and without light we cannot live. It is the very essence of our being. There is no creation without light. The seven rays have to do with this knowledge that light is at the essence of life – the light in your heart, the light in your life, the light wherever you are going.

When you consider light as the very cause of our life and being, it comes from the Sun – you know the radiation of the sun makes our earth alive through light, and this light goes through all the different layers that are around our earth. We have the same in our own personality – different layers around us.

You know that light changes its colour according to the substance on which it is shining, from which it is reflected, and the seven rays are the seven colours according to the breaking of the light in the different layers of different substance. This is a fantastic vision – that the very cause of our life is light, and the differentiations of the different performances are the different colours.

The seven colours are scientifically the spectrum of light. The spectral colours are the seven colours. When you see a rainbow it contains these seven colours. We are dealing with these seven colours, with these seven differentiations of substance in different layers in which the seven rays appear.

This is very important – that you know that when we are dealing with the seven rays we are dealing with light, with love and with life. This life is such that it is so important to know something about it! We have our being there in this entity of space and light and rays. The rays are beyond astrology in a way. The seven rays and the *Treatise on the Seven Rays* are esoteric insights. When you deal with this differentiation of the seven rays on the different levels it gives you a lot of knowledge about human beings, about life in the universe, about your life individually, and about the life of our whole planet.

Universal and Analogical Thinking

You see how it works completely and holistically. Esoteric knowledge is built on the hermetic law of 'as above so below', or 'as within, so without'. This is so important. As astrologers you know all about this analogical thinking. Without analogical thinking you cannot deal with astrology, and you also cannot deal with the seven rays.

Esoteric and the seven rays is every enlargement of your consciousness, which is expansion into the whole universe. Otherwise you will not have any knowledge that you can use when you enlarge your consciousness to the whole universe. 'As above, so below' is a basic saying about esoteric and the seven rays.

When we speak of the rays as an entity, this is something that you can subtly and feeling-wise understand what it means. Space is an entity, and the rays are entities. When you see the light is going through all the seven layers of our existence and changing their colours, changing their impression, changing their symptoms, then it is fantastic to understand that this is not only interesting for me, but for my planet and for the whole universe.

This law of the seven rays is creating everything in life, it's basic stuff, it's principle as Bruno said, it's inner stuff, not outer thinking but universal thinking.

Universal thinking is included in astrology too. We are dealing with the stars, the signs and universal influences, and the rays further differentiate the kind of knowledge we already have through astrology. These seven different qualities or colours are also divided into seven again.

In the *Treatise on the Seven Rays* Alice Bailey deals with more universal thinking, therefore it is difficult to understand and bring it down. On the other hand, when you are dealing with the seven rays you have to enlarge your consciousness into universal thinking, otherwise you will not understand your life according to the knowledge of the seven rays. We have first to break through our barriers of thinking in a way, to look for a different frame of reference in the seven rays manner – the seven colours, the spectral colours, the light, life and love. This is something which we can feel – that this has to do with the experience of being of the entity of space.

**Without analogical thinking
you cannot deal with astrology,
and you also cannot deal with the seven rays.**

The Solar System and the Seven Lords

Now we come back to esoteric knowledge. The seven rays are the seven lords before the throne of god. In the bible the seven lords are nothing other than the seven rays. Can you follow me analogically? The number seven runs through the whole thing, even the bible.

Then we have a different saying of Alice Bailey, which I considered over many years and could not understand. She said that our planet has its own ray, our sun has its own ray, and we have a solar system which is on the second ray. What does that mean – a solar system on the second ray?

Then she explains that we are one solar system in seven solar systems. These seven solar systems are involved in linking up with each other. This is a kind of work of communication between them. Ours is the one which is on the second ray. Because our solar system is on the second ray, at the end of evolution the second ray will win the battle – love will be manifest everywhere! (Love is the second ray – love and wisdom.)

It was when I was thinking about this, when the world was so dirty, and everything was speaking of wars, when all the brutal stuff was happening in France[2]. When you watch television sometimes it's difficult to believe that love will win the battle in our solar system.

On the other hand, I was thinking about these seven solar systems from which we are the one on the second ray, the earth will be on the third ray, and humanity will be on the fourth ray (I give more detail on this later). Figure 3.1 helps to understand this better.

You see there the seven cosmic lords before the throne of God – these are the basic rays 1,2,3,4,5,6,7. The first ray is creating one solar system, the second another, the third another, and so on. This kind of analogical thinking means that all these seven rays are analogically the same in many many manifestations. These seven rays are going through all the universe – at the basic seven rays, and then they will go down and have a lot of seven solar systems. I have put here one for each ray, but you could put hundreds – the universe is so big.

This is just to give you an idea that our solar system is on the second ray. There are different solar systems in the universe which are on the first ray, others on the third ray etc. It means that the evolutionary goal of the process of growth and development for our solar system is to have pure second ray qualities at the end of this cycle; in a first ray solar system the first ray has to be similarly developed.

This is only a trial to bring down this analogical thinking of seven, which is going down from the highest plane, from ADI[3], from the throne of God where the seven lords are linked – and they manifest the

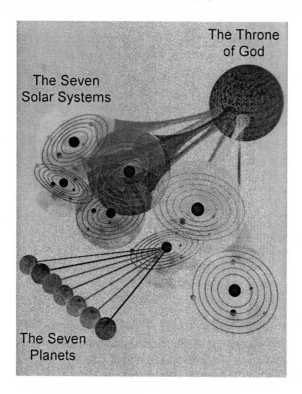

The Throne
of God

The Seven
Solar Systems

The Seven
Planets

Figure 3.1 Seven Solar Systems

same thing in many many forms. As above, so below. Universal thinking means that we have to think in micro/macro-cosmic dimensions. This aims to give you the understanding that space is an entity in which we live and have our being, and that the rays themselves are entities.

Now we make a jump to our earth ray. The solar system and the solar logos are on the second ray. We have the seven planets, each of which is on a different ray (according to Alice Bailey). We as the earth planet or the planetary logos are on the third ray, and humanity is on the fourth ray. This gives a mix of many possibilities, and it is difficult to discriminate between all them.

I have tried to give you an understanding of the rays, which are energies, which are qualities, which are colours, which are entities – that they pervade everything we know. They go through you too, building up your physical body, your emotional body, your mental body, and your causal body. This is something you cannot deny to know about. Alice Bailey says that the knowledge about the seven rays is the psychology of the new age, because it goes through everything, makes everything alive.

Etheric Level and the Planetary Logos

As we've already seen, the physical body is the dense body, and living 'in' and pervading the physical body is the etheric body. The etheric body is linked with the etheric plane of the whole planet. At the etheric level we are linked with all life, with the group, and even with the place in which you live. On the etheric level you are 'floated through', you are unlimited, we are all connected with each other. This is a fantastic idea! On the level of planet earth, one layer of the planet is the etheric layer in which we have our life as human entities.

Kingdoms

On a different layer the kingdom of plants has its own living. More different even is the mineral kingdom, which also has life from the planet. The kingdoms have life from the planet differentiated by the rays. The mineral kingdom is ruled by the first ray, plants by the second ray, animals by the third ray, and humanity by the fourth ray[4].

Planetary Logos

We are living in the etheric plane of our planet. We are linked to each other on that level, but I have in my etheric body a different ray from you, and this makes me different from you. From an energetic point of view it is the life of our planetary logos 'in whom we live and move and have our being'.[5]

The planetary logos is built up the same way as me. He also has seven levels. The astral level of the planet in which I have my feeling nature, according to my own ray on the feeling nature, is not the same as the planetary logos has, and is not the same as you have. Still, on the astral level I am linked with all of you too.

On the mental level we are living in the mental realm of the planetary logos. I have my individual mental body, but I'm also part of the whole mental level of the whole planetary logos. This is micro/macro-cosmic thinking 'as above, so below'. It is a consequent logical following on.

The Seven Rays

Shamballa – First Ray

Now we go on with the seven rays, summarised in Figure 3.2. This is knowledge from Alice Bailey and the Tibetan that the whole planet is built on the same rays – as is every human being and the solar logos and the seven lords before the throne. It's always the same thing.

The Seven Rays

Crosses, Temperaments, Planets

Major Rays

1. Will and Power	Cardinal	♇	☉
2. Love and Wisdom	Mutable	♆	☽
3. Active Intelligence	Fixed	♅	♄

Minor Rays

4. Harmony through Conflict	Water	♀	
5. Concrete Knowledge	Air	☿	
6. Devotion and Idealism	Fire	♂	
7. Ceremonial Magic, Ritual and Order	Earth	♃	

Figure 3.2 The Seven Rays

As I said before, we have humanity on the fourth ray. We also have the spiritual hierarchy of the planet on the second ray. And we have in our planetary realm a very important point of power and energy – Shamballa, where the will of god is known. Shamballa is on the first ray[6]. The first ray has to do with will, the second ray with love and the third ray with active intelligence.

The Shamballa energy corresponds with the first ray of will and power. According to the Great Invocation[7] the will of God is known there. And on the second ray, the love principle, we have the spiritual hierarchy. And we have humanity, with the third ray as a physical approach, the earth being third ray. This is again mixed up as the fourth ray is humanity and the third ray is the earth. This is again something where you have to think 'why?' – I want an explanation!

Shamballa is on the first ray and the Shamballa energy is transformed by the hierarchy on the second ray level, in order to bring it towards humanity, so that they can use the energy of the first ray. The solar logos is on the second ray, so we are aimed to develop towards the second ray - this is our destiny at the end of evolution.

But with the first ray level we always have a little feeling of will and power. Who is putting his will on me? I don't like it. We have gone through the war, we have gone through the Hitlers, we have gone through all these totalitarian regimes and stuff. We don't want their willpower any more, and politics is rubbish, so we are not so much interested in politics and power stuff! We always have bad feelings when somebody is putting power on us! This you understand. Only when you are the one who puts the power towards others!

Shamballa has in the long term such effect. The will and power of the first ray are to destroy old stuff so that the movement of life is guaranteed. Everything that is stuck, everything that is not the aim of the plan, everything that hinders evolution will be destroyed by the first ray. Therefore Alice Bailey said that at the last war the first ray was directed towards humanity, and the result of this direction was the second world war and also the atomic explosions. This is not so comfortable to know – all this destruction is also to do with the rays and the planes and evolution.

We love the second ray much more – love and wisdom. I think you have the same feeling as me, that at the end of evolution we want to become all brothers and sisters, and we love each other, help each other and support each other. This is much more human-like, especially when you are dealing with universal things like the seven rays. You are on the second ray line. Even when you are not – maybe you are first ray as a personality – but still these people who are first ray have to develop the will to love, according to the solar logos second ray aim. Isn't that a fantastic idea?

This is something which is not just hopeful. It is also giving you the permission that you are in the right space, that you are on the right lines, or on the right side – when you deal with love, with understanding, with forgiveness, or whatever aspects of love you have in you.

First Ray: Will and Power

The first ray is the ray of will and power. Analogically, it's the cardinal cross. Remember the principle of the cardinal cross which is will, impulse, movement, aiming for something, breaking through barriers. This is the first ray; this is the cardinal cross. So you as astrologers already have an understanding about the first ray when you think about all the possibilities of the cardinal cross. This is basic stuff!

This is the first ray. It is very much needed when you are aiming for a goal, when you have to build up something, when you have to change something in the world. When such change is necessary the first ray always has to come in, because it has the power to push away all the hindrances! In order to build something new you have first to get rid of all the rubbish!

The first ray is not only destruction but also rebuilding. This is very important to know. The first ray has two sides. It is needed to get rid of the rubbish, and it builds up new stuff when the place is cleaned up. Always these two sides.

> ## The first ray is not only destruction but also rebuilding.

Second Ray: Love and Wisdom

The second ray is love and wisdom, and has to do with the mutable cross. We explain the mutable principle with love and wisdom as the contact cross, the cross on which you meet people. The related planets are the Moon and Neptune.

This is again clear for you, that this has to do with the second ray, the love business, all that is involved in humanitarian and social attitudes. With the mutable cross you are able to love people, to be interested in their needs, to support them when their needs are not met, to help them, to educate them. The second ray is the great educator in life. Everybody is learning a lot through other people and through communication and all these things, and the second ray is for that.

The need to be loved, like the Moon – the Moon ego always needs somebody who loves him, and sometimes at certain periods becomes very egocentric – "I want to be loved and I love you because I want you to love me". This kind of reflection is always possible on the Moon level because the Moon is a reflector. It does not have its own light and is only seen when the Sun shines on it. We have the same on the second ray Moon level too; we always need the other for being worthwhile or being loved or being secure or whatever. The love-wisdom ray deals with this interchange between people.

Third Ray: Active Intelligence

The third ray is related to Uranus and Saturn. This is active intelligence, skill in action. Third ray people often have high intelligence, but are very skilled to use the means in life for their own sake, their own profit, their own wealth, etc. They are very good in money, earning, economic things, economic setups, economics.

The chaos in the economics in German politics at the moment is to do with lack of the third ray – when there is something really wrong on that level not functioning any more, when the third ray is not there. There are too many first ray people in politics. For example the nice guy Tony Blair – he's very intelligent. With the third ray you can really bring things down to earth so that they function correctly. This is the principle of economy and the third ray with their intelligence, skill in action, diplomacy and taking care that everything will function.

Functioning is the world of the third ray and active intelligence. When you only 'blah blah' and speak and speak and speak, the third ray says 'let's do it', 'let's do it'. That's the third ray - active intelligence.

We've seen the three major rays 1,2,3. Alice Bailey says that the other four (minor) rays come out of the third ray. This also made me think a long time – the third ray and all those four coming out of this Saturnian fixed cross stuff. My goodness! In this way the third ray gets so much over-valued. This is something you have to think about. I liked the idea of the second ray solar logos and now the third ray gets so much…

And Saturn gets out. You know that Saturn ate up all his children in mythology? Uncomfortable feeling – the third ray! For a long time I didn't like the third ray, till I found out that I am on the third ray!

Fourth Ray: Harmony through Conflict

Now we come to the minor rays. The fourth ray is associated with Venus and the element water. This is very difficult because the fourth ray is harmony through conflict. This is also something that is not so comfortable – harmony yes, but conflict nein! This is what we don't like so much!

The fourth ray is the ray of artists, of equilibrium and balance. And it is always falling out of balance, all the time. Because when there is only balance and equilibrium, when there is always harmony, then it gets so annoying – nothing is happening any more. An artist who is painting nice pictures and there is no pepper in it, then it's not so interesting any more. The fourth ray has to do with this pepper, to do with conflict. It's needed so we learn through conflict.

Now you see why humanity is on the fourth ray – we learn through conflict – it's our way of learning. The fourth ray is the ray of humanity and we have to learn through conflict all the time – it is our destiny.

Now you look differently at the fourth ray; you do not avoid conflict any more, because conflict is needed so that the energy is again coming into flow. It has a different meaning when you understand it, when you accept that it is part of the evolutionary process that we have to go through conflicts all the time.

At the end you are looking for conflicts! I know fourth ray people who create conflict all the time. They appear in a group and suddenly everybody is nervous or provoking or whatever, but they themselves

> ## The fourth ray is the ray of humanity
> ## and we have to learn through conflict all the time
> ## – it is our destiny.

think they are doing right – they have a kind of enjoyment! But I get nervous when they appear!

The fourth ray has to do with artists, also creativity. Creativity comes only when there is something that you have to master – then you have to become creative, because when there is a crisis or conflict or whatever you have to think about 'what can I do to help' etc, and you can become creative. Even in counselling sometimes fourth ray people create conflict, make you aware of something that is problematic in you, that you have suppressed and at the end they give you a 'plaster' to dress the wound. This is their method.

Fifth Ray: Concrete Knowledge

The fifth ray is associated with Mercury and the element air. It has to do with concrete knowledge. Do you know where you find a lot of people with the fifth ray? At the university – the academics and scientific people. This is the fifth ray person who is analytically very skilled. He can determine everything, can integrate everything, can think dialectically, logically, and whatever. And they can tell you all the things that belong together – a wonderful ability to build thoughts, but they are very strict and concrete and thoroughly knowledgable.

When I come with my intuition they do not understand me at all! When there are not 1,2,3,4,5 points made then they will not understand it. Their very concrete knowledge means that they have to be systematic and didactic. Teachers are very skilled in the fifth ray, and the fifth ray is needed.

Alice Bailey said that she hoped there will be more esotericists with the fifth ray in the new age, because in esoteric knowledge the fifth ray is needed. When esotericists are on the sixth ray level they are mystical and romantic, but the fifth ray brings the esoteric into a thought form that you can deal with, that you can give to others, that you are able to share with others. Education – the fifth ray.

Difficult combinations of rays are fifth and second, fifth and first etc. You have to learn the combination of the rays too to have the psychology of the new age in your pocket.

Sixth Ray: Devotion and Idealism

The sixth ray corresponds to Mars – devotion and idealism. This ray has a lot of power because Mars is a powerful planet. It's our energy pool, our adrenaline shooting, idealism, activity, something which needs devotion, which needs your whole being, which needs a goal you have to go for, the commitment – all these things come from the sixth ray.

Now we have to make a jump again, because again 'as above, so below', this hermetic basic rule. Let us look at the whole of humanity in time, in history. You know the new age is coming and now we have to make a big change. At the time when Christ was born 2000 years ago, the sixth ray was manifesting, for a whole period of 2100 years. In our days the sixth ray is going away, and the seventh ray is coming into manifestation for the next 2000 years.[8]

A lot of happenings are explained through the sixth ray. When Christ came how was his life? The first Christian people were persecuted and died for their ideas. This power of dying for the idea is sixth ray. Devotion and idealism are needed to die for an idea. Through all the centuries you can see the development in different cultures where sixth ray power was coming through.

Even in our days we still have the sixth ray power in fundamentalism, fanaticism, terrorism, sectarianism etc, all the things that are now popping up so much in the media. We see it all around because the sixth ray is dying out and therefore the worst energy still remains (the death throes). Now do you understand why in our day, the last ten or twenty years, this kind of thing has popped out so much all over the place?

Seventh Ray: Ceremonial Magic, Ritual and Order

It is very interesting that we have the changing from the sixth ray to the seventh ray, because the seventh ray is also very mysterious. It is called ceremonial magic, ritual and order and is to do with Jupiter, and the Jupiter energy. We know something about Jupiter energy, and the corresponding temperament of earth.

The seventh ray and the earth temperament. You know that all the temperaments have the ultimate manifestation with the earth – it must come into earth, into form. That is the magic of the seventh ray – it must come into form, it must manifest, now it's the end.

That is the magic of the seventh ray
– it must come into form, it must manifest.

You start in the first ray and end in the seventh ray. The first ray, the will of god, gives the impulse for development, for manifestation, which culminates in the seventh ray. And the seventh ray is kind of tail of the snake, when the tail and the head come together (ouroboros). The seventh ray is to do with the end of a long period of development – a kind of circle.

What does that Jupiter earth temperament mean? Jupiter is the central stuff, the lord of our senses, our essential appearance, our life experiences, etc. Now in this seventh ray period human beings have to become more and more sensual-conscious.

Now, at the beginning of the seventh ray period, sensual experience is very evident, for example with youngsters in discotheques and dancing. The seventh ray has to do with dancing too, with movement, excitement, ecstacy. When the senses are getting excitement and love and sexuality and all this stuff, this is seventh ray.

We recently saw street parades when they were dancing in the street – this is seventh ray stuff. This is something so new we older ones have trouble to look at it even sometimes – it gets too much! This always happens when a ray first begins to manifest, and when it's dying out – it gets over-emphasised. In between, over the last 2000 years, it did not stand out so much, was not so obvious or overdone!

The seventh ray is to do with ritual and group consciousness, according to Alice Bailey. When you think about group experiences when people come together with similar ideas, such as astrological people, you have the same ideas on the mental level – not only the same ideas but also the issue of your mental body is the same. Then you have a kind of feeling of unity – "Ah you feel the same way as me, how wonderful!" This is a Jupiter-like enjoyment when we are all on the same wavelength, in a way a kind of erotic experience on the mental level!

The seventh ray is also very much able not only to bring something down but to organise things – well done organisation, such as when the organisers of an event prepare and plan thoroughly, looking for all the things that could happen, or could hinder, searching it out – planning so correctly that it will come alive.

This is seventh ray, and it will change the whole world in a sense! Because in our economic situation in different countries, people are so aware of confusing energies everywhere – the money and stuff – that they have to change their economic behaviour so that everybody can live securely, without sickness, without deficit, etc.

This is the goal for the seventh ray in the 2000 years ahead of us – that this will happen for all humanity – that food will be divided right, all humanity will become one. There is kind of an experience of a new brotherhood, like Beethoven was saying in the ninth symphony – that all people are brothers.

Global Transformations

In our days we have a global transformation, according to Alice Bailey, not only the changing from the Piscean Age into the Aquarian Age, but also the changing from the sixth ray to the seventh ray, as I said before.

Agni Yoga/ Violet Flame

We have also a changing, when you think universally about your consciousness, as the whole solar system with its seven sisters and brothers on the solar level is moving in the whole space of the universe from the blue light into the violet light. Can you imagine this? This is happening at this time too, because in the whole universe the seven rays are also working as entities, and violet is the seventh ray and blue/ dark blue is the sixth ray – according to the spectral colours.[9]

So we are moving into the violet flame. The Agni Yoga[10] movement works with the seventh ray Master Rakoczi and with the violet flame. With the violet flame you can heal, dissolve karmic conditions, change your physical radiations...

Soul Kingdom

Then we have another thing happening now that Assagioli was very much concerned about. This is the manifestation of the fifth kingdom. I told you that the fourth kingdom is humanity, the third is the animals, the second is the plants and the first is the minerals. The fifth kingdom is the kingdom of the soul, and this kingdom is now also able to manifest because of the violet flame, because of the seventh ray, because of the ending of a large cycle with the seventh ray, etc. The fifth kingdom is manifesting in our days – the soul kingdom[11].

This means that when you think of the dimension of the soul, or the realm of the soul, you want to vision this, and the fourth kingdom and the fifth kingdom are coming together. When they merge, when they become one, then we will in 2000 years really have a new humanity and we will become all brothers in a way.

The soul in its own kingdom is very much concerned with the manifestation of the second ray. In the same way that human beings have a primary motivation for survival, the soul has a primary motivation for love and service, nothing else, just these two things.

Love and wisdom, the second ray on the soul level is manifesting now. It has to do with the solar logos, which is on the second ray, and the soul kingdom is linked with the solar logos.

Global Transformations

1.　　Changing from Pisces to Aquarius Age

2.　　From sixth ray to seventh ray

3.　　From blue to violet light

4.　　Manifestation of the fifth (soul) kingdom

5.　　A cosmic initiation of our planetary logos

6.　　Third initiation for many disciples

7.　　New holistic methods

8.　　Pluto in Sagittarius two years ago

9.　　Year 2000 as MC for humanity

Figure 3.3 Global Transformations

Therefore when the manifestation of the fifth kingdom is taking place we are dealing with psychosynthesis. Roberto Assagioli wrote a small leaflet about the manifestation of the fifth kingdom[12]. In his egg the Higher Self means nothing other than the manifestation of the soul kingdom. To become whole, to become healthy, to become harmonic, and soul-like happiness.

Assagioli said that during the time of the sixth ray and the last Piscean age 'sacrifice' was the seed thought. The seed thought of the new age will be 'joy.'

Sacrifice – martyrs! Also in those 2000 years there were monasteries, where mystical people were sacrificing themselves and their sexuality, suffering until they were so pure that they could get a place in heaven!

In the new age this is no longer the way – you do not have to sacrifice to get a place in heaven, you have to use all your substance, all your potentiality of the soul, to create in the world a new paradise in a way. To do something for others, to do something for all the hungry people in the third world. This is social rapprochement, a different thing.

During the last Piscean age
'sacrifice' was the seed thought.
The seed thought of the new age will be 'joy.'

To bring the soul kingdom into manifestation means that we have to love each other, to serve each other, to support each other. This is the New Age time. This is the new seed thought of the New Age – joy.

And you participate with pain – this is also something Assagioli told me.

The sacrificial attitude meant you thought you had to give something to a transpersonal God. In our days you no longer have to transform your ideas in this way, but you have to bring it down to earth. This is seventh ray – to bring it down to help people, to bring paradise on earth, to build a new world.

It has already happened in certain degrees. On the physical level we now have comfort in living, medical improvements, alternative healing, convenience – we push on a button and the washing machine goes. This kind of improvement in our civilisation already makes physical life easier than 100 years ago. We have to see that this is good stuff. Many people do not have to die any more because of medical advances, surgery etc. This is what you have to look at – the good stuff that is popping up now too, not only the negative things.

Initiation of our Planetary Logos

Then we have a very interesting fifth point. Our planetary logos – the big entity in which we live and have our being – Sanat Kumara himself is taking a cosmic initiation in our time. Alice Bailey speaks about this, but she didn't tell what kind of initiation he is taking[13]. She says only that this means that when the planetary logos is initiated in more cosmic knowledge then the whole of humanity will change, because we have our living in him. When he has developed a little bit more into cosmic realms then the whole humanity will profit from it.

This is again macro/micro cosmic consciousness needed to understand this. Aaaah! When I was looking through this I was so happy, because I knew deep in me that he will take this, he will pass this proof or this initiation! Because initiation is only to do with the lessons you have to learn. He will, I am so sure he will! So we will all profit from this bigger view.

Maybe therefore we are dealing with the seven rays at the moment because of that. Because when humanity, or you, or me enlarge our consciousness we can do this only because of him. We cannot go further than he has gone. Can you follow?

Wow! And I know that he has done it, that he has passed it, because we are able to think now more in terms of seven rays and entities and cosmic realms and stuff, and blue flame and violet flame and the colours. It's new, it's so new. And we have in our day in the last ten years a lot of knowledge about colours and healing and all these many insights in energy lines and whatever. Wow! This is the hope for the world.

Third Initiation for many Disciples

Alice Bailey also speaks of many people taking the third initiation[14] in our days. You know the first initiation is to do with Saturn, and the second with the Moon and the third with the Sun. The third initiation means that the disciples of the New Age are very many in our days – no longer three or four or five. Once, she said, in earlier times only five in a whole generation took the third initiation. In our time now hundreds are taking it.

This means the same thing – that it will enlarge, expand. And when a lot of people are taking the third initiation this means the same thing, that they can deal with the seven rays as the new psychology of the New Age. They can deal with cosmic dimensions, they can think cosmically, and then humanity is safe because all the time the disciples of the third initiation have been inspiring the masses of men – all the time.

You understand, all the great people in history who have given something very special towards humanity – even Napoleon – all these privileged people, you can count a lot of them. They had the third initiation. They were doing a task for evolution. They had to give something of themself so that evolution goes on. We say that they serve the Plan. In different words they have a link towards Shamballa, because under certain initiations you have to knock on the door of Shamballa; otherwise you will not get the vision of the next step you have to do for fulfilling the Plan.

They are linked with the mind, with the wisdom, not with the solar plexus. There are a lot of people who want to know about the plan, but they are only ego-like and have only ego-interests, but this is a different question. So the third initiation is going on.

Holistic Approaches

We also see in all the different fields of humanity – astrology, education, sociology, economics, whatever – that they are conscious now of looking for holistic methods. In medicine, in psychology, all over the place, you always hear that we are trying to get a holistic approach towards human beings. This is when it comes down to the seventh level and this is where it becomes visible – you hear it and see it – that's the changing of the world!

Pluto in Sagittarius

The eighth point is that Pluto entered Sagittarius two years ago. This means that on the mental level (Sagittarius is our own thinking ability) we have to expand our consciousness too. Pluto helps us to get this kind of vision of the divine plane, to understand why we are going through such and such crises. Pluto in Sagittarius gives us the answer to the 'Why?'.

This is Sagittarius. Sagittarius is always looking for the truth. He's always looking for the answer. He's asking 'why?', and only when he understands it is he quiet again. While he doesn't understand it he's looking, looking, looking and asking 'why, why' until he finds the right answer, the right solution, the right vision, and the right philosophy.

Year 2000 at MC

Then we have a ninth point. In my opinion we are now climbing up to the MC of the Year 2000. 2000 for my vision is the MC in the chart cycle for humanity. You know when you go with the age point towards the MC – that's age 54 for an individual – you can become a self-sustaining individuality, because that's the individuation point. It has to do with this climbing up to the year 2000 that we will come over the MC and look into the new millennium with all the new vision I gave you now. Then we will be on the safe side.

But before the MC you have this kind of stress situation, you know, you are out of breath because you have to climb to reach it. We are on that point now, so we always have this kind of feeling that we will not reach it, a kind of fear that we will not come over it, or something will happen, or the world will break down, or whatever they prophesy for this happening. People are full of fear at the moment.

But we know that the Solar Logos is on the second ray, and love will remain, love for all humanity, with all the responsibility, with all this MC-like attitude that we feel responsible also for the lower ones, for the one who has nothing to eat. I think we will take this consciousness over to the new millennium, with the seventh ray, and with the Planetary Logos.

And the fifth kingdom will be the result.

Questions

Audience: We know that in the esoteric studies we read a great deal of controversial material, some of which seems to contradict various things, but in the end it all somehow or other comes together. One of the things we have learnt in esoteric studies is the relationship of the rays to the planets. Some of them differ from the ones that you had on the board. Could you reconcile them? For instance, according to Alice Bailey and her students, the Sun is a second ray planet, Moon is fourth ray, Mercury is fourth, but Venus strangely enough is fifth, leaving Mars which is sixth, Jupiter as second ray, Saturn as third, Uranus as seventh, and Neptune as sixth, with of course Pluto being first. Could you try to reconcile these contradictions at all at this stage.

Bruno Huber: Well. The point is that Alice Bailey presented there a scheme. It is very probably not Alice Bailey who did this, but that it was the idea of the Tibetan who dictated this stuff.

Whenever it comes to structures or models there is some appropriate thing in it. This is done with intention in order to hinder the pure logical intellect – to put up something. So you are forced to sort of go deeply into it, also with intuition, with meditation, and deep sort of mentally and spiritually hammering about it, and slowly sink into it. The Tibetan wanted this process, and he describes it in many places. His trick was to constantly put in things that are not logically right.

In fact Alice Bailey had no notion of astrology. She mixed up for instance Mercury and Venus. She had the wrong definitions. She got some faint definitions from Dane Rudyar, who was a friend of hers, but she didn't know anything about it, and she mixed up those two. That additionally makes for a distortion.

Now there is a further thing to think of. What Louise presented here were different frames on different levels. Now wherever you stand with your mind, on which level you stand, makes you look at things differently. For instance, the Sun in one point was quoted to be second ray; in another reference frame Louise said it's fourth ray; but then suddenly in still another frame humanity was fourth ray. All these remarks are right, but they are seen from different levels.

If I look from the level of humanity the Sun for me is fourth ray; if I look down from the Sun to humanity, humanity is fourth ray, and so on. It's a question of proportion and perspective from where you've got or from where you look. That's the point. If you try to find the logic of the system of esoteric learning and knowing you will constantly have a high complexity of views from different levels which you have to sort out. You cannot just make it mental.

For instance, later I will present you with how to find the rays out from the chart. This is then a model that is strictly seen from the level of human personality. Whatever apparent contradiction you find to other remarks that Louise said, or that the Tibetan said or etc, is not in contradiction to that. For the rays which you want to find out about personalities of human character that is the yardstick.

So, it's all a question of relationship from where, and that's the puzzling thing to a strict logical mind. Somebody who only thinks logically will ever get puzzled by such changing viewpoints, where the same structure suddenly looks all different.

4

Finding the Rays in your Chart

Bruno Huber

Personality Rays

• Personality Ray •
• Example - Bruno Huber •
• Rays of the Three Bodies •
• Combinations of Rays •
• Questions •
• Example – Albert Einstein •
• The Moon Nodes and the Rays •
• Questions •

Soul Ray

• Soul Consciousness •
• The Soul Ray • The Causal Body •
• Primary Rules – Major Ray •
• Secondary Rule – Minor Ray •
• Questions •
• Summarising the Rays •

Discovery of the Method of Finding the Rays

The Seven Rays in the Individual Horoscope

Personality Ray
shown by the signs on the main house cusps.

Find out the CROSSES at the two Main Axes: AC/DC & MC/IC:
- if both are in the same cross, it is a Major Ray
- if you find different crosses, it is a Minor Ray

Major Ray		Minor Ray	
Cardinal:	Ray 1	Cardinal + Fixed:	Ray 4
Fixed:	Ray 3	Fixed + Mutable:	Ray 5
Mutable:	Ray 2	Mutable + Cardinal:	Ray 6

If AC or MC is in a border degree (29°– 1° of sign): Ray 7

Body Rays

			Etheric Level		
Mental	Sun	Mind	Manas	Uranus	Meditation
Astral	Moon	Feeling	Buddhi	Neptune	Identification
Physical	Saturn	Body	Atma	Pluto	Contemplation

If planet is in sign of main cusp, take the crosses:
   Cardinal: Ray 1   Fixed: Ray 3   Mutable: Ray 2

If not in contact with main cusp, take the temperaments:
   Water: Ray 4   Air: Ray 5   Fire: Ray 6   Earth: Ray 7

Notes

The etheric is not an independent body (aura), but consists of the 3 subtler of the seven sublevels of the physical plane. Through these Uranus, Neptune and Pluto can become the etheric entrances to the levels of the soul. If not cultivated they are automatic antennae for the ongoings in the surrounding world and also function as channels to the Collective Unconscious.

Intercepted signs and Low Point planets are possibilities of admission to the soul (ray of the soul may come through). If not realized (over compensation), the respective house may lead to suffering or failure.

Cuspal planets tend to over-identify with wordly success (extraversion; Karma?).

Signs with two axes imply overexploitation of energies because of compulsive efficiency (self examination of motivation necessary) incentive to grow, "stimulus to evolution".

Figure 4.1 Personality and Body Rays

Personality Rays

Now we come down to the nitty gritty – how to find out your rays from the chart. It's a bit of an intricate system and requires some new ways of looking at the chart.

First, let's discriminate – we have several different rays in the whole of a personality that can be very different in their qualities. There are three major rays and four minor rays and there is a certain familiarity between some rays, a certain grouping. It's very simple to know – rays 1, 3, 5 and 7 go well together, and rays 2, 4 and 6 go well together.

So if you have a 5 and a 6 this doesn't easily fit. Whilst if you have a 4 and a 6 that fits easier. It's a very simple scheme. Just the even and odd numbers.

Personality Ray

Now, looking at a chart we want to know the personality ray – that is the totality of personality, which has its own ray. We will come later to the rays for each of the three bodies – the mental, emotional and physical bodies.

The method is shown in figure 4.1. The first thing to do is to look at the angles in the chart – AC, DC, MC and IC. Look to see in which cross these four angles stand. Now you have two possibilities, either the axes of the two angles are nearly at right angles to each other and therefore in the same cross, or you have a situation where they are not nearly at right angles and the two axes are in different crosses.[1]

If both axes are in the same cross you get a major ray 1, 2 or 3. If they are in two different crosses then you get a minor ray 4,5,6 or 7.

Major Personality Ray

If you have both axes in the same cross your personality ray will be either 1, if it's cardinal, 2 if it's mutable, or 3 if it's fixed.

Intercepted signs don't matter. The important thing is in which signs, and therefore in which crosses, the angles stand.

This is important because it shows that the personality ray is based on the four angles. And what does it show? It shows the world into which you have been born. Angles are functions of the house system, and the house system indicates surroundings, not the surrounding itself but your sensitivity to the surroundings. You are selective. When you were born you selected a certain surrounding by the sheer act of being born, because you were born into that particular surrounding.

That's the first and major imprint on the personality, one that lasts for life, for sure. But it's not very conscious because this surrounding is a big lump of separate factors that come together and make a certain atmosphere so to speak – the general atmosphere into which you are embedded for the first years of your life at least. And this is an imprint on your personality consciousness that goes deep down, and is afterwards little or not conscious. But it leads you through life much more that you ever think.

It's not the same as, for instance, the aspect structure that represents a motivation or purpose that you brought with you. What you see now with these angles is what you perceived first, so that on entry to this world it was your clue as to how to handle this world. It's a very basic, but also very general clue, and that's why it's not so conscious. There's too much in it to enable you to perceive it clearly. So you just have a basic summary quality.

Minor Personality Ray

If the axes of the main angles fall into different crosses you have one of the minor rays. With one axis in cardinal and and the other in fixed signs then it's the fourth ray. With fixed and mutable combined then it's the fifth ray, and with mutable and cardinal it's the sixth ray.

Now, from what you know already about these rays and their qualities, try to understand for yourself that combining the qualities of cardinal and fixed make for a fourth ray. Cardinal is active, going at things; fixed is the opposite, holding what's there. This is a strong contradiction so, in order to get that together, you have to develop a strong harmonic sense, to get those extreme polarities together. Right? That's the way it functions. With the rest it's the same. Try to do that, try to think it out, how it comes about.

For instance, fixed and mutable makes for the fifth ray, and the combination of mutable and cardinal makes for the sixth ray. Now there are six rays, which means there is one missing – number seven. It's a special kind and a special rule applies to it.

Example – Bruno Huber – Seventh Ray Personality

It says in Figure 4.1 that if one axis is in a 'border degree' then it's ray 7. I'll show you an instance - my chart (Figure 4.2).

If it were not so I would probably never have found out. You see, one axis, the AC/DC is ¼° into Pisces - actually 13 minutes of arc. So that is a 'border degree'. 0° to 1° and 29° to 30° would be border degrees.

You know that planets, for instance, which come into such border degrees have a lower amount of energy at hand and they experience mixed qualities of the signs involved. Now, if you have AC or MC in a border degree your personality is seventh ray. Think about the fact that the personality ray is an overall quality that goes though your whole life as a largely unconscious and strongly functioning quality.

This means that you have to begin at zero – everything you do, or want to do you have to start from scratch. Begin at zero and build it up

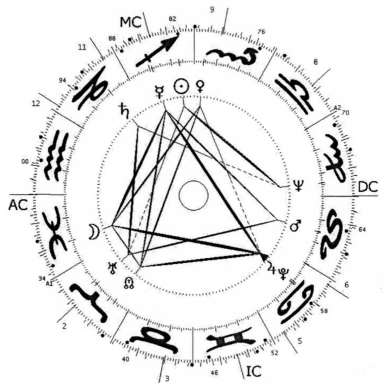

Figure 4.2 Bruno Huber
29.11.1930, 12.55, Zürich/CH
Rays 7 227 (624) 1

entirely on your own, so to speak, entirely out of your own inspiration and insight – and nobody will help you. But that means a completely empty field where you can build up something absolutely new. That's the advantage of it.

The seventh ray is a builder in the sense of bringing a creation to its final form so that it can exist. But it is not the seventh ray that can then take care of it. There are other rays for that. It creates it to the utmost perfection possible – nobody's perfect! Not even the seventh ray! And then it's usable. It can be used, it can be exploited, it can be done by routine. Even routines have to be developed so that they can be handled more easily. It must be something practical in the end.

It was so with Huber astrology. I started from scratch with my astrology. It may be in one big thing you do in your life where, in your

**The Personality Ray is an overall quality
that goes though your whole life as a largely
unconscious and strongly functioning quality**

younger years, you start something from nothing and build it up, or it may be a thousand little things that you start, but every time you start something new you start from scratch. So that's the seventh ray. It's a very tricky one. There is a special magic about it.

Audience: *What is the difference between having a major personality ray and a minor personality ray?*

Bruno Huber: In practice, none! It doesn't matter, but mostly the major rays have more power of 'pushing through'. But they are normally less practical. The minor rays are more in the line of practicality. But that's the only difference you can perceive by living a ray. There might be a spiritual differentiation which I wouldn't really be able to name right away. But I'm sure there must be some, though practically speaking it's not important.

Audience: *You say the minor rays are more practical, does this mean that there is a greater sense of idealism in the major rays?*

Bruno Huber: Idealism is not the right term, but you've got the point. Its more to do with aiming at principles, whilst the minor rays keep talking about 'How to do it'.

Rays of the Three Bodies

Now we go on to the three bodies: mental body, emotional or astral body, and physical body. The rules for the three are the same, in the lower part of Figure 4.1.

The body rays – you can see that the mental body is shown by the Sun, the emotional or astral body is shown by the Moon, and the physical body by Saturn. So look at the three major planets in your chart – where are they?

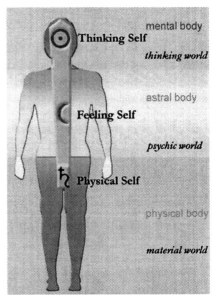

Figure 4.3 The Threefold Personality

Take your Sun. If you find your Sun in a sign where a major axis is located, ie AC, DC, MC, IC, either before or after the Axis (its not important which) – as long as it's in the same sign as a major Axis, then again its a major ray. You take the cross in which that Sun is to identify which major ray. So, again, cardinal is first ray, mutable is second ray and fixed is third ray.

If its not in such a sign, where a main angular cusp is located, and has no relationship, signwise, to a major cusp, then it's a minor ray, and you take the temperament, or element to identify the ray. It's a minor ray. This is the second rule.

Water is 4, Air is 5, Fire is 6 and Earth is 7. You should try and understand this association between the temperaments and the minor rays. From an understanding – not from me telling you! I don't want you saying 'Huber said', you should try to understand it, to feel it.

I don't want you saying 'Huber said', you should try to understand it, to feel it.

Water and fourth ray. Take for example Venus, which is the same principle again. Water, Venus and the fourth ray – always the same principle. And so on. You know the correlation between the temperaments and the planets: Water – Venus, Air – Mercury, Fire – Mars, and Earth – Jupiter. So you have this combination of three, a temperament, a planet, and a ray – they correlate and have the same quality, but of course in different functions. So, if you find your Sun in a sign which has no contact with a major axis, then it's the temperament that gives you the ray, a minor ray.

The same applies for the Moon, the emotional body, and for Saturn, the physical body. And you will see, mostly the three bodies are in different rays. Or maybe two are in the same and the third is in a different ray. It may also occur that they are all in the same. Of course, all possibilities are open.

Combinations of Rays

Now, of course, this may give you certain problems. If you have, say, the mental body in the second ray, with the emotional body on the fifth ray, you can perhaps imagine what kind of problems might occur. Your feeling nature always wants to be very logical and always wants to explain itself – that's fifth ray. But the mental body says 'Oh, that's all too smallish stuff – that's not the right argument, it's bigger, it's wisdom, and anyway I love it.' The second ray is more a feeling quality and not a thinking quality. And the fifth ray is a thinking quality, so they might fight with each other.

Mental body fights with the emotional body! That's sometimes very funny, you know, because they come to different conclusions, or want to go about things in different ways. So it is important to know these rays of the bodies because certain problems can arise from such contradictions, or seeming contradictions.

Nature doesn't really know contradictions in that sense. It knows polarities that can be more difficult to resolve, but then they may be more fruitful and creative, because there is more tension, and then you have to work harder to get something out of it. That makes for more creative possibilities.

For instance, a person with the above combination, second ray mental body, fifth ray emotional body, might go and successfully write fairy tales. Can you imagine what quality could be the synthesis of these two? Because telling tales, putting fantasy into words needs the fifth ray. Mercury, remember, words are his tool. Formulation is his art, but the fantasy comes from the second ray, from the mental body.

The mental body has visions, sees scenery, and then the emotional body has to express it. That's for sure because it is emotion that formulates it, is very flowery, very mobile, proportioned, intensive, etc. And that makes for good fairy tales, right?

Questions

Audience: My Sun is in the twelfth house which is a water house, but the sign it is in is Sagittarius. When I look at the temperament to find out the ray, do I look at the sign or do I look at the house?

Bruno Huber: The sign! Never look at the house quality in this case. Always look at the sign. That is what is important – the sign and the temperament of that sign. The house cusp is not important if it is not a major (angular) cusp. Actually for both considerations, main cusp or not main cusp it is always the sign. In one case its the cross of the sign (major ray) and in the other case its the temperament of the sign. It is always the sign in which the planet falls.

This says a very important thing. If you look at these major planets, the personality planets that make the bodies, we look at them in the sign and the signs indicate something you brought with you to this life. It's not coming from the surroundings, there is no imprint from outside. The major cusps are the strong imprint of the surroundings on you, they give you the personality ray, which is a summing up value. But the bodies are defined by inheritance, the genetic background. That's what you bring with you into life.

The bodies are defined by inheritance, genetic background – what you bring with you into life.

And then the personality is sort of 'put on you', on that total, to give it a link with the world and to give it direction. There are fantastic mechanics at work here, you bring your three bodies to life and the world puts something else on top as a summary quality that tells you how to approach the world, and how to move in the world. The personality ray is not a specialised thing, it's a channeling value that gives you orientation in this world. That's why esotericists say human personality is an illusion.

Bodies are real. You bring them with you, but the personality is an illusion of this world. It only comes as long as you're here. Then it's finished, which of course takes a lot of air out of certain businesses in this world, which build on personality!

**The personality is an illusion of this world.
It only comes as long as you're here.
Then it's finished.**

Audience: If you find a body ray which is the same as the personality ray will they operate easily together?

Bruno Huber: Yes, that's right. If you find the personality ray is the same as the body ray, then you will find that that body will be more controlled by the personality and they will correspond easily because they have the same quality. One could think it over and wonder whether it's not reverse and it's that body which controls the personality! That's also possible, no? This means it could be changing, sometimes the personality rules that body and takes it as a primary tool of self-expression, and in other situations the body takes over and controls the personality, with its own rights and its own needs. This may change within a life, or even with a day it may change because you go into very different situations. There are very interesting stories you can build from that.

Audience: Does this relate to the integration process?

Bruno Huber: Yes, of course. It has strongly to do with that. Using the rays is an entirely new way of looking at people, at personalities. It gives you insights that you cannot otherwise easily gather from the chart.

That's why it also needs new tools, to look for the rays. These rules I have given you now are new to you. You never considered such things, it's not the normal way of looking at a chart, but it's needed for the rays, and the rays therefore give you a still different insight into the personality. You can come to an understanding of certain problems which you won't find or explain with a normal chart reading. So, that's esoteric. You are nearing the answering of the question 'Why?', which you cannot properly make out from the normal chart. So, that's very important.

Audience: Could you say something about the body rays that are on ray 7, which I understand is obviously earth, because something has to be manifested.

Bruno Huber: Yes, I have it there too. Saturn in Capricorn but the MC is not in Capricorn it's in Sagittarius, so it has no connection with a major axis. It's in earth, which makes for seventh ray. Now, this needs bringing down to earth. Bringing things down to absolute reality, manifesting things in a form which stays in the physical world.

Like building up a school. But if you go away it will still go on – if you have done well! Because other people can take it over. There is a form, a structure which can be handled. It is physically existing. If you do well it will be the case. We are faced with that too, you know. We are getting older and we have built up a school for 30 years. We have helped a lot of people to take over – not the school itself in the form that exists legally – but in the same way there will be many little Huber schools, because we have very good teachers now. So it's built into a structure that has physical consistency, that can remain and can be taken over by others.

> We are getting older and have built up a school
> for 30 years. We have helped a lot of people to
> take over. There will be many little Huber schools,
> because we have very good teachers now.

This is one of the main aims of the seventh ray, to produce something that goes beyond the person who has created it, that persists longer and can be used by others – this is very important.

And of course again, for the personal life, it's your physical body that is seventh ray. It means that you have to constantly find your ways of handling your body. You will experience that your body changes politics. It suddenly starts manoeuvering in different ways, and the old yardsticks you used to handle your body don't work any more, or partly don't work any more. You have to find new routines with your body, to handle it well. So these are the people who are no good for doctors because doctors have rules and for them bodies are bodies.

But the seventh ray body is today a different body from yesterday, and the Doctor will say 'Why do you now behave so?' or 'These symptoms are no good, they don't fit'. I mean, I know I've over-expressed this now, but it's a rule of such bodies that they are fluid, moving through all kinds of possibilities of physical existence. They may change their rhythm, their ways of eating and sleeping and all that stuff that's so basic to the physical body. So, you'd better follow it – find out day by day, so to speak. That's a very personal side of that seventh ray body. But they are that fluid because they have to adapt to the constantly changing conditions of the world, in order to be fit to always, at any given moment, create that which now fits and works.

If you're producing something which you've probably worked on for years and it's still at the stage when you first started to work on it, then you're out of time. You miss because you're creating something for yesterday, not for today. That's why it has to be fluid, changeable, adaptable – and you must not mix that up with mutable or the mutable cross. It's very rational and the mutable cross is not very rational. We very often call it irrational because it has ideas and is more at home in the business of consciousness and fantasies and stuff like this. It reacts to changing situations in a similar way to the seventh ray, but doesn't normally take it physically, rather takes it as an emotional or consciousness function. The seventh ray makes everything physical. Everything must at least be thinkable with your physical brain.

Audience: *It seems to me that the seventh ray is like a cutting edge, a leading edge, which is looking for something new all the time.*

Bruno Huber: Yes, you must never get stuck, or your shouldn't! If you present something of yesterday you're off the beam, and people will tell you. If it's the Sun they **will** tell you, and that's the difference from the physical body, they won't tell you, though they might object that you have changed again!

Audience: *When I worked out the personality ray I got a five which I quarrel with because I know I have a seventh ray personality. Then I went back to what you said originally, which was to do with how the entity enters the world. So I then flashed back to early childhood and I can quite see that I as a youngster would have a ray five, but I have moved on to another ray.*

Bruno Huber: You certainly have, though there must be some fifth ray still there. But you handle it in a progressively different way. A ray can change in a lifetime but these are things we cannot read from the chart. A change would happen mostly due to your own work in raising your consciousness. You're striving towards more understanding, and so on, so changes may come about. More often in body areas, less often in the personality, and hardly visible at the soul level. Those changes take lives, not one life. A soul has a much longer life than a personality.

Audience: *If you have two people in a relationship, or several people working together as a team, could it be useful to look at their rays to see how they would interact?*

Bruno Huber: Sure! Though of course you should not use normal evaluations such as sympathy and harmony and stuff like this, but rather how do they match in a very neutral way, so to speak. Any ray will go with any other ray in principle, but you can evaluate. Suppose you find two astral bodies on the same ray or at least on the same quality line, that is both having, for instance, odd number rays, then the going is easier, the understanding is more straightforward.

Whereas if the rays are on two different lines then there's always some translation work to be done, or explanation or definition. In some situations this makes it difficult and a bit more complicated. But the rays mustn't tell you 'this is good or bad', it should tell you how it is so you know what you're faced with. That's the important thing, not an evaluation of whether it's easier, or right or wrong and so on. That's not what it's all about – the rays don't tell that.

Rays have no value judgement as a possibility. They are quality measurements, not quantity, not empathy, or anything like that – they are just qualities, basic principle qualities – seven only. They permeate the whole world, they permeate every action or function you can think of, so value judgements are absolutely off the beam. Don't try to say 'Oh, that's good' or anything like that.

If you find two Moons in the same sign then you might say 'Fabulous, fabulous', though in fact it might not be fabulous. It may be very heavy, it depends on the situation, on how willing the two personalities are to use that link-up, and what they make of it. So, that's very important – not to value judge with the rays.

Audience: *Is the personality ray what we've come in to this life to learn about? For instance if its ray 2 have we come here to learn about the qualities of love?*

Bruno Huber: Surely there is learning there but this is not the aim of it. The aim is that, in case you have a situation that might get out of control, or is overwhelming and you need some additional energy to handle the situation in the right way then this personality ray will turn up and function. Normally you don't use the personality ray consciously, because mostly you're not aware of it. But in difficult situations it turns up by itself and gives you a hand. And there is learning in that. Each time it functions in this way you learn something more, but that's not the aim of it. The aim is that, as a personality, you can survive in this world and take a path that fits that quality of your personality, and gives it a certain fulfilment in this world.

This is what I would call a passive way of learning, an automatic learning – you can't help it. You learn something by every experience you have with that quality.

Audience: I would want to add something there – guides, spiritual guides – are they in any way connected to the tasks of the personality ray?

Bruno Huber: Well, there are different possible guides on different levels which are difficult to discriminate from a personality consciousness. But that's one possibility, that you suddenly, by way of your personality ray, know in a situation that you should do so and so. Or that's not important. This may amount to the impression of a vision of sorts, and then you have the feeling that a guide gave you that direction.

But there are also guides on higher levels that may come through and feel the same way to you. The personality is not so easily equipped to discriminate. But so what? I mean, what the personality ray tells you, or makes you able to do, is anyway good! Whether you call it a guide or not is not important because it helps you a few steps further on your way.

Audience: I have a first ray Moon in the twelfth house. It feels difficult being in the environment of the twelfth house.

Bruno Huber: Well of course, because that Moon has got little or no education of manifestation towards the outside. As a child you have been left on your own, too much, eh? You have been told too little on how to handle the world, so of course it's right to say the first ray is not so easy to work out. In a way, you always have to shout, symbolically speaking. To make yourself perceived by the surroundings you have to do something special. But the first ray also gives you the power to do it, strong pushing through.

Anyway the twelfth house doesn't demand, say, physical manifestation, but only to be heard, for instance, or to be seen. That's enough, to impress, because it is an impress function to give pushes to certain people or to certain situations. So, that should work.

It's not the type of, say, 'standing on a stage' behaviour. It's working from behind, so to speak. But that's the demand of the twelfth house, not to appear on the stage, but rather make things move. Anyway, for the twelfth house that's always true. With the first ray you can push through – sort of 'get' the person – 'Hey, listen to me'.

Example – Albert Einstein

Now, lets look at one example of how this works in the chart of Albert Einstein (Figure 4.3).

First the personality. We have MC in Pisces, mutable cross and AC in Cancer on the cardinal cross – two different crosses so it's a minor ray – cardinal and mutable – sixth ray. What does this mean? His personality must function in a sixth ray way.

You know what Einstein did? But it's a question of how he did it, because it's a minor ray. How did he do it? I mean everybody knows the formula now – you even see it on posters! But how did he do it? He was working as an officer in the Patent Agency, he had to check if everything was right with patent applications that came in, and he found it very dull. So he looked for that famous formula that could sort of explain the world, make understood why the world 'ticked'!

And he took many years. All the time nobody knew what he was doing. But he was going strong on it, till he had it. Then he came out with it and the whole academic world said 'Ah Ha'. Nothing more! It took 25 years of telling people and lecturing all over the world, trying to convince people, with his flamboyant and enthusiastic way of being all for it – you know sixth ray stuff – until it reached general recognition. Nowadays everybody loves to speak about Einstein, as though they'd discovered the formula for themselves!

That's the function of the sixth ray, to get an idea and then go at it with full conviction and with all the power of your psyche, and stick to it until you have it. And then go through and push it and push it, until finally it gets accepted. It needs a lot of commitment, being eaten up by it, obsession in a way.

Audience: *Would that be Uranus in that Intuition Quadrant? Because I remember reading that he said that he was lying underneath a tree when he had this hunch, and it was from then that he went on to finalise the formula.*

Bruno Huber: Well, that's the special tool then. Uranus is the Tension Ruler of the whole structure. It stands out, so that's right. That's the tool for it. But the sixth ray tells him that he must stick to it until he solved it. It took him something like 30 or 40 years, from the beginning of the original vision to acceptance by the world. But he stuck to it. That's what the sixth ray can do. So he did something Uranian, which you would probably expect more from the seventh or fifth ray. That's what he did, but he did it in a sixth ray manner. If he only had the Uranus stuff it would not have been enough. He would probably have given up long before he succeeded in even finding the formula.

He also has the Sun in Pisces on the MC – second ray. The Moon is also in a mutable sign, but no relation to a major axis so it's the fire temperament – which is sixth ray. And Saturn in the fire sign Aries, no

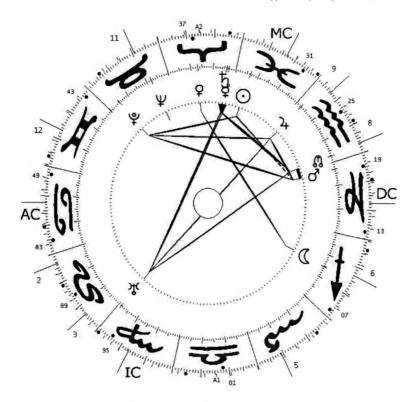

Figure 4.3 Albert Einstein
14.03.1789, 14.30, Ulm/D
Rays: 6 266 (277) 3

link with a major axis so, once again it's the fire which counts, another sixth ray. Quite a sixth ray package this man had! Three times sixth ray, amongst them personality ray, and then a mental body which works with the qualities of love and wisdom. That's why in the end he said 'I shouldn't have done it'.

That's my wording but that's what he meant, because from that came the atomic bomb. He made it possible, but thought it absolutely inhuman – typical second ray. Inconceivable that what I did enabled people make the atom bomb to kill thousands and thousands of people. It nearly killed him. That was the reaction of a second ray to the result of sixth ray engagement, and pushing, and working hard, and sticking with it. In the end he has to say 'My wisdom says it's no good'. That's hard, but such things happen.

We sometimes have to find contradictions in ourselves that are not easy to solve. But again, try not to evaluate in the sense that it is good or bad. Try to find out what it brought, what it realised in the world, what it added to the world, because the energies of all the rays want to create something in the world, want to move the world, want to form the world. That's the positive aim.

All the rays have destructive sides. All the rays can also destroy, can kill if it's necessary that something must get through for the future, in the course of development of humanity, society, and so on. So value judgements are off the beam again. If Einstein was nearly depressive at the end that was his problem. He had to do that, we needed that, not only for making atom bombs. We needed that for science, and its part of progress into, for instance, very deep space, and so on. All the highly complicated calculations that astronomers make today wouldn't be possible without Einstein.

And many inventions made since are based on that formula. OK, the atom bomb was one result, but many other results were more positive, or even very positive, and in summation much more than that atom bomb.

That's how history judges things. Rays have to make something come to life, create something, and they may destroy. As nature shows us clearly, nature kills, but not by aiming at killing but by aiming at growing. So the minor things have no space any more, it's the sound things that grow. That's the rule of nature. Nature doesn't kill, but it outgrows. And so with the rays – they follow this absolute rule. If it's time for something to happen now, or to be created, there's no way of stopping this – and some things have to get out of the way.

To us this may appear as death, or even as bad killing, or whatever, but this is too small a scale that we use there. Esoteric thinking, generally, is always on a large scale, not on a small personal scale. It hurts me, or something like that, which is sometimes still difficult to bear.

Einstein is a nice example of a seemingly very one-sided person, in a way. But there is his mental ray which strongly contradicts the other three rays. This second ray, the mental ray, also hindered him to a certain degree – for instance stopping him from coming out too early with a not-quite-finished thing. It must be perfect because it must not hurt or do harm, that is what the second ray demands. It must be human, it must be wise, therefore this elongated the process. It had to be driven to absolute perfection in order to have its way out in the world, and this took a lot of time.

Audience: If you're looking at a chart and the planets and how they operate in the signs and houses and so on, does the information you then get from the rays always give added information that is nearly always supportive or complementary, or can there sometimes be a conflict.

Bruno Huber: Complementary in a way, but this is a difficult term because the rays are on a different level to what the chart says. The chart has to do with the concrete personality in this world; the rays say

'What's behind it, what is driving this personality on a purpose level?' So the rays give us a further insight, not on the same level but from a level 'above'. This is a different kind of judgement. It brings out meaning. Information on the personality level may be functional – you can define, name and function with it. The rays give an understanding of why that person is built that way. Therefore many insights which you make from the chart are complementary. Others may be contradictory and may pose a problem, which you have to solve in order to live your own real life.

The idea from the rays point of view is that your life should be a self-expression of your inner being. Not of your outer personality as it's judged and valued by the surroundings, but rather of your own qualities that you can say 'Yes, that's me', and that should have expression. The rays can help you because you understand that 'inner me' better. It gives a quality evaluation, not a quantitive evaluation as the world normally does: 'He's so rich', 'He's so powerful' etc. These are value judgements of a quantitive way of thinking, which is normal in our world. The rays give qualities, and therefore meaning and understanding as to why the personality is built that way, as shown in the chart.

> **The idea is that your life should be a self-expression of your inner being. Not of your outer personality.**

The Moon Nodes and the Rays

There's one further thing to add. We can look at the Moon Node ray-wise as well, but this is a simple business. The ray of the Node is a summary value. As you know, we do a Moon Node chart, which sums up past lives – not a particular life, but all the past is summed up there. What remains of your deeds and strivings, whether good or bad, is marked there as qualities that you have dealt with.

In the North Node one could say we have the dharma – that is all the "goodies" that you have worked out may be called upon there. That's why the Node functions as a help when you are in difficulties or insecure about decisions etc. You look at the North Node, and it tells you "Do this!" and you get further. That's a very simple clue to it.

The South Node also shows "goodies" of the past, but goodies you shouldn't rely on, because if you indulge in them, you will get stuck. It's mostly perceived as a very easy way, particularly by people who have a planet there, in opposition to the North Node. It's easy to go there, and to function, but you shouldn't indulge in that. It's good for a holiday, for relaxation, but it's not good for extended use because it makes you stuck. It hinders your development. So you can use it when you have a need for it, but you shouldn't be proud of it or indulge in it.

So in this respect now, with the rays, the North Node is a very simple statement of quality that is there at hand from your past, and it can tell you, in cases of difficulty, use this ray quality. The same way as we normally already use it, but it's only useful to use the major rays for that.

The North Node is a simple statement of quality that is there at hand from your past.

The actual finding of the ray is simple – you just look in which cross the Node stands, in which cross of the sign. It's either cardinal fixed or mutable, so it's first, second or third ray. Forget about the minor rays. They would complicate the business and would not give you more information.

The chart can give you the practical things which follow from looking at the Node – it shows the Node in a certain house, then in a certain sign, and there are aspects that can tell you a further story, how to go about things practically. In extreme situations in life, when things really get hard and tough and seemingly insurmountable, then you should use the quality of that major ray that the Node indicates.

For instance, I have no first ray in my chart. But in a few cases in my life, when things were really confused I suddenly started using first ray power, and it worked! Louise can tell you, it works!

Use that quality if things really go wrong, or really are absolutely blocked and you can't get through. Use that quality. Don't think in terms of energy, but think of the quality of that major ray which you have at hand there. If you understand that quality, suddenly things will loosen up and you will get through.

That's what it's good for – it's just a general qualitative help, not quantitative. The quantitative things you can draw from the chart and the position of the Node there.

Questions

Audience: My North Node's in Scorpio and I'm looking at the fixed cross?

Bruno Huber: Yes, that's right. The house doesn't matter. The house matters when you go to the Node in your chart, where it is very important because it gives you practical clues of what to do. The house gives you the practical know-how, so to speak, while the ray, which is on a major axis, only tells you the quality which now is important. You are up against an insurmountable situation because your attitude is not the right one. You have to rearrange your attitude, the quality of your present being. That has to be in line with the nodal ray, and then it works. Then things loosen up, and you find ways, and you can make decisions.

Audience: What happens if the North Node is 29 degrees 47 minutes in one sign. Do you use the qualities of both?

Bruno Huber: You can be exact here, because it's a qualitative thing and has nothing to do with amounts of energy available.

Audience: What happens if you have a planet conjunct the North Node - can that help?

Bruno Huber: It will help, of course.

Audience: I don't understand, because surely the South Node will have the same, and that's where you said to watch out that you don't get stuck.

Bruno Huber: Yes, that's why the North Node is a summing up, also of the South Node which belongs to it. It's one system, it's in the same cross. Again it's not a question of how you do it, because it might become dangerous if you have a planet on the South Node, in opposition to the North Node. That's not the question – the question is the quality of that cross, or rather of that ray. That quality is important, not as a way of doing, but a question of my attitude. How I have to re-regulate my consciousness to be on the right wavelength, so to speak.

Audience: We begin an adjustment through the ray, and the planets help to fulfil that.

Bruno Huber: Right. Generally the chart, with the positioning of the North Node by house and sign, aspects, planets that work with the aspects etc., gives you the practical clues to what to actually do.

Audience: The way you stated that the Node is where we look for what to do next, it looks like, from an evolutionary point of view, the most important point in the chart – because the Sun and Moon and Saturn have to conform to the voice of the Node.

Bruno Huber: Yes, in a way that's right. They are tools, but of course, Sun, Moon and Saturn are "own" tools that you have brought with you.

Audience: From an evolutionary point of view, not like from a level of working now on the integration of the ego planets.

Bruno Huber: It's above it. Seen that way, it's more important because it's superseding the rulings of the planets. But of course it's only quality, it's not action, it's not form that you deal with – it's an attitude, of your mind or your consciousness.

The Soul Ray

The Aspect structure shows the Causal Body

Form key	Line	1
	Triangle	2
	Quadrangle or Polygon	3
Colour key	Red	1
	Green	2
	Blue	3

Primary Rules

If one of the following rules applies, the soul corresponds to a major ray (1,2,3):

Whole of Aspect structure	Ray
one-coloured	Ray 1
two-coloured	Ray 2
figures of ALL 3 TYPES	Ray 3
one colour DOMINANT	Ray according to **Colour key**
whole form clearly 1 TYPE	Ray according to **Form key**

Definitions:

one-coloured: may include 1 other colour (if up to 7 aspects in total);
may include 2 other colours (if more than 7 aspects in total)
two-coloured: 1 colour is totally missing.
Figures of ALL 3 TYPES:
if all three form types are contained in the structure.
one colour DOMINANT:
if 50% or more of the aspects have same colour (colour key)

Secondary Rule

If none of the above rules fits, then add form key + colour key and find minor ray:

POINTS correspond to RAY

6	4
5	5
4	6
3	7
(exception) (2)	(1)

Nota Bene: The rules given here for the Soul Ray are by no means final. There may be hesitations in judging, and therefore mistrust in the rules given. In the face of the supreme importance of the matter to judge, this is fine, as it is doubtful that mathematical measurement could be an adequate means. This may set you to an in-depth search of self-discovery, which can last your entire life.

Figure 4.4 Finding the Soul Ray

The Soul Ray

Soul Consciousness

Now we consider the soul. This is not so clear! The soul is a the term largely used in esoteric writings, and is said to live on it's own level. Of course soul consciousness is difficult to have with your daily consciousness. Mostly people use forms of meditation to try to get through to that consciousness, and it's absolutely right – the soul is on a level that is difficult to conceive of from a normal human framework of thinking, because our thinking is tied to material, realistic things of this world. So the soul lives on its own level, in it's own world, or whatever the terminology will be. The meaning is that it's difficult to get there with our daily consciousness.

Soul Infused Personality

There is the other term that Alice Bailey uses often – a "soul infused personality". It refers to persons who are ruled by their soul – their thinking, feeling, and physical behaviour are infused by soul quality, consciousness, will etc.

Soul Ray

The soul has its own ray, but it is inconceivable that sheer mathematical rules can pinpoint that quality. I've tried for something like 30 years to pinpoint that soul ray. I haven't been able to. I have nearing values, which are in Figure 4.4. Using these rules, which are not easy – they are difficult judgements to make – you may come to a conclusion where you have a contradiction on your hands.

So what? I mean, if your consciousness is not yet prepared enough to understand soul quality, then you will get some sort of difficulty in pinpointing the ray, which is not a bad sign! It's a rather normal human state of being! Our consciousness is constantly tied down to this world, day by day, hour by hour, minute by minute, so it's difficult to step out and look at things from such an aloof point of view.

Now I explain these rules.

Form Key and Colour Key

The first thing in Figure 4.4 is two keys – a *form key* and a *colour key*. You know that our charts show aspect colours. This is not for the fun of it, or to give manufacturers of coloured pencils some work, or to make computer programming more difficult!

The soul has its own Ray, but it is inconceivable that sheer mathematical rules can pinpoint that quality

The Causal Body

As the sentence at the top of Figure 4.4 says, the aspect structure shows the "causal body", which I will explain using Figure 2.3 Amphora on page 19.

You recall the realm of personality generally from the bottom of the Amphora up to the level of concrete mind. With some people, this upper line would be a bit lower, with others, a bit higher, but it's in that area, where our daily thinking can work and function.

As already said, you can be happy in life with the possibilities within there, you can get rich and powerful in worldly terms. But it is only in the higher levels that spiritual qualities begin to come into consciousness, in the upper mental level of abstract thinking, Manas, in the Buddhi level and in the Atma level – the three aspects of the soul[2]. Anything spiritual is always trinity.

You have a still higher entity above, the Monad, which is again a trinity, but of a still higher level. With this we can forget about charts and trying to get rays and stuff. It's much higher and there is no way our measuring mind can try to get hold of it; it's way out.

Coming back to the soul, as we know from esoteric writings, the soul remains on its own level. It doesn't incarnate itself because it is not in a state of being. It is not constructed to survive in this world. It has no tools for this world. It is a pure entity of consciousness on its own level.

We can draw from that, if we're lucky, if we're successfully meditating and so on, but the soul itself cannot do anything in the world. By going into an incarnation, it creates a causal body. "Causal" means a body that creates – causes – personality in the world. A tool that in essence lives a number of incarnations, but then at one given point, that also has to be dissolved in order to get further, and a new causal body has to be built. In other words, it is partly formal in its nature, and we can see this formality in the aspect structure. The aspect structure is a picturing of the causal body.

This is again a trinity. It contains the three so-called permanent atoms of the three personality levels, which are located on the highest sub-level of each of the three personality levels. They are nourished, stimulated and directed from the causal body. The causal body is therefore what interests us, because this is a mirroring of the soul.

The causal body persists for a certain number of incarnations. We don't know exactly how many. It is the entity that causes each next incarnation, prepares it, chooses the possibilities and conditions needed for the next step in evolution.

Audience: *The Akashic records come to mind. Is it these that hold form?*

Bruno Huber: No, the Akashic Chronicles are found on physical etheric levels, in the etheric body of the planet. This is where the personal aura is also to be found. The causal body is not there, because that is an absolutely individual quality, on an individual level. The Akashic Chronicles are a collective thing.

Let's come back to that copy, in a way a thinned-down copy, of the soul – or we could call it a soul-quality combination that is also clad into formal material that can have effect in this world. It's the aspect structure that shows us these very individual qualities.

That's why, in the aspect structure we have that purpose of this life. We can understand why this person is built that way now in this incarnation, what meaning that has and where that drives towards – and what is the needed quality of development on its way forward in it's own evolution.

Going back to the rules in Figure 4.4, we're dealing entirely with the aspect structure. Nothing else interests us, because that's the only "hold" we can get on the soul in the chart. To make that clear, it's not the soul itself, it's its mirroring in the causal body.

Now we can use *form key* and *colour key* – the two things that make up the aspect structure. With the form key, Linear aspect patterns are first ray, Triangular patterns are second and Quadrangular patterns are third ray. With the colour key, red is first ray, green is second ray, blue is third ray.

These are clues, but there are superseding rules which, if they apply, it may be that!

The aspect structure is a picturing of the causal body.
The causal body is a mirroring of the soul. That's why,
in the aspect structure we have the purpose of this life.

Primary Rules – Major Ray

In Figure 4.4 there are five primary rules which, if satisfied in the chart, indicate the major ray of the soul. Otherwise the soul can be on any ray, and then we have to work with the clues in the secondary rules.

Let's look at these funny rules, which may seem very unsystematic. There's no system visible; they seem sort of accidental. I cannot tell you how long I needed to find these accidents!

One-coloured rule

The first primary rule relates to a one-coloured aspect structure. 'One colour' means that it may include one other colour. Say there are all red aspects, and there is just one blue, then it can be considered as 'one colour'. If there are more than seven aspects, there can even be two other-coloured aspects, and it's still considered to be a one-coloured structure. That will make for a first ray, which is logical in that you have one dominating colour!

Colours make for life quality! Forms make for working with life forms – there's a difference. So a red, one-coloured aspect structure is a simple hammer, and that might apply to the first ray! There is enormous energy there – strong, pushing-through energy. The first ray doesn't constantly work, it works "in case" – in case it's needed, but then with full power, full drive, and mostly with success.

So a first ray soul will probably, in the extreme case, only actually function through with it's hammer once in a lifetime. More is not necessarily needed in some cases; in others it may come more often. Very seldom do people with first ray soul quality have it constantly coming through. I think they would be unbearable for humanity! They would be so pushy, unbearable.

Two-coloured rule

Two coloured means one colour is completely missing. The second ray is indicated here. It's very sharp! With the first ray, one thinks it's very sharp, but no, there's some space to manoeuvre. One aspect may have a different colour, but two-coloured must be two-coloured, no third colour. The second ray, that feels so soft, is very tough in saying "no". So it's just two colours: red and blue, red and green, green and blue – three possibilities that are always second ray.

Figures of all three types

The next is not three-coloured – that would be logical! One-coloured, two-coloured, three-coloured. No, forget it, because most horoscopes show three colours.

No this refers to figures contained within the whole aspect structure being of three types: that is, there are linear elements, triangles and quadrangles or polygons. If all three types of form exist in the aspect structure, then it's a third ray. But the three types must be clearly identifiable. Don't take a quadrangular structure and then take it apart to have a triangle as well – that's cheating!

One colour dominant

Next rule – one colour is dominant. "If 50% or more of all the existing aspects in the structure have the same colour." It's like the shares in a company. If one has 51% he rules the business! He needs only 50%, that's enough. Then with this dominant colour you take the *colour key* to find the ray. So 50% of blue aspects would indicate third ray.

Whole form clearly one type

The final primary rule is already a bit diffuse, because it's diffuse to see. If you look at the chart from a distance, or screw up your eyes so you don't see sharply anymore, then you see the entire form. Then you don't see the details and how exact aspects go to each other, just a rough form. If that rough form looks quite clearly either linear, or triangular or quadrangular/polygonal to you, then you use the *form key*. For example a clearly quadrangular form would be ray 3.

This is clearly somewhat diffuse because it's a question of how you judge it with your eyes.

I have not found further rules. These primary rules are pretty precise in definition. The last one is already dependent on the onlooker. One person would say it's a quadrangle, another would say "mmm, not really, not at all, no, no, not a quadrangle, it's another figure". It's a question of judgement.

But look at the whole thing from a distance – two metres or so. Or screw your eyes up. You don't see sharply any more, it's darker than if you have your eyes open, and then you will see the figure more clearly. You miss the details. That would be the right way to use this rule properly.

Secondary Rule

If none of this applies, then we have the secondary rule, using the two keys: *form key* and *colour key*. Again this is not definite and sharp, it is a question of judgement. You have to look at the chart again, diffuse – what could it be as a whole?

Now you could say "Well, as a whole it's not clear, it's so many different things, it's pretty spread out, but probably it might be that, for instance, there's a pretty disparate figure, biggish all round but with a lot of triangles in it, single figures that are triangles". Then the triangle is dominant in that structure, and you could say "OK, triangle". That would be second ray. But in this case, it's not yet the ray, it's a number, the *form key*, which you later have to add. It's number 2.

Then you look at the colour to find the *colour key*. Again, what colour dominates my view? It mustn't be a dominant colour in the formally defined sense of 50%, but many figures make the impression "Oh, that's more a reddish, or more a greenish or more a bluish colour". It doesn't reach 50% but anyway, for instance, it can be that the blue aspects are very thick lines, and the red and green not so precise with thin lines, and that's why the blue jumps out. Maybe that one triangle or one quadrangle is made of one colour is made of strong lines and jumps out, so that is your evaluation. You can take the colour that jumps at your eye at the first look, by first impression.

Add the *colour key* to the *form key*, and you have a translation table at the bottom of Figure 4.4. The number on the left is the points you have reached by addition, and on the right you have the respective ray. These are all minor rays.

There is, of course, an exception, as to many rules! Addition can be 1+1=2, and that gives the major ray 1.

Questions

Audience: When you were talking about the colour, you said which colour actually looks the most dominant not in terms of the ratio, not in terms of the ideal ratio? I mean, when you're looking at a chart normally you look at the ideal ratio.

Bruno Huber: No, don't look at the numbers of coloured aspects, look with your eyes, because it can be one figure, or two or three aspects out of ten, or fifteen, that stand out because they are so thick and have the same colour. Then the picture is dominated by that colour visually. Don't go for counting the numbers of red, blue and green aspects. That would be misleading.

Audience: If you have figures of all three types and one colour dominant, would one take precedence over the other?

Bruno Huber: Yes, that's one of those "un-sharp" areas! As I warned you beforehand, this is a trial to get some hold of a soul quality, which is, in itself, a doubtful undertaking. By sheer mechanics, which our mind can do, this is not the way of consciousness of the soul, therefore you might get it, but how far you get it is not sure, not safely establishable. It gives you a clue for which direction to look for your soul quality.

It helps you, but it may be misleading. In rare cases, as far as I have found up until now, it may be misleading, but then we have that case, which you mention, that two of the major rules apply. This may mean something else, that is that you are probably changing soul ray. This is taking several lives, I am sure. You're under process, therefore you still have some of the old soul ray and you already have some of the new soul ray, and they show both.

So then it's your decision from which ray to change to which ray! It doesn't say from the rules – that's all I can say to that.

The soul changes its way slowly, slowly though the experience of a number of lives and therefore you're in a suspension of decision for several lives! And it's your choice, but not of the little personality, only for that life it may be this choice. It's a choice of your soul, sort of meditating constantly on the next ray to take. So from your day-by-day consciousness you are only partly in this business.

Audience: *If you look at a whole chart with a large quadrangular aspect figure, and you also have a couple of small linear aspects to the side, would you say that the quadrangle becomes dominant and clearly one type?*

Bruno Huber: Yes, again close your eyes partly, or look at a distance, and look at what dominates your vision. Normally if you have a quadrangle and other small things, the quadrangle stands out – that would be your choice. With the aspect structure that you know already from working with charts, you always have the visual angle that can lead you to a judgement, but it all depends on how you look.

Different people look at things differently, and you probably know for yourself that if you talked about a certain chart with other students, you would probably hear "No, I think it's not that – it's this", and you thought it was that! So it's a question of how do you look, how do you perceive visually?

This "un-sharp" business in reality has to do with the subjectivity of the human being. I look, for instance, at my chart with my eyes. Somebody else looks at my chart looks with their eyes. If there is no chart, they look at me with their own eyes and judge me differently from how I judge myself. So that's human!

Finally, in the soul area, it's only my judgement that really counts. Even if it's wrong, it counts, because it will need my next step, probably for a whole incarnation, and this surely is meaningful, beyond what I can understand.

We are moving in an area where normal human thinking gets to loose ends again and again, and that in itself is meaningful as it pushes me to go deeper, to stick to trying to find out more clearly. That's fabulous! It's a thrust, a push that makes you grow. That's the basic idea. of the whole thing. Esoteric thinking always has to do with development, with growth, with evolution.

Audience: *I suppose that a being with the soul that's moving from second ray to third ray, would then be moving into the New Age, into the rays more consonant with the earth's and humanity's development?*

Bruno Huber: Yes, but if it's vice versa, then it doesn't move out of actuality, but looks at it differently, and probably some souls are needed to look at things differently. It may cause a certain hardship for that person, because he cannot run with the masses. It's very often these people who move the world, or correct something to some degree which, if it were not corrected, would go on.

Audience: When you were talking just now to the lady who asked you about a dominant shape and linear aspects, were you talking about a secondary rule, or a primary rule?

Bruno Huber: Both. Whenever a chart has to be judged, this would be with the rules: "figures of three types" or "whole form clearly one type". If you miss with that, then using the *form key* it's also true. Only with the first four primary rules, do you have clearly defined results; the fifth rule is a judgement.

Audience: It's quite interesting because if you do it with the secondary rule, it will come out to a particular ray, then if you apply the first bits of the primary rule, it's like the sixth going on to the second.

Bruno Huber: If you find a primary rule fulfilled forget about the secondary rule. It's very important – that's why I call it the primary rule! If you find correspondence, and it's fully, clearly there using a primary rule, forget about looking at the secondary rule, because the primary rule overrules.

Audience: I just felt I'd got half of it on the primary rule, so I should stick with secondary because it's only half clear on the primary rule.

Bruno Huber: If the primary rule is not clear, forget about the primary and go the secondary to get more clarity. The rules are easier, wider, and you get something clear. If you go "un-sharp" with the primary rules it would be betraying yourself. So be clear, and clear-cut at least with the first four primary rules. If they are fulfilled, forget about the rest. If they are not clearly fulfilled, forget about those, and go to the secondary. Then you are always as near as possible.

Audience: I've almost got it on the primary rule in two cases, and they both come out on the same ray, but it's not exact, it's very close. They're both coming out in two different definitions but on the same ray, so my feeling is that that's the ray. I could go on to the secondary rule and come up with another one.

Bruno Huber: Yes, that could be, but anyway I say that if the primary rule counts, is fulfilled, forget about the secondary. Spare that work! If you happen to see that it corresponds, it gives you the same result, then it looks very good, I mean very safe in a way. Two different rules saying "yes" to it, OK, fine! It's a confirmation.

Audience: When checking for a one-colour dominance you presumably take all the aspects and ignore the four degree rule? Or would you take that into account?

Bruno Huber: That doesn't count because you have to look "unsharp".

Audience: I find it difficult thinking in terms of consciousness. I experience my surroundings through my personality, so what's the use of the kind of development with both rays and these qualities to the soul? I'm a Taurus - how do you understand it and use it in daily practice? Consciousness is composed of many different parts. It's confusing in a way with your mind or not with your awareness to grasp the soul quality and that ray quality.

Bruno Huber: That's a good point. Let's put it another way, to make simple sense. All these other rays of personality and the bodies are the tools the soul has in this life. So if I try to understand the soul quality, that cannot be for handling purposes, for telling me how to go about things. It is question of influencing my state of mind by a certain quality, which of course, is an aiming quality – "aiming" in terms of evolution of mind. I am on my way to a quality and that quality is clearly named by the soul, because the soul is the collector of all these achievements of growth.

Therefore, looking at the soul ray can help me to permeate my state of consciousness which I have at hand every day, with that aiming quality. It needn't be that I constantly formulate that quality in my mind all day, but I might, for instance, use it in a daily meditation which I do as an aiming quality. Not as a tool to handle the world, because for that I have all these tools which we have dealt with before. It is a quality pervading my consciousness in the course of time. If I keep to it, that makes me react differently with my tools. That's the idea!

> Looking at the soul Ray can help me to permeate
> my state of consciousness with that aiming quality

Summarising the Rays

We have a standard way of summarising the rays. The arrangement is that you write up one number for the soul, then leave a space, then one number for the personality also standing alone, and then you write up three numbers for the three bodies, then in parentheses the three numbers for the spiritual planets, and then at the end one single number for the Node ray (see eg. example charts).

Well-developed Huber programs[3] will print these out for you, apart from the soul ray. I have forbidden the programmers to include soul ray information – it would be a shame to say to a machine "Tell me my soul ray!"

Discovery of the Method of Finding the Rays
Louise Huber

The knowledge presented here on finding the rays is very special. For 40 years we looked for our rays, and were never sure of mine. We got information from the Tibetan's books and Assagioli's instructions, but were never sure if what we found from this and our observations of ourselves and the reactions of others was true. There is little advice in the books on how to handle it, how to bring it into reality.

I was at an astrology congress some years ago, where a lady gave a talk about the seven rays. Afterwards you could go to her, and from your birth date she looked up your rays in a table, even the soul ray. I was shocked!

I said, "My goodness, I tried for years to find my rays and I was never sure, and she's just giving out all the rays! I have to go to her!". So I went to her talk. She had a kind of method looking at when the Sun comes up on the horizon, when you are born, and certain colours, and when there is a red colour it's a first ray and this kind of thing. She had a technique to find the rays from the birth date and time, and something else… Then she told people their rays.

I said to her "I come from Switzerland, and I'm also an expert on the rays, but I will never allow myself to tell people their rays like you do". She said: "I got advice. Inner guidance told me to give out the rays! I cannot keep them on the shelf any longer, and now the time is right to give them out".

This was the appeal for her – to bring it out. What method and techniques were used did not matter. It was just that she was getting the advice to bring it out. No truth or responsibility, just bring it out!

Back home I thought to myself... I'd bought her books and was building up all these tabulations. I'd collected a group around me and asked them to help me to research if they felt good with these rays. For one year we looked and looked, but we were not satisfied – doubt was always with us.

For years I had known that the rays are not easy to find because the books of Alice Bailey say that only after the third initiation will you find your rays. So I thought to myself that I had not got the third initiation, so I will have to wait to get to know my rays.

Because the lady who gave the talk was pushing me with the advice that the rays have to come out, I was driven by the thought that I too had to bring them out. So I put on our programme a seminar on the seven rays, with all her tabulation stuff. But I did not feel good about it!

Two hours before the seminar starts, Bruno came softly – he's second ray – and brings out the new techniques presented here! It was so simple and logical! Immediately when we started with the seminar, we gave out all this knowledge and the students experienced it and were all happy. It was a real good experience for them to find out about their own rays.

Now we had a real technique to find out about the rays! That's what Bruno gave you.

5

The Effect of the Rays
on the Personality

Louise Huber

Psychosynthesis Typology

• Psychosynthesis Typology and the Seven Rays •
• Assagioli's Background •
• Psychology of the New Age •
• Experiencing the Rays in Daily Life •

The Threefold Personality

• Rays of the Physical Body •
• Rays of the Emotional Body •
• Rays of the Mental Body •
• Rays of the Personality •
• Rays of Famous People •

Psychosynthesis Typology

I now enlarge on the subject of the seven rays in more psychological terms. Roberto Assagioli was the founder of psychosynthesis and we we spent three years with him learning about psychosynthesis and all that he had to offer on esoteric psychology. His Psychosynthesis Typology in Figure 5.1 directly relates the rays to psychological types[1].

Assagioli's Psychosynthesis Typology

1. Will Type	1st Ray	Will and Power
2. Love Type	2nd Ray	Love and Wisdom
3. Active-Practical Type	3rd Ray	Active Intelligence
4. Creative-Artistic Type	4th Ray	Harmony through Conflict
5. Scientific Type	5th Ray	Concrete Knowledge
6. Devotional-Idealistic Type	6th Ray	Devotion and Idealism
7. Organisational Type	7th Ray	Ceremonial Magic

Figure 5.1 Psychosynthesis Typology and the Seven Rays

Assagioli called the first type the Will Type. When you watch people, maybe you can understand that there is this differentiation between the Will Type and the Love Type - not by the planets in the signs, but by your impression of the person. Can you discriminate this when you look at certain people who are powerful, who are strong in life and reach their goals etc.? These are the Will Type.

The second type, the Love Type, are easy to spot too. They are softer people, receptive and sensitive. You have probably met people like that too. So you have to think about this kind of relative discrimination, without astrology. As I told you yesterday, the seven rays are the basis of differentiation of our life qualities. You can practise discriminating these qualities in the people around you in daily life.

The third type is the Active-Practical Type. Do you know people in your surroundings of this type? They are the business-like people, those who work a lot, those who have a lot to do from the morning through to the evening. They're always occupied, they have no time for different things, they are full of activities, meaningless activities sometimes, but they can also be purposeful.

The fourth type is the Creative-Artistic Type. Can you think about these people, on television for instance, or actors. There are different sorts there of course, but usually the creative artistic types are something very obvious. When you contact them you feel that they are always in a kind of ambivalent or chaotic state, and you cannot rely on them

– they do what they like. One day they are full of effervescence and the next day they are very depressed etc. – you see the ambivalence? These are very interesting types and have to do with the fourth ray of harmony through conflict.

The fifth type is the Scientific Type. Can you think about people that you know – professors in a university, for instance? The people who deal with science think that everything you live for has to be proven, has to have evidence. They only believe in things that they can grasp and that can be seen. They prove scientifically with material stuff, formal stuff. This kind of person is very concrete; it must become concrete or it's not true. Such people are mostly not in our circles and don't deal with astrology, for instance, because they only want to deal with things that they can grasp and understand!

The sixth type is the Devotional-Idealistic Type, demonstrated through the sixth ray. This is a special type. These people always have something in mind and need an ideal, something for which they want to fight or to which they want to commit themselves. And they need not only ideals but also a kind of leader or guru, something philosophical or religious. When they fight for their ideals they feel good.

The seventh type is the Organisational Type – the seventh ray. The seventh ray has to use organisations, which means that these people are very able to bring things down to earth. They want to organise forms and lives, which they deal with so precisely that what they want will become properly functional. This is also a creative type, such as a researcher – one who looks for the laws and rules behind the material world, which are used to make things useful and functional.

Assagioli's Background

At the time when Assagioli wrote his books, he was always concerned to divide the work into the exoteric knowledge and the esoteric knowledge, and there must between a holy wall of silence between them! At that time, at the beginning of the twentieth century, there had to be discrimination between the scientific, which was accepted by society, and the esoteric, which was outside society's acceptance.

These days we know that Assagioli was a disciple of Kuthumi[2] and a friend of Alice Bailey, and he got a lot of his knowledge from the Tibetan's books. All the things he brought out about spiritual psychosynthesis were linked with the books of Alice Bailey. Now we can say this, but in his time the holy wall of silence was necessary.

Assagioli was a companion of Carl Jung, Sigmund Freud and the other pioneers of the early development of psychology. It was hard enough to get the psychological ideas accepted, without the esoteric connections. So for Assagioli it was very dangerous to have the seven rays brought into psychology.

But today esoteric knowledge is on the street – in bookshops and libraries etc.! Now it is not necessary to retain the holy wall of silence. We can now speak about this frankly and openly.

Psychology of the New Age

As the seven rays are said to be the psychology of the New Age they must be linked to psychology too. It must not remain "up there" in the Alice Bailey books, which are very esoteric, highbrow, cosmological, universal. To bring it down is the task of the disciples of the New Age, like you and me! We have to bring it down to make it usable, to make something out of it in daily life, and to use it also for psychological treatments and counselling. In my opinion this is part of the New Age, and it has changed a lot since we started with the seven rays in 1958, already 40 years ago!

Therefore it is also interesting to combine it with our knowledge about astrology, such as in chapter 4.

When we use our chart for self-recognition and for self-understanding, then the seven rays enable more effective understanding of the qualities of our own being. It is a quality thing with the seven rays, helping to realise yourself and to experience yourself in reality. It is a kind of experience, it must be living, it must centred in feeling, otherwise you can forget it. It's not a mental knowledge, which you can computerise; it is live experience of ourselves. Therefore to combine the seven rays and astrology is the right path.

It is a process also – you have to walk into it, it is not just seeing, you know – "I have a fifth ray emotional body" and that's it. That's not it! You have to experience it.

Experiencing the Rays in Daily Life

In Alice Bailey's book *Discipleship in the New Age*[3], the Tibetan speaks to his own disciples. He gives a lot of advice on how to find out about the rays through observation of daily life. Through observation you find out about your rays because you watch how other people react towards you. It's a qualitative thing too – you cannot measure this.

You know that when you appear, for instance, with the fourth ray, as I told you yesterday, then people sometimes get into conflict! You do not aim for conflict, but they come into conflict because of your appearance. When you enter a group some conflict starts, and you think about why is this so? Maybe you have no answer for it. You do not want to bother them, it's not something that is done on purpose, it's a qualitative thing.

Through observation you find out about your rays...
you watch how other people react towards you.

The Threefold Personality

I now want to go into the effect of the rays on the personality and its bodies. Figure 1.1 on page 7 introduced the human constitution, showing how the different bodies of the three-fold personality fit together. And Figure 4.3 on page 54 shows Sun, Moon and Saturn corresponding with the bodies of the threefold personality

Rays of the Physical Body

The physical body is not a cosmic principle. According to the esoteric knowledge it is a dense material thing, which only becomes alive when the etheric body, the living body, the light body, enters it. When the etheric body makes the dense physical body a living thing, this is the same thing as when you are born and die. At death the etheric body goes out of the dense physical body. This is this energetic thing, so the physical ray is not the dense physical ray, it is the etheric ray. It has to do with the etheric body, because the physical itself has no quality, it is dead matter, formal – bones, cells etc. The brain also works on that ray of your physical/etheric body, because the brain is a physical thing.

Saturn corresponds with the physical body in the three-fold personality. Saturn is the physical principle, symbolising matter, the real form that you live in. The physical ray is not the physical appearance, it is the quality of your physical body. That is a little different.

The physical ray is the quality of your physical body.

When you feel into your body and find out how it reacts to food, to smoke, to sickness or whatever you can gain a lot of knowledge about the physical responsibility for your own body. With the seven rays you get an even better tool to feel into your body and ask it what it needs, what is wrong and how it reacts. Because the seven rays give a key to how you can become healthy or how you can feel better about your physical reality.

I now consider the quality of the physical body on each ray in turn.

First Ray Physical Body

According to Alice Bailey, it's rare to have a first ray physical body. When somebody asked the Tibetan[4] why he had the physical body on the first ray, he said: "Because in earlier times, there was much more need for a first ray physical body, they had to work hard". Can you imagine that the physical first ray has a kind of a powerful expression to handle matter?

The first ray is always will-orientated. The first ray on the physical level needs immediate results. He looks neither behind nor to left or right. He just looks towards the goal he wants to reach, and pushes towards it. It is an idea – he physically "thinks" and when he's working you can see this is a first ray power. You can see this in how he takes things, how he moves. With a single movement he does things swiftly, whereas a second ray first looks at it, maybe taking it in. You know the difference, physically? The first ray line is the masculine line, and the second ray line is the feminine one. (Rays 1,3,5,7 are all pushy; 2,4,6 are receptive, feminine-like.)

From the physical aspect of how you handle matter, it's important to discriminate between them. The first ray on the physical level can push out a lot of energy. For instance, a forester felling trees needs a lot of physical power. On the physical level the muscles on the 1,3,5,7 line are much stronger than on the 2,4,6 line. The muscles are much softer on the feminine line.

With the physical body on the masculine line, you have much more resistance, much more ability to overcome sickness. For instance, a first ray physical body can overcome sickness very fast. A first ray can immediately get rid of things when he's directed towards the goal of getting rid of it and when he's conscious of it, so that he can use his will for his physical defence mechanism.

With the first ray on the physical body it can sometimes create difficulties. Every ray has two sides. When you act too quickly, on the first ray physical level, then you are not physically very sensitive towards others. Can you imagine that there is an insensitivity in the body? You have no patience, can't wait until things are ripe or ready, can't wait until something happens by itself, which would be more of a second ray attitude.

Sometimes you can shoot before you know it's necessary, because the first ray also has destruction in it. The first ray is needed, as we have seen, to clean up the rubbish. There is danger, too. You can cut your finger very quickly because you don't look first – you grasp the knife and so on... You can have accidents on the physical plane. Then you are not in control of the first ray on the physical level.

Second Ray Physical Body
With Saturn on the second ray of love and wisdom it is different. When this quality controls your physical body you need comfort, warmth, being taken care of. The second ray is the ray of Love; you love your body and don't want to be hurt.

You also get a little physically weak sometimes, and maybe your defence mechanism is not so strong. With a first ray physical body you can defend yourself immediately, but with a second ray body you wait until somebody comes to protect you. You need somebody who says "I'll take care of you, support you, love you." And so the second ray body can sometimes become dependent on somebody who protects them, and takes responsibility for their physical body.

Most of the time with a second ray physical body, you will have somebody around. We call this the magnetism of the second ray. He attracts the things he needs, which make him feel good or comfortable, which give pleasure. Mostly the second ray has a nice-looking physical body.

The second ray is not only magnetic, there is another side. The weakness of the physical body can sometimes hinder them in taking responsibility for their own body.

The second ray body can give a kind of caring and caressing and warmth to others. There is always a kind of back and forth in the contact situation, because the second ray has to do with love. When you have this you can give love and you will get it back.

Third Ray Physical Body

On the third ray at the physical level we have active intelligence. With this active intelligence on the third ray you are able to find out a lot of details about how to live properly, and there is great concern for gathering information about healthy lifestyles. There are many things you can gather information and knowledge about for the physical level – health, food, medicine etc.

But the third ray has trouble as he may get lost in the multiplicity of information available. So he has to decide on something, and the physical body tells these people what they have to do. They really have to listen to the intelligent part of the physical body, because the physical body itself has a kind of third ray intelligence. That intelligence has to be listened to – you have to hear what your body tells you.

But sometimes it can be the reverse. You have a third ray physical body and you refuse things very strongly. It's Saturnian-like, the third ray – the fixed cross. When there is something you don't want and don't like on the physical level then it's rejected. The third ray can utilise this kind of refusal, and most of the time he is very healthy because it enables him to avoid things and protect himself.

The security drive of the third ray and Saturn and the fixed cross similarly comes out in physical intelligence. He knows exactly what he needs and what he wants and what he doesn't want. Being on the first ray line he has power, and the first ray power also goes through the third and the fifth. Refusal – you do not take in anything that will damage you. This is self-protection.

On the other hand, people with the third ray body can also have such an urge for movement and action that they become lost in senseless activity. From morning to evening they have a programme to be filled, and after a day of this they get tired and ask themselves if what they have done was the right thing or not. Their activity and work is also physical.

With the second ray activity includes periods of laziness; it's not driven by a lot of energy; he can sit and dream, or wait until others do something. But the third ray is always doing things by himself a lot! The multiplicity can also drain off a lot of energy, so he can also have physical breakdowns. Economy, on the third ray level – Saturn, fixed cross, economy – to use your energy correctly, this is the work of the physical existence level. So this must be intelligence, as used by the third ray.

When intelligence is driven by something, for example fear or security needs or whatever, you can damage yourself too, but yourself, not others. Right use of energy, skill in action with the physical body – listening to your own physical voice.

Fourth Ray Physical Body

With the physical body on the fourth ray, the fourth ray has a similarity with Libra, always looking for balance. It is concerned from morning to night to balance everything, so with the physical body on the fourth ray, you balance physical things all the time. You are so concerned about it that you miss out on some of the joy in life sometimes because there is a fear of conflict or losing your energy or getting something wrong or conflicting, or worrying that somebody does not like you, or your body is not nice enough... So you stand for an hour in front of the mirror as you are very busy with physical things with the fourth ray physical body.

Such people have to balance this dilemma, because the fourth ray is Harmony though Conflict. They aim for balance, but they will never reach it because they think that harmony will last for ever when this is physically oriented. And no harmony lasts for ever! Our life is eternal movement, always changing.

When they want to have things stable, they will be kicked somehow – perhaps getting some sickness, stomach trouble, headache etc. There is no possible stability in harmony, in the physical sense. So they are very concerned to look after themselves – they have one pill for headaches, another for the stomach, and they always have to be balancing things out. If something is not quite right, they can always take a pill! So they gather a lot of knowledge about the physical. Medicines, for instance, can be homeopathic, or teas or infusions, or alternative medicines and therapies, such as chiropractic.

They are very intelligent, because the fourth ray is creative. It is artistic, and these people have a fascination with their own physical appearance, like stars on the television. We look to them because they are so beautiful and so nice, and they have this kind of magnetism, because second and fourth rays are the feminine side.

Fifth Ray Physical Body

The fifth ray is the ray of science, research, gathering knowledge, so people with a fifth ray physical body have a good analytical mind about physical things. Their physical appearance is refined. They have an attitude of thoroughness. They keep very clean, are very conscious of their physical appearance. Their hair must be just right. They are precise in all areas, so physically there is a Virgo-like precision. They are able to put things together well.

Sometimes they are afraid of disturbance on the physical level, as order is very important for the scientific mind. Everything has logical effects, and if this order is disturbed they have the intelligence to think ahead and be aware that danger might arise, so they take precautions against this for their own physical sake and safety.

They can also take this on for other physical bodies. It is interesting that when we have a ray in our body that we have lived through, then we can use this quality for taking care of others. For instance, a medical doctor uses his analytical fifth ray knowledge for other bodies. He can diagnose sicknesses, having all this knowledge at hand and knowing what to do.

Sixth Ray Physical Body

The sixth ray physical body is again on the feminine side, and it has devotion. How do you feel when your physical body is devoting itself to something? Idealism about your own body – you think your physical body is pretty or nice. Maybe you take a lot of care of it because idealism needs an ideal. Maybe you want to become the nicest or the strongest or the most beautiful. These could be the people who say the body is a temple of the Holy Spirit.

The sixth ray physical body is sometimes difficult to have, because of these ideals. When the physical body is not a temple of God, and not healthy and pure or not beautiful, then they feel unhappy. They feel depressed when they get sick. I know people with the sixth ray physical body who get unusual sicknesses. It's as if this idealism attracts something very special.

So they are sometimes dependent on other people. Whether they get sick, or something happens to their physical appearance, or they lose touch with reality, they depend on somebody else, because this is the 2,4,6 line. This is again the feminine line and it is contact experience that we need – we need someone to take care of us. Some find it is easier to live when they are always sick, because then they have someone to take care of them.

Physical dependency can also lead to dependence on drugs or alcohol. When physical pleasure is missed, when there is pain, the sixth ray can be like martyrs. There is a kind of self-punishment, holding the ideal that the physical body is bad and must become a pure temple of God, then this is the reverse of health. It is sometimes masochism.

The sixth ray with its devotion and idealism can become a 180 degree reverse in a fanatical way. It's the ray of fanaticism, not only of idealism. Like in America recently there were 1,000 who sought death because they thought that intergalactic things were happening on Sirius and that they would be beamed up safely after they had committed suicide. They are driven by silly ideals sometimes – like sects, for instance. Terrorists are to do with the sixth ray, and on the physical level, you can imagine it's not so easy to handle, whereas the third ray physical body is very self-sustaining

Seventh Ray Physical Body

The seventh ray is on the first line again, with a power and will-orientation. He can help himself, he can stay on his own feet, he is grounded. Jupiter belongs to the seventh ray. He can organise his own life but has a tremendous individualistic attitude towards his own body. When you say he must eat salad because it's healthy, he never eats salad. When he does not want salad, when it's not the right thing for him, then he will never do it. The will refuses all indoctrination from other people.

It's really a creative ray on the physical body – they experience themselves, they try this and that. They have experience of the things which are good for them, and then people with other ideas are wrong. They say "It's my right – I do my own thing."

Rhythm also has something to do with the seventh ray – the cyclic processes in life. The cycle of sleeping and waking, working and not working. In controlling and organising daily life they do what they think is right for them. They don't depend on anybody, and don't listen to anybody else. This is the 1,3,5,7 ray line. They have this kind of will from the first ray in them, so you must not tell them what to do.

For instance, Bruno has a seventh ray body, and he's never listened to me! Never! You know this salad business – he never eats salad, and he smokes – when he thinks it's right, he takes responsibility for it. Bruno has a seventh ray body; I also.

They need to find their own rhythm of sleeping and work. When they are put into a situation where they have to get up at six o'clock in the morning, and be at the office at eight, finishing for the day at five – with this kind of routine stuff they get sick. They cannot stand it. They need a different kind of rhythm – their own rhythm. In our society where you have to fit into the whole process of working who has the freedom to find their own rhythm? It's very difficult.

These people take the risks and responsibility on themselves, even when the doctors say go away and we won't treat you any more. It's fantastic – these seventh ray physical people – but they are also irritable when they get sick. When you take responsibility for yourself, when you refuse all this healing stuff, you are still sick, and you can only heal yourself. It's as simple as that with the seventh ray.

The third and first ray, of course, are the same. The first ray person is able to heal themselves very quickly. Recovering, regeneration for the first ray and the seventh ray is something very similar, because, as I told you previously, the first ray is the head of the snake, and the seventh ray is the tail. It's the ouroboros – so the seventh and the first come together in a way. They can understand each other very well.

I am a first ray physical and Bruno is a seventh ray physical. We tolerate each other completely now, but we first had to learn about the rays – this was needed, as we tried to superimpose our own ideas on the other.

Audience: I've read a book in German giving remedies for each Sign, connected to the rays.

Louise Huber: I don't know whether they know something about what we call the rays This is quite new what I'm telling you now about the connection with health and medicine and so on. But you yourself could find out if this writer is on the right track – we are all researchers! Astrologers are researchers. You have to research these books for yourself and see if they are true according to the rays.

Rays of the Emotional Body

We go on to the emotional body. It has such a tremendous feeling nature because everybody has their own feelings, desires, ideas on how to be loved and how to fulfil their visions and so on. It is a large field of activity – contacting people, communicating, understanding, feeling for others, having a kind of exchange with others at the feeling level.

First Ray Emotional Body

With the feeling nature on the first ray, can you imagine that these people are very strong in their radiation, their presentation. They have power in their psychic approach. They can approach other people on the feeling level when they want something badly. They can make you do what they want.

This is the first ray, and the first ray is the one-pointed disciple as the Tibetan says. With the feeling nature when you have a goal in your mind, then you go for it! When others do not want to come along with you, they will be pushed away. This kind of feeling nature is not liked so much, but a person with the feeling nature on the first ray is not aware that he will hurt people with this kind of attitude.

It's sometimes very insensitive, without sensitivity. Reaching a goal is the important thing. This person doesn't want to hurt anybody – that is not his goal. His goal is to reach something important for him, and that you "get out of the way!"

This kind of feeling is there for people who are just going for their own ideals, for love and exchange. It is sometimes very difficult to deal with a person like this.

They do not get a lot of sympathy. Even when they have cultivated the feeling nature, know about the first ray, and know how to expand their consciousness. Even then, when they want to reach something, they have to be aware that they don't hurt anybody with their own will power on the psychic level. This needs a lot of awareness and a lot of working on yourself.

It's also the will to love, the will to tolerate, the will to understand, to be sensitive, to be nice, so they need a kind of ideal of humanitarian attitude, according to their own power – they can really do damage with their own psychic stuff.

On the other hand when you have first ray astral body you can also bring energy into something which has almost been dying. When somebody has no energy anymore, no joy in life, and he's dull and depressive – along comes a first ray astral body and revives his energy. You can also give energy to others so they can breathe again – that's something! To spread around a lot of fiery psychic energy so they get excited and animated again. They are very good for mass influences.

They can give a good talk. With a first ray astral body they can carry you along on a wave of enthusiasm when they want it! But this is sometimes difficult for love, because in love you need a kind of exchange.

On the astral level with the first ray you can also become angry, and then you destroy other people. You hurt them, because you have the power to hurt. You can reject them, push them away when they are not willing to love you anymore. This kind of feeling nature is not so easy to have in contact situations.

Second Ray Emotional Body

The second ray feeling nature is very lovely. It belongs to people who are very nice, very sensitive. They wait until they are asked for, they are not pushy, they are really pleasant to make contact with, and they fit in well. In groups they show sympathy and have magnetism, calmness, understanding and so on.

But they can also become very demanding when they feel that they have this kind of allure which others respond to – they can then suck others. You know, they have this lovely attitude and because this is so pleasant, other people give them what they want, and they want a lot! When they feel that they might get some feedback, whether materialistic or physical or emotional, then they can take in a lot.

They can become very egoistic when they find out how easy it is to get all they want. So they have to transform, and with the feeling nature we always have to transform. This is the law of the feeling nature.

You know that the astral level is a reflection. You can read about it in *Moon Node Astrology*[5], about projections, egocentric love and the ego stuff. And the Moon is so egocentric sometimes, especially when it becomes intelligent too. Then love and wisdom, the second ray, can become very cool, without forgiveness – the reverse of the second ray.

The Tibetan differentiates between the love line and the wisdom line on the second ray. People on the love line have a kind of dependency on others, and taking from them what they can get. They give back something but they take in more than they can give.

On the wisdom line they can become very snobby, cool, cold. Then when you have so much wisdom – all this feeling stuff, you know, there's this kind of knowing too much about the ins and outs of the feeling level so they are beyond it, in a way. They are in an ivory tower and sit at the top looking down, and when you try to get love from them they give you a little bit and say you are nice again, so they manipulate. On the feeling level we are always in polarity. These can be good, and they can also be egocentric.

There are nice things about the second ray nature when they are in a position of contact, such as humanitarian, social and psychological interchange, and counselling. When they work in an area where this exchange on the emotional level goes back and forth then they are wonderful!

Third Ray Emotional Body

The third ray astral body is intelligence. The third ray is on the first line so it's masculine, and the astral body on the third ray is very clever. You know all about economy and how to get things. You are a very good business man and you can handle the wealth of others. You can even sell them fridges in Alaska!

They can handle their emotions so intelligently and nicely, according to their plans of course. On the third ray level you always have a goal in mind, and then you may do lots of things, but you have to reach this goal, you have to get this money. So you are clever, you play this very skilfully, like a pianist on a clavier or piano, and at the end you get it! You get it because active intelligence is able to gather all kinds of psychological knowledge. They have it in themselves, because intelligence in the astral body means they already have this intelligence, to be able to handle things and to handle people and so on.

In partnerships they can sometimes feel pain and suffer, because when they are so manipulative on the love side, then at a certain point they are no longer satisfied.

You know when Moon is on the fixed third ray it can be Saturnian – crystallisation. When it is too fixed then there is no life, no joy, no real love anymore, so they suffer. The matter is there, the money is there, the brilliance is there, the change is there – you have all these things around you, but inwardly, it's dead. Crystallisation, death. You have too much of everything. Too much form shapes the love into structure, or makes it demanding, or gives it rules, or whatever... Then love is gone.

The third ray astral body can sometimes reach the barriers, and then they have to break through the pain and through suffering about love. But then they have to open up for real love again.

Fourth Ray Emotional Body

The fourth ray astral body is again very undeveloped, because the feeling nature itself is very ambivalent. The Moon level is mutable, reflecting, polarising. Its experiences are of polarisation. On the feeling level you only feel yourself when you are in contact with others, otherwise you don't feel yourself. This is dependency on the view of others, and on their love.

With the fourth ray emotional body you are either saying "Hallelujah!" or you are depressed. You say "Hallelujah" because tomorrow you will experience love and excitement and all kinds of nice things, and then, when the next day comes, it is gone again.

The feeling nature is not stable at all, it's very unstable and there are a lot of quarrels and a lot of desires. The Tibetan[6] says that sometimes the fourth ray can handle this as if he were a first ray. He can push things through powerfully. With the fourth ray you can create conflicts, you can fight, you can push others away, even with the feminine line, because this ray is Harmony though Conflict. It's something which you cannot control. It runs out of control very easily.

On the other hand, it is the artistic ray, and the intuitive ray as Alice Bailey says. The fourth ray is the intuition, and if the emotional body is on the fourth ray you can open up for higher visions. Your own feeling nature can become very demanding – some very transpersonal things can come through.

In the arts and the creation of beauty the fourth ray astral body can reach the soul level, the buddhi level (see Figure 2.3 Amphora). When the astral body on the fourth ray reaches up to this buddhi level, then he can bring beauty down. He can bring healing down. He can understand all the other people who are suffering about love. He can bring harmony and healing and wholeness. And he can also contact the highest buddhi level and bring down something about love which is not from the world – the healing power, fourth ray.

Sometimes when you look at the paintings by the great masters, something comes out of the picture and goes into you, and makes you whole again. I don't know if you've experienced this? Beauty is such healing stuff! It's wonderful to have beauty around! And to bring beauty into our world is something very special, it's culture, it's uplifting, it's music – it's the fourth ray astral body.

Fifth Ray Emotional Body

The fifth ray is of course scientific. When you love science and how it works, this is when your fifth ray astral body is in love. I cannot find out how it works! Scientific use of the power of love. Maybe you are a researcher into the psychic. Maybe you want to find the ins and outs of the human psychology. You want to find out about love and contact in a scientific way. He is a scientific person who is dealing with feelings in this way. Maybe he's very critical. But to love such a person means that he's always analysing feelings. I don't know, but I can imagine this. I am trying to understand the fifth ray astral body.

As with the third ray and with the first ray on the emotional level, love has to be experienced, and this is more of the second line. So with the fifth ray, they're missing something which has to do with this feminine receptiveness and waiting and warmth and this feeling stuff and so on. Maybe they have to learn it, and maybe then they can use it as if they have it.

Audience : *I think that's absolutely true. I've spent ten years getting in touch with my feelings*[7].

Louise Huber: But they are highly intelligent and they can write books like Richard Llewellyn did when he wrote the training manuals for the Huber School in England. With this fifth ray emotional body, he took out of us all this knowledge in a way, but on the feeling level. His intelligence is in his Moon. Because the Moon is a reflector and maybe he has ability to draw into his feeling nature this knowledge which we have given to you, and he brings it down, and structures it, so you could learn about it.

Richard is all on the masculine line – third and fifth – can you imagine now that he founded the Huber School in England. He wrote down all the knowledge that he got from us so beautifully. And I have had this translated in Switzerland back into German! This gives an understanding of a fifth ray astral body. He can suck in, absorb it, feeling-wise. This is also an explanation for you – that you tried for ten years to get more knowledge about your feeling nature.

Sixth Ray Emotional Body

Then we have the sixth ray. People with a sixth ray astral body are always in love! They always need somebody who will adore them, as they are very idealistic. This is the sixth ray, very much devoted to somebody on the emotional level. When they have somebody, they stick with them, because there is fanaticism behind it, and this means that they stick at it, bind themselves to the one who is in love with them. They bind the ideal of this love to themselves, because they cannot function without ideals. And in love, you need somebody whom you can adore. When you love him, then it's the best thing in the world, because the sixth ray emotional body is very devotional. He gives everything but he directs his feeling nature towards somebody.

It can be so strong and so fantastic, so caring... until something happens, such as him being refused or rejected by somebody who has had enough of this emotional stuff and doesn't want any more! For instance, when you have a fifth ray or first ray astral body with a sixth ray one then you kick him out! "Don't come near me!" Then you can imagine this devotional sixth ray stuff – it's very first ray-like. They are touched by something very strongly and they grow into this attachment. They become obsessed, with ideals, with love, with the person, with the children, and so comes this whole business about letting go – they do not want to let go! This is because they live from the ideal of love, and without this ideal they have no right to live.

It's fanaticism. Fanaticism in love can sometimes be a tremendous burden. They have to learn to let go.

Seventh Ray Emotional Body

The seventh ray emotional body – these are the single people. As I said before, with the seventh ray physical body, they want to decide by themselves how they look after their health and so on. At the emotional level the seventh ray can also become very independent, demanding freedom and space – they do not want closeness. Don't come too near – once in a while is OK – yes, and this is the kind of feeling they have with the emotional body on the seventh ray.

The sixth ray is impressing and pleasing others, but the seventh ray always has this kind of distance, and a kind of respect for the barriers and boundaries of others. It's very nice with the seventh ray astral body, but when you have the sixth ray along with the seventh ray in your partnership, then it's difficult. You want closeness, even to become one with him or her.

With the seventh ray astral body, nein danke! No thank you! I want to remain myself, and contact and relationships and Moon and all these feeling experiences must be in rhythm, according to cycles, organised and so on. It's the same in love, and I tell them "For you it's better not to have a partner for daily life, but you need a partner for Sundays!" Then it works!

Rays of the Mental Body

Can be determined by the position of the Sun in the horoscope.

First Ray Mental Body

The first ray mental body makes for a dynamic mind – someone who creates his own world according to the motto "you are what you think". The first ray thinker has a powerful intellect and nearly always gets what he wants and what he focuses on. He can direct all his mental powers on starting something and meeting his goal, ignoring everything that is not relevant. He often exerts a strong, almost sinister, influence over others, and can use them to achieve his goals. First ray thinkers only have their Sun in a cardinal sign on the AC, IC, DC or MC.

That makes the first ray thinker strong-willed and bossy. He feels personally responsible for everything that happens. He controls events with dynamic single-mindedness. He is the perpetrator, who even creates his own problems, and puts all his effort into managing them. His personal development is very rapid, because the intensity of the first ray spurs him on and enables him to successfully negotiate any changes he may encounter on his way.

They can be writers or political thinkers. They are often politically powerful characters who can use their mental powers to get things done, with either good or bad intentions. In the negative case, they can be dictators or black magicians, who have realised that they possess this power and use it to satisfy their own ego. The first ray thinker is aware of his inner power and magical ability. When bent on destruction, he can be very dangerous and destroy his enemies or anything standing in his way. In the positive case, he can immediately eliminate mistakes and create new and better conditions. The first ray can be constructive or destructive, depending on its motives or on what kind of changes are required.

Second Ray Mental Body

A person with mental body on the second ray already possesses a certain wisdom, love and psychological understanding. A second ray thinker is a teacher, an educator. He reaches out to people and can lead and guide them with love and insight. The second ray thinker has tact and foresight, he proves to be an excellent ambassador, a first-class lecturer and teacher. People with a second ray mind have the ability to influence others with their views, and to show them what is good and healthy for them. They have paedagogical and educational abilities, and a lot of credibility. People like to listen to them and take their advice. While the first ray thinker puts others down, the second ray thinker persuades. He teaches lovingly, with care. His eyes shine with this loving attitude and the motivations and principles that support it.

Third Ray Mental Body

The third ray thinker actively uses his intelligence in order to meet his goals. He uses his intellectual powers to calculate his logical chances of success and knows exactly what he has to do to succeed. He is capable of utilizing all his economical and business talents to guarantee profit. Most managers have the third ray in the intellect. They use logical arguments to persuade others and realise their interests, which also benefits them. When a third ray thinker manages a business, it gives others a certain economic security. The third ray has access to both the fixed cross and the quality of Saturn. That is why it controls matter intelligently and is nearly always successful. A third ray thinker thinks of profit and success, a second ray thinker thinks of love.

Fourth Ray Mental Body

With the fourth ray mental body, the mind is geared to harmony. It is creative and wants to represent the positive side of life. A fourth ray thinker can intuitively focus his wisdom on greater connections and reveal new solutions. Such a person has a natural understanding of life's opposites, which often means he finds himself in conflict and arguments. He knows the problematic nature of polarities, the difference between good and evil and uses situations of conflict to develop himself.

As a creative, intuitive thinker, he can also become a writer because he is good at describing life. He can enthral his readers with his stylish, brilliant descriptions of conflictive situations. These people are poets and writers; people who see polarities and turn them into a philosophy. They know that conflict is necessary for progress to be made, which is such a reasonable, logical and beautiful conclusion. They can often be very interesting people who are capable of communicating things in a loving way.

Fifth Ray Mental Body

The fifth ray thinker is usually very intelligent and geared to concrete knowledge. Alice Bailey says: "We need fifth ray thinkers in esotericism, because these people can explain it in a form that is logical and comprehensible. Today this is still a mystically and emotionally loaded subject due to the influence of the sixth ray. Fifth ray thinkers can put their thoughts into words and give them a scientifically acceptable form. If this happens, then the subtle bodies, such as the etheric body, will come under scientific investigation."

There have already been many attempts to research extra-sensory perception. Alice Bailey wrote a whole book about the etheric body[8] which is particularly important for fifth ray thinkers. We need them to research these kinds of frontier areas in a scientific manner and also to reveal the order in astrological precision and accuracy.

Sixth Ray Mental Body

The sixth ray mental body produces thinkers full of idealism. They need an ideology that they can feel committed to and that they can communicate to others. They can be inspired by all kinds of ideals: philosophical, esoteric, universal or religious. If they do entertain such ideas, their intelligence is stimulated and vitalized. If not, or if they have to deal with financial matters, people with a sixth ray mind are often unsuccessful. Many everyday duties remain undone, and mistakes creep into their finances or economic policy.

In the Age of Pisces, when the sixth ray was very active, factories were destroyed, there were pioneers, and people who were inspired by an idea and prepared to make sacrifices for it. This includes the brave people who climbed onto the barricades in the French Revolution. One idea to improve circumstances can take off. Ideas stimulate the intelligence; the energy and strength necessary to turn ideals into reality are made available. The sixth ray thinker can also be very stubborn, especially when forced onto the defensive.

The ideas that they have thought out must be put into practice. Anyone opposed to them or stepping out of line is considered an enemy and is condemned. There is an element of fanaticism in the sixth ray thinker. They can become so convinced by their version of the truth that they demonise anyone who thinks differently. They are even jealous of those with a different opinion. Some are so convinced of their ideas or their love that they are prepared to die for it, for example the martyrs who die for their faith.

Seventh Ray Mental Body

People with a seventh ray mind are powerful characters with sharp persevering minds. They search for truth, not resting until they have found it. The seventh ray enables elevation of thought to the highest level, expansion of consciousness into the universal realm. The seventh ray word of power is "The highest and the lowest meet" (see page 124). Touching the highest and seeking the lowest covers a lot of ground. It is the hermetic principle "as above, so below", universal macro and microcosmic thinking, characteristic of the seventh ray thinker.

These people can expand their consciousness and are able to see contexts easily. This enables a great ordering principle to be revealed, explaining many things and allowing deeper meanings to be recognised. They cannot rest until they find this meaning. They want to find the essential and the meaningful. They investigate and search until they have found the highest connections, at which point the seventh ray starts to think creatively. The span of their thoughts can be so wide that there is often no longer any difference between above and below. Sexuality is below and above is the noble and sublime, the inspirational and the intuitive. Their thoughts merge both energies to produce something quite original, and even unique.

Rays of the Personality

When we talk about someone's personality ray, we must bear in mind that he also has the three body rays within him. Although in some people the personality ray has a certain dominance, in others the rays of the different bodies are more noticeable. It is obvious that this depends on the level on which the person is already polarised, i.e. has gone through learning experiences.

In reality, most of our lives are spent just functioning, working and struggling for survival. We then live mainly in the physical self and need its physical ray. In love, we live in the realm of emotional relationships, enjoying the company of people who are good for us, in which case the Moon is the polarisation point. When we think and research, learn and listen, then we live in the mental self, which can acquire knowledge by concentration, alertness and attentiveness.

According to our experience, the personality ray is best expressed when you need all your powers in a difficult situation. The personality ray is then able to co-ordinate all three rays. For example, if the house is burning down, the alarm goes off and you must quickly salvage the most important things, and for a while all your efforts are integrated. Or when somebody falls into the water and you have to jump in to save his life, then at this moment all the rays must work together and you need to act as a whole personality for one moment and the personality ray comes in. Directly, purely, in such situations. The same applies when you must make a decision or find yourself in an argument. In these moments you act as an integrated personality.

The personality ray therefore usually only functions when we are forced to act as an integrated ego, when there is a demand for all our powers. It is associated with integration, with holistic awareness and the well-developed ego, which possesses awareness on all three levels. It has particular importance with regard to the integration of the threefold personality and the transformation into the soul ray.

We describe the different personality rays below:

First Ray Personality

The first ray personality is charismatic. He can dedicate himself completely to achieving his goals and is dynamic, active and independent. He creates new things with dedication and joy, cleverly defends the truth and does not let himself be distracted from his ideals and visions. His well-developed willpower can move mountains and he aims to create things of lasting value that are useful for as many people as possible.

He devotedly defends the tasks that matter to him. If they correspond to his inner ideal, he is ready to act resolutely. He possesses the power to face up to life and its tasks without shirking or doing things by halves. His motto is: "If I want something, I can get it!"

This resoluteness makes him a role model for others, arousing their enthusiasm so that they immediately set about achieving their own goals. Sometimes this attitude is also perceived as ruthless or stubborn, as he tends to cling to a particular idea, feeling or point of view. This is not the case though, as the first ray is actually flexible by nature and fascinated by the new. It is a vital force and not a function or a role. When a new goal direction presents itself, he is willing to make himself ready to act and to leave behind or eliminate the old. This usually makes him intolerant of unnecessary things. He wants nothing to do with people whose superfluous emotions, thoughts or words delay the achievement of his goals. He always gets straight to the point, avoids beating about the bush, and goes down his chosen path looking neither left nor right.

In the personality, the lively first ray energy ardently seeks independence. This kind of person wants to be in charge of his own life without restrictions from those around him. He strives to control his environment and aims to get everyone to fall in line with his own plans. It is typical for the first ray to be prepared to do whatever it takes to achieve his goals. This again involves the ability to keep his mind on the job in order to find the best way to meet his goal.

Concentration on one thing also comes from the fact that a strong-willed person does not pay any attention to things that are beyond his control. He is perfectly in control of himself and therefore of everything within his sphere of influence. As his will is subordinate to his self-control, he is also able to put his plans into practice. He controls himself with inner strength. For example, if he decides to fast for health or ethical reasons, he will do it almost at the drop of a hat.

First ray people are therefore prepared to actively collaborate on the implementation of large-scale projects, and are often leaders of organisations that need a firm hand.

Second Ray Personality

A second ray personality radiates love, sensitivity and a keen interest in the affairs of others. Their activities tend to involve relating, love and understanding. These are predominantly qualities that come from the soul, which shines through their personality and make them magnetic. Their goal is to establish greater understanding between people and real human relationships. They feel empathy for others, including those in need, and want to help them to live a happier life.

When they think of another person, they are not interested in how they can benefit from this relationship, but they feel connected to them by a subtle sensation in their consciousness. They are just as interested in the other person's life and ambitions as in their own. The scope of this sensation will extend further and further the more a person opens up their spiritual quality.

Second ray personalities are really prepared to help others, not just to talk about it. They give themselves to the world with all its imperfections and mixture of joy and pain. They feel called upon to make a creative contribution to evolution and try by their own example to be good and helpful people.

Many with a second ray personality search for the meaning of life and try to look for the causes of suffering. They are interested in alternative healing methods and recognise a process of ongoing human development in the theory of evolution. From this point of view, destiny resembles a learning process, which enables strokes of fate to be explained and accepted. This fills them with positive energy, which they express in their devotion to and love of other people. It gives them a good feeling and enables them to be a real help to those in need. It is the law of love that manifests itself in life through them. We should remember that our Solar Logos, representing the final goal of evolution, stands on the second ray. The second ray ultimately brings people together, merges them into a whole in consciousness. At the same time it makes their union with others stronger and stronger, thus unifying things that used to be different.

At the ideal culmination of evolution, law and order will triumph over chaos and darkness, and love will conquer all. To be part of this stream of consciousness is a joy for people with a second ray personality. They feel obliged to continually improve themselves.

Third Ray Personality

A third ray personality is above all an economical thinker; these people act according to the laws of give and take, offer and demand. They are very busy getting the information they need in order to find the best way of successfully implementing their plans. The third ray is driven by its active intelligence to combine the goals of the first ray and the sensitivity of the second ray. It wants to control matter and show how useful it is. They have a special instinct for knowing how things should be arranged so that they can be implemented as smoothly as possible. They have brilliant organisational and planning ability, and know how to make things successful. They only act when they are sure that everything has been thoroughly thought through and is running smoothly.

A person with a third ray personality is versatile. He has a good intellectual grasp, but is often bored by how much has to be taken into account to be able to make a decision. He really does not like to settle, restrict or deny himself. He wants to participate in everything that life has to offer and uses his intelligence to get everything he needs. This shows how skilful he is at managing circumstances and matter. He exercises mental control to structure matter. He can devote himself to business, natural sciences or to art; his versatile talents enable him to succeed at everything he touches. If he manages to focus sufficiently on one thing, he can attain what is normally called a successful and fulfilling life in many fields.

He plans his steps very carefully, first thinking intensively about how best to proceed and then comes up with a perfect plan. In a certain sense, he instinctively understands how things are connected and knows what has to be done to get the most benefit and profit from them. This is what makes him successful in business. He has a nose for gaining advantage because he spots connections and possibilities.

While the first ray indicates the goal and gives people an orientation, the second ray perceives unity, brings understanding and inner contentment. On the other hand, the third ray shows the purpose and provides security by reaching the goals. The coaction of the three main rays can therefore be seen as a developmental process.

Fourth Ray Personality

The fourth ray lies between the first three and the last three rays. It therefore has a connective function and mediates between pairs of opposites. It vacillates to and fro and is not really sure where to turn. It often goes through phases of instability, moodiness and imbalance until a state of harmony has returned, so that it can be optimistic and look to the future again.

His task is to achieve harmony between inner and outer. He only rarely manages this, which often makes him unhappy. He suffers from the imperfections of this world and must constantly try to understand everything and find a place within himself where he can feel in harmony with himself and with the world. In his life, he feels the need to express an ideal. This makes him creative and artistic. It is precisely this discrepancy between inner and outer, between the imaginary world and reality that awakens his creative powers in order to create a balance. His task is to find ways of overcoming this discrepancy.

With the fourth ray, harmony is achieved through conflict. Although he wants to avoid conflict, he is constantly finding himself in this type of situation, where he must learn to judge correctly because he cannot ignore the middle ground. He has an overactive conscience, which is troubled when extreme emotions force him off balance. Basically, he longs for a state in life in which he can bring his inner and outer affairs into a constant, functioning harmony, in which the laws of outer and inner growth are merged. He is only happy and satisfied when this merging has been achieved.

This process of harmonizing the inner with the outer is a life task for the fourth ray personality. This process is ongoing, comprehensive and constant. Occasionally, there is even a flash of intuition that helps him clearly see the middle way between opposites. This awakens creativity and aestheticism, which find expression in his work.

When someone with a fourth personality ray reflects on a problem, he does not dwell on the details. His emotions assess the situation and suddenly the solution comes to him intuitively, opening up new perspectives to him, which get straight to the point. He has the ability to imagine; he can expand his consciousness and intuitively establish greater connections. There is something very alive and organic in this process. Writers with these qualities have a great treasure of figurative language. They can express their ideas well and have a particular gift for analogy. As the inner and outer are harmonised, the above and below also come together. These people's analogous thinking enables them to pick up on graphic images from universal sources, and they have wide flights of thought that correspond to an all-encompassing world view, which allow them to help others to have the same insights and visions.

Fifth Ray Personality

This ray directs his interest toward the material world. What counts for him is the scientific demonstrability of things. He values only that which can be measured, weighed and touched. He therefore focuses on demonstrable truths, recognises his dependency on the material world and wants to structure it as perfectly as possible. He concentrates on what is feasible and searches for scientific truths. Someone with a fifth ray personality is determined that no errors from the 'unprovable' side of life will destabilise his material world view. He often draws a separation line between that which can be learnt and known and the experiences on subtle levels.

He feels very secure when everything runs with scientific order and regularity. He does not trust new things and needs a long time to come to terms with changes. They must first withstand constant checking and prove themselves in daily life. He himself is not inventive and it would never enter his head to change the order of things according to his own ideas, so perfect do the organisation and functioning of his world appear. Once he has accepted something as a fact, it is hard for him to be convinced of another opinion. He looks for durability and structures his life around rules and forms, law and order. Routine makes him happy; he needs a stable environment that he can rely on. He does not believe in changing anything without good reason.

The fifth ray personality can also focus his concrete perceptive faculty on spiritual matters. Whenever he does manage to create something new, or to enter new dimensions of thought, he tries to find more provable things there and to explain what is there convincingly. This is his special ability, to devote himself with precision and patience to the improvement of matter. For this reason, he is constantly learning, so that his knowledge becomes richer and more comprehensive as it is used in an environment that it must adapt perfectly to. A person with the fifth ray uses his knowledge to bring a deeper understanding of the living truth. He makes it clear that for the wise person, everything that exists is essential and worth taking time to look at in more detail. This is his creative contribution to evolution.

Sixth Ray Personality

While the fifth ray perceives the world by knowing and thinking and wants to prove everything scientifically, the sixth ray perceives, classifies and evaluates it with his feelings, without really thinking about it. For him, the main thing is to feel whether something is good or bad. It is a kind of all-embracing love, whether animate or inanimate. He gives himself totally if something interests him. He penetrates the energies that emanate from a person or a situation with his emotions, can identify with it and thereby "know" its essence.

The person with a sixth ray personality needs an ideal to live by. He can find this in a philosophy, a persuasion or even in another person. This kind of devotion is not blind, but intelligent. It recognizes the value of a world of good and feels called upon to support goodness and to defend it wherever necessary. For a person like this, it is important what we perceive through love, not through our thinking or making things with our hands. His devotional nature means that he judges his fellow men and himself according to motivations of love and helping.

He is suspicious of exploitation and claims to power. He stands up for the fair distribution of goods in the world and his ideal is for everyone to be happy and have enough to eat. He is troubled by poverty and hunger, he feels personally responsible for them and wants to do something about it. This can make him fanatical, and he can be overwhelmed by feelings of pity. He feels helpless and can no longer tolerate reality as it actually is.

The personality can experience devotion in several ways. He can be devoted to a loved person, thereby feeling valued; or he can devote himself to an ideal task, sacrificing himself for it. Another possibility is religious devotion to the divine principle. He defers to God in all things and is satisfied with what happens, for better or for worse. He accepts it as the best way for life to improve. This religious devotion is not naïve credulity, but serves as an example of the noblest and most valuable feelings a person should cultivate in his devotion to the Highest Being.

The sixth ray is also concerned with deciding what is really good for a person, which requires wisdom and the other ray qualities. Active participation in improving the world requires more than just a developed feeling of devotion and idealism. The spiritually inclined person is aware of this. He usually joins a group of like-minded people and tries to do good things with them.

Seventh Ray Personality

In the description of the seventh ray, the term "ceremonial magic" can be approached in several ways. For a seventh ray personality, all life is ritual, hence the association of group events, dancing and also religious ceremonies with this ray. In public group events, ceremonies evoke sensitive perception and a mood of meditation which are usually created by mantras, chants, colours, sounds, music, decoration, coloured robes, etc. This vibration and energy moves us and gives us a feeling of joy that can even lead to ecstasy.

The seventh ray requires order and a certain ritual in its daily activities. This makes it difficult for such people to accept the instructions or commands of others. They ardently pursue their own plans and goals, create their own rules and take responsibility for what they do or do not do. They cannot bear to be restricted by others, need their own free space within the possible parameters and live according to their own individual rhythm. When they do attain this freedom, they can become creative and set out to make sure that everything happens in the safest, best and most organised way. When they are able to decide freely and act spontaneously, they can achieve wonderful things. They do not like taking orders as this blocks their creative flow.

It is fitting that the last of the seven rays is concerned with finalizing and completion. In the universal sense, this means the implementation of the divine plan within the given limits and possibilities. This generates creative stress, which is the source of the seventh ray personality's creativity. With great commitment, endurance and concentration, he tries to present his ideas in a form that expresses beauty and perfection in an absolutely realistic way. Many have artistic talents and are receptive to beauty. They are fascinated and inspired by creativity and artistic expression. They are convinced that everything must run smoothly, and act accordingly.

This is the ray that creates form in order to express life perfectly. He glorifies ideal beauty, which he wants to be materialised everywhere. He is interested in beauty and perfection and devotes himself to them. He is also a perfectionist. If something does not correspond to the established order or ritual, he is rattled and sometimes even angry. In particular, he expects good performance from all technical appliances, and can become aggressive if this is not forthcoming.

The seventh ray personality is also interested in neatness, not because he likes order or cleanliness, but because he wants to eliminate disturbance, pain and deficiencies that detract from perfection, beauty or his own well-being. He puts a lot of effort into feeling good physically. The modern emphasis on physical awareness is caused by the influence of the seventh ray.

Rays of Famous People

As examples, here are the rays of some famous people:

Roberto Assagioli	6 226 (575) 3
Alice Bailey	4 511 (777) 1
Sigmund Freud	7 755 (747) 1
Albert Einstein	6 266 (277) 3
Carl Gustav Jung	7 333 (333) 1

It is interesting that Carl Gustav Jung (Figure 5.3) has a seventh ray personality. On the three personality levels, he has the third ray three times! In my opinion, this must be an outstanding personality, a real third ray personality, with all the intelligence needed to bring out a new psychology, as Jung did.

Figure 5.3 Carl Gustav Jung
28.10.1975 19:32 Kesswil, CH
7 333 (333) 1

6

Transformations

Louise Huber

The New Age and the Seventh Ray

• Heart and Mind •
• Synthesis – The Highest and The Lowest Meet •
• Transformation of Consciousness •
• Invocation and Evocation •

The Constitution of Man

• The Amphora and Alice Bailey's Diagram •
• Gap in Consciousness •
• Soul Consciousness •
• Building the Antahkarana •

Initiation

The Soul Ray and the Personality Ray

• Transformations of Rays 1,2,3,4,5,6,7 •
• The Rays of the Masters •
• Ray Words of Power •

Shamballa, the Plan, and the Hierarchy

• Cosmic Evolution •
• Living the Soul's Purpose •
• Sacred Planets •
• The Monad •
• Closing Thoughts •

The New Age and the Seventh Ray

Heart and Mind

Each ray has a related seed thought, mantra or 'word of power'[1], given in Alice Bailey's last book[2]. These words of power give you a very strong connection with the quality of the ray. As we have already said, the rays are not forms but qualities. Quality is something which you can only grasp with your heart.

With the mind you can grasp all the form stuff, the methods, the techniques etc. In astrology you can also grasp with your mind, but with the heart this is something different. You have to become sensitive to the quality or the radiation or the "vibes" of a person. With the seven rays we have the possibility to become aware of the inner quality of the other person. This is a kind of communication on the level of heart.

Heart and mind have to come together. The sign Aquarius has the special facility of being be able to bring heart and mind together. In astrological psychology, we always deal with more than one sign. When we deal with Aquarius, we immediately see its polar opposite Leo too. Leo and Aquarius belong to each other on the whole axis. This is a holistic approach, and we know that Leo has to do with the heart, and Aquarius with the mind, and so mind and heart are coming together, and Leo and Aquarius have to do with bringing the seventh ray into humanity.

> With the Rays we have the possibility to become aware of the inner quality of the other person. This is communication on the level of heart.

Synthesis – The Highest and The Lowest Meet

It's interdependent, linking up with the signs, the rays, and the changing of our time. Remember what I said about global transformation? Every transformation has to be considered in our time, because now a lot of things are coming together. It's not only in Aquarius that this starts, it's also the violet sphere that we are entering, the third initiation of the planetary logos, and a lot of other things that are coming together at the end of this millennium. And this "coming together" is happening from the highest to the lowest beat – it is the mantram of justice happening – it all comes together.

I remember when I met Bruno, 40 or 50 years ago – I forget to keep count now. It's the "Eternity ray"! He was always telling me "I have a vision. I want to bring heaven and earth together, and they are such large things to reach – all this height and depth – and to bring them together." It was always his vision to bring them together. He's a seventh ray personality – he has a seventh ray physical body and also two other seventh rays. I have a seventh ray, so we fit together with this kind of manifestation of this vision. This is the seventh ray – the manifestation of visions. "The highest and the lowest meet" – it's the mantra of the seventh ray.

When I have the theme, as now, of the transformation of the ray of the soul and the personality, and the ray of the soul is the highest, and ray of the personality is the lowest, and they have to get together, this is some work. It does not come together all alone. The seventh ray brings it together, with its mantra. It is a kind of inner goal in the seventh ray entity, which we are now entering. But still we have to co-operate with this mantra. This is something else, and to co-operate with such a powerful word of power, you first have to know a lot about heaven and earth, the highest and the lowest. And it also has to do with synthesis.

Did I mention that the Avatar of Synthesis[3] is coming nearer to the earth, as Alice Bailey put it in poetic words? The Avatar of Synthesis is coming nearer to the earth. He has already reached the mental level, now he is coming down into the astral level, and at a certain point he has to come down to the physical level. This is again the highest and the lowest meeting. When he comes down to the physical level, then, in 2,000 years maybe, we will have reached this synthesis of the highest and the lowest. It takes a long time to bring them together! But in our time, we have the help of the seventh ray, and that offers the possibility of bringing in new consciousness – the soul and the personality together. This is the same thing that the seventh ray is aiming for.

As already mentioned, the manifestation of the fifth Kingdom – the soul kingdom – is happening in our time too. Now we can really try to reach the soul! In the Amphora[4], maybe you can grasp this idea with your eyes – not only with mind and heart, but also with the eyes and your sensual awareness. Then when we have sensual awareness, brain, and heart together, a three-fold approach.

Three always brings the kind of synthesis we are aiming for: three-dimensional, three worlds, three levels, three personalities – three is a number of high quality which runs through all existence. When you grasp the idea about three and four, as in chapter 2, the seventh ray is easy to understand. "As above so below" is also the seventh ray, and so is the micro/macrocosmic consciousness.

To bring the highest and the lowest together is also something that is obviously difficult in our days. We have to transform our attitude towards physical experience and existence, towards our physical body. We have to change, transform our attitude towards sexual drives. We have to transform a lot of wrong ideas – not inherently wrong ideas as they have been right for 2,000 years of the Piscean Age and the sixth ray. But in our days, this changes.

A lot of things change – you are aware of this, you are not blind! You are living with open eyes, I hope! You see what's going on in the world, and that a lot of people who wallow in making judgements have changed. And the moralistic stuff with the sixth ray, and fanaticism and purification and mystical transcendental stuff, or whatever, is not so much "in" now.

Now, physical, sensual experiences are more "in" – this is what youngsters are looking for, not escaping into Nirvana. This is an idea maybe some youngsters still have, but on the other hand they are driven by a lot of sensual experiences. They want to mate together, and they also have a different attitude towards sexuality. This has to do with the seventh ray. Sex is seventh ray, it's creation, it's excitement, it's ecstasy. You can experience all this with the seventh ray when the lowest and the highest meet.

"The highest and the lowest meet." You have to meditate on this seed thought, the word of power. Then maybe you will have insights into the happenings of these times we live in, and you will have a different judgement about them. You will not judge according to the moralistic sixth ray attitudes of the past, you will judge differently now when you know that this is to do with the seventh ray, and this is the New Age, and this has to do with the Avatar of Synthesis. You know, when you can bring it into a larger frame of reference, then your consciousness changes immediately.

Transformation of Consciousness

This is what the rays and astrological psychology want to bring to you – the enlargement or transformation of consciousness. You have a different view towards life, evolution, your partner, your children, your friends which changes with consciousness.

When you transform your consciousness then you are linked in with the Plan. Being linked in with the Plan means you are aware that you have to make a contribution, a creative contribution to evolution. This is already a different life motivation.

When you live only with the motivation to have a good life, to have money, drink, friends, sensual excitements and so on, then this is what you will get. But when you have transformed your consciousness into a high area, a higher overview, when you are linked in with the seventh

When you transform your consciousness then you are linked in with the Plan, aware that you have to make a creative contribution to evolution

ray, or the entity of the seventh ray, or the Avatar of Synthesis – these are very high, powerful entities which are in a different dimension. You cannot say "Hello, here I am!" No, this is something much bigger than we are. These are beings, space entities. When you understand this linking up with the New Age, and have dedicated yourself to give a creative contribution towards evolution, then your life motivation is changed completely. When your motivation is changed and you want to contribute something for evolution, then the whole universe is with you. Then you are linked to the higher source of life power, and all the angels are with you. Because they wait until somebody is awakening and co-operating. They wait for it – in the bible you can read the sentence about meeting half way – do you know this?

Audience 1: *There's the parable of the Prodigal Son, when having reached the lowest part, would eat of the husks swine would eat. He then makes his way back to the father. The father then meets him halfway.*

> When your motivation is changed and you want to contribute something for evolution, then the whole universe is with you

Invocation and Evocation

Alice Bailey says that the Law of the New Age is invocation and evocation[5]. Invocation is demanding (asking) things, and evocation is the answer. This is the Law of the Approach towards the higher world. We first have to struggle for it, aspire for it, long for it, put all our energy into reaching it, and at the moment when we have put out this kind of energy then we will awaken to the answer. The stronger our prayer or invocation is, the more energy we will get back. But first we have to take the first step to awaken the soul consciousness.

Now I have my theme again – personality and soul linking up are the things I wanted to say, but I always like to start with an overview, so you know why we have to struggle to get soul consciousness.

Many people nowadays want this, because now is a time of ripeness, of opportunity for doing this. With the rays and the words of power, I tell you, you can link up with the ray of your soul quickly. For instance, when you have a seventh ray soul, or a seventh ray personality, the mantra "the highest and the lowest meet" is effective. This is something which opens up a lot of information, inspiration and intuition. Suddenly you know all about it! It comes in inspiring you, when you reach this entity of the seventh ray, with this fantastic quality.

> With the Ray words of power you can link up with the Ray of your soul quickly.

The Constitution of Man

I now refer back to the Amphora in Figure 2.3 on page 19 because it gives insight into the diagram used by Alice Bailey (Figure 6.1⁶). You can look and look, but it's very difficult to get information out of this diagram! I don't want to get into it too much – Alice Bailey's is a different frame of reference, and it's sometimes difficult to make sense of it.

There you can see the three points of the permanent atom. This is one of Alice Bailey's terms, but in Huber terms it is Saturn, the Moon and the Sun. This is easier for you to grasp than "permanent atoms"! What does this mean? "Permanent" means it's about continuity, something which is there all the time, but we know that Saturn is the physical body, the Moon is the astral body and the Sun is the mental body. Also, this is the three-fold personality. You can see the physical, emotional, and mental levels in Figure 6.1, grouped under 'personality' on the right hand side, and we work on these three levels of the chart all the time. When you deal with the chart you are dealing with these three levels.

Then we have the centre of the chart, the circle, through which we do not draw aspects. This centre of the chart symbolises the soul, the inner being, the source of your existence. The soul lives in eternity, and manifests for this incarnation for a certain time into the three-fold world, and then you need the three-fold vehicle.

During the birth process you build up the three bodies, mental, emotional and physical kinetic to operate in the environment. This is what we deal with in the chart, only with these three.

This is not much – when you look at Figure 2.3 there is much more above, if you want to understand what the highest and the lowest means. So we have to also get an idea about the highest, and the highest is the monadic energy – and in between is the spiritual triad, which is also a triangle – so we have a three-fold entity there.

Between this and the threefold personality, there is also a little triangle, and this is the ego triangle, or the causal body, which is represented by the aspect structure in the birth chart. You've made the link? Analogical thinking! You see the aspect structure, which gives you an insight into your life motivation, has to do with the triangle of the causal body, and is closest to the circle in the centre of the chart – this circle which we leave free. It's always the same thing – you have to link with analogical thinking to get the highest and the lowest together.

The centre of the chart symbolises the soul, the inner being, the source of your existence.

The Constitution of Man

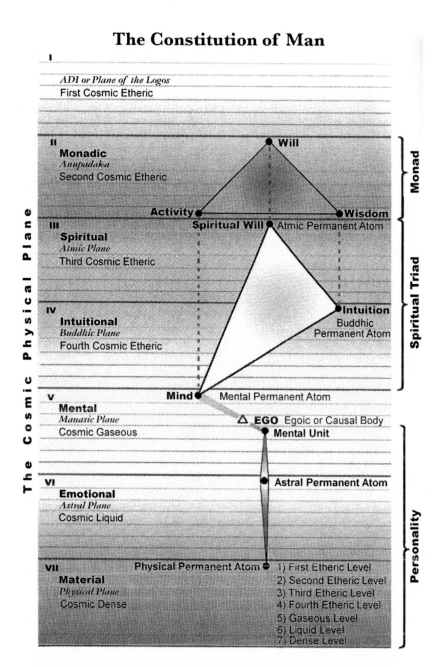

Figure 6.1 The Constitution of Man

Gap in Consciousness

Between the lower nature and the higher nature there is a gap – a gap in consciousness. To make the highest and the lowest meet, you have to do something, otherwise it will not come down! With this gap, you have to work on developing something which links it up.

In the Arcane School, the esoteric school founded by Alice Bailey, you are trained to build up the antahkarana[7]. Antahkarana is a Sanskrit word, also known as the *Rainbow Bridge*. Now this links to the rays again. A rainbow is a spectrum of colours, and we already noted the relation of the seven rays with the spectrum.

When you think according to the seventh ray, you always have to include different viewpoints, not only the Huber Method, but also Alice Bailey, psychosynthesis, transpersonal psychology. You have to find out the way these different approaches link up, and this is analogical thinking. If you do not think in analogical terms, you cannot grasp anything.

With intellectual, dialectical and logical thinking you are off beam, you will not follow my thoughts – you cannot just follow this logically, analogical thinking is necessary. This is the hermetic law of "as above, so below", and like inwardly, outwardly – it's the same thing.

When it does not click in your mind, when it is not meaningful for you inwardly, then don't go for it. For the highest and the lowest to meet in the seventh ray, you must gather everything, and what doesn't belong to the whole thing, you have to kick out. We have to select, we have to eliminate, we have to refuse.

In the Alice Bailey books you read about the Laws of Refusal[8] – what does not belong has to go. It is a purification on the mental, consciousness level. You have to enlarge your consciousness and connect with the inclusiveness of everything. This is love in cosmic terms, when you find those things that go together, that belong to each other. Wow! When you are in one ray, feeling this unity and synthesis, feeling a wonderful understanding that "Yes – this is the same as me", it is an experience which comes from the soul.

Soul Consciousness

This is soul consciousness, when you feel this inclusiveness, when you feel that it's right, when you feel as a whole, when you feel this is **mine and yours**, and we are all in one – this is the Avatar of Synthesis. This is the highest being which is now coming to the earth.

Oneness has to do with the heart, with the enlargement of the heart, and also with the consciousness of your heart power. The heart meditation – I don't know if you have ever done it – tells you how it feels when you connect with synthesising and inclusiveness and cosmic experience of love.

This is something else, with love, on the Moon level. Can you imagine? The highest and the lowest again means this word of power to bring these together – to bring together what belongs together, and kick out what doesn't belong to you. This is a kind of process of unification of the seventh ray, of the New Age, of our work and also the work of psychosynthesis.

Roberto Assagioli was dedicated to this work; this was his vision too. He was a disciple of Kuthumi[9] - a second ray disciple.

When you reach your soul level with these kind of inner experiences, then you know the ray of your soul. According to the Tibetan, when at last you are coming home to your inner being, to your inner ray – then you will be linked up immediately with the rays of all the souls who have the same ray. This is fantastic, I tell you! You are never alone anymore. You are coming home, you are linked with the rays of all the souls with the same ray. This gives a powerful inner security and sense of yourself. You belong to something which is your source – you came from there and you want to go back there again.

Then you really and fully accept the inner and outer, and the highest and the lowest, and you stand in the middle and are linked with all things, everywhere. This gives a good experience with the rays.

Building the Antahkarana

Bridging the gap. I want to give you an insight into my own experiences of the building up of the antahkarana. In the Arcane School you have to meditate every day for 20 minutes to build up the antahkarana. You get meditations and forms, and there are three levels of course. Then you have to visualise this building of the antahkarana, and sometimes you can bridge the gap and get something out of soul consciousness – meditations when you get into a state of unification with the soul.

But most of the time you are sitting down, in your personality level, and trying to get up there *(Louise jabs upwards towards the ceiling)*. I've been doing it for 50 years now, and I am a Taurus and therefore have the ability of perseverance – going on and on, often without result. But I've worked harder because sometimes you get a little bit of it.

In some good meditation in the mornings I got really inside there. I got this feeling, that excitement which is a kind of peak experience, then of course it was after 10 years work on it, and maybe some experience which gave me a good feeling and real experiences, like initiation, on my own. But then, for two years, nothing happens!

As the Tibetan says – I don't like these words but I will tell you – the soul is most of the time in deep meditation, sleeping, it's not aware of the personality stuff down there. And I was very angry because I wondered "Why is my soul always sleeping every morning?" I wondered "How can I awaken the soul and get it interested in me?"

According to the work in the Arcane School, the motivation of the soul on its own level is only love and service. It will only be awakened or interested in your stuff when this motivation is involved. Service is happy mothers, contributing something to the evolutionary process, something where you have to work from morning to night for the manifestations of some visions or ideals, and love. When you love somebody, maybe you have this kind of experience, or ecstasy, or euphoria. When you are in love, maybe the soul will be interested in participating! Love and service is the only motivation of the soul.

Alice Bailey says the antahkarana is built up best when you are a servant of humanity and you are working hard and doing things where you have the right motivation, and you are dealing with the manifestation of the Plan. Then the three threads you have to build up will be built by themselves. With the meditation, building up the antahkarana means getting soul-consciousness, and you learn a lot. You learn tremendously, and when you do 20 minutes meditation every morning, something happens inwardly. You are not sleeping during that time, you are working, you are doing, you are aspiring. Something also happens in your meditation to build up the antahkarana.

Very slowly, but I gave you the example of my own 50 years work, and I can give you a little bit of my own sensual experience to encourage you to go on, and not to stop, and keep going. This is to encourage you not to stop in spite of apparently getting nothing out of it – this is what I mean. And in the Arcane School this a long process of aspiring and so on.

Looking at Figure 6.1, when you reach the higher triad, the spiritual triad as Alice Bailey calls it, this is soul consciousness. The little triangle of the causal body is only a little mirroring. But when you reach this point – then, my goodness! This is when something of the higher triad comes into your consciousness. This is a kind of peak experience, as Roberto Assagioli called it.

Love and service is the only motivation of the soul

Initiation

Peak experiences – initiation – this is a different word for the same thing, the first initiation, second initiation, third initiation etc. When you read Alice Bailey you always hear about initiations. Sometimes she mixes up the first initiation with the third planetary initiation, and with the cosmic initiation. I got so mixed up at the beginning with all this one, two, three and four, five, seven, and the rays! Now I know about them because I've thought about them a lot.

I discovered something very interesting in the chart about the first initiation using our astrological concepts, specifically the threefold personality: Saturn, Moon and Sun. In our diagram of levels of the planets (Figure 6.2) we have the personality planets in the middle, and above them are the transpersonal planets. Above Saturn is Uranus, above the Moon is Neptune and above the Sun is Pluto. These correspond to three initiations, the transformation of these three personality planets to the transpersonal level. This is initiation. These are the three initiations Alice Bailey speaks about. This gives me a key to understand the Alice Bailey books better, otherwise you can get very mixed up.

♅	♆	♇	Transpersonal
♄	☽	☉	Personality/Ego
♀	☿ ♃	♂	Tool
Fixed	Mutable	Cardinal	

Figure 6.2 Types of Planets

The first initiation has to do with getting some knowledge about atma, buddhi and manas[10] first (see Figure 6.1 The Constitution of Man). These terms come from Helena Petrovna Blavatsky[11], as part of the explanation for the disciple who is trying to further himself in evolution. This is used in training in an esoteric school, such as the Theosophical Society, and Rudolph Steiner's anthroposophy – he and Alice Bailey were both pupils of Blavatsky. So it's all the same Ageless Wisdom, and Figure 6.1 comes from Blavatsky, and manas, buddhi and atma are from Sanskrit.

Manas – Uranus

Manas has to do with the Uranian quality; this is the higher intellectual ability to think which we call Uranus creative thinking, creative intelligence in our diagram.

When Alice Bailey or Helena Blavatsky mention manas, then Uranus is what is meant. You always have to make an analogical linking up with all this wisdom, then you will get a whole picture, when you can link this up with these other things. You understand, you get a key, and without a key you will not understand anything!

Buddhi – Neptune

Buddhi has to do with Neptune; it is love on a higher level. Krishnamurti called this unconditional love. I thought for years about these terms, wondering what does that mean – unconditional love?

The astral, feeling nature, the Moon, has to do with love and you can transform it into Neptune. When you get a little bit out of Neptune you will move into the buddhic sphere. Buddhi is a wonderful yellow! And you reach this in meditation sometimes. There is oneness, unconditional love, warmth, and in your feeling level, you are on the second initiation according to Alice Bailey.

I am jumping from Alice Bailey to Blavatsky to the Hubers and to Assagioli – they all reflect this Ancient Wisdom, otherwise you can kick it out! The seventh ray again has to clarify these things, or has to use the Law of Refusal to kick out rubbish.

Remember this first ray business – 1,3,5,7. On the seventh level you really do have to purify your consciousness. You know that this is the truth, and nothing else, and the truth must become whole, and you have to link up with everything. It must click with you, otherwise it's not the truth! This is the seventh ray – the inspiration ray – and it brings this into the world, into every field, into your own experience.

Atma – Pluto

Above the Sun in Figure 6.2 lies Pluto, the divine will that represents the evolutionary plan comes from Shamballa. In the third initiation, we have a vision of the divine plan and discover what personal contribution we can make to it.

That is a relatively simple explanation, which will suffice for this context[12]. It is the task of the seventh ray to present these things as simply as possible and to clarify misunderstandings. Anything that does not belong should be weeded out. This is how we learn to separate the essential from the non-essential, the genuine from the false and the transitory from the eternal. The consciousness is purified of superfluities during this initiation phase so that only the simple truth remains. The inspiration of the seventh ray helps us in this process, bringing this knowledge down into the world of concrete experience.

The Soul Ray and the Personality Ray

Synergy between the personality ray and the soul ray is brought about by our own will. Only when a person starts to take an interest in his own soul does he start to adapt to the soul ray. It is important that he knows his soul ray. Only then can he consciously carry out the necessary transformations. This consists essentially of transforming selfish personality motivations into humanitarian soul aims.

Every transformation or change of awareness starts with a crisis in which angst, rejection or a compensation reach their peak. By stepping beyond this peak, we can break through into a new dimension. In order to reach a higher state of awareness, we can also consciously construct the so-called antahkarana or rainbow bridge. This is usually done by means of a special daily meditation and a life of service. Over time, a direct, conscious link to the soul and the soul ray is developed. This is followed by the ascent to the monad, the divine self or the higher triad, whereby this ray also becomes effective.

Transformations of the Seven Rays

In the transformation processes, it is always advantageous to know the transformations within the rays. We explain them below, using keywords corresponding to the three astrological cross qualities: cardinal, fixed and mutable.

First Ray   "Will and Power"

Cardinal Cross – Sun

People with this ray are strong-willed, grabbing, go-getting and grasping. They are always at the centre of things and never give in; they concentrate all their energies on one goal. These people are powerful and strong-willed. They can also have a destructive effect on their environment when they are power-hungry, ambitious, ruthless and domineering and cannot tolerate anyone around them.

Transformation

In the transformation, they must develop the will to love, renounce personal power and work vigorously for the divine plan. Complete devotion to higher goals, dedication to the planetary logos, ceaseless activity and always performing creative contributions to evolution – nothing else counts any more. Then their influence is decisive.

Second Ray "Love and Wisdom"

Mutable Cross – Moon

Such people possess the gift of love, but they also want to be loved and want comfort, tenderness and warmth. They automatically attract what they need and possess a natural magnetism. They long for material and spiritual comfort, want their wishes to be realised and use others to that end. They are often self-absorbed and separatist and hide the light that is within them.

Transformation

The rejection of separateness – giving love, not being loved. The construction of dwellings that bring comfort for all, an all-encompassing feeling of belonging. Longing for wisdom and truth, inner compassion for all creation. Forward planning, making plans, healing, teaching, educating.

Third Ray   "Active Intelligence"

Fixed Cross – Saturn

Clever use of intelligence for personal gain. Intensive material and mental activity, clear intellect, cautious approach, emphasising the essential. Intellectual arrogance, coldness, lack of attention to detail. Longing for fame, beauty, material goods and possessions. Absorption in delusions, conceits, illusions.

Transformation

Stillness, restraining the urge to act, cultivating peace, learning to be silent. Developing the love of truth. Striving for the correct use of energy to encourage plans, seeking ordered harmonious activity and collaboration with the whole world, trying to do the right thing, showing integrity, honesty, magnanimity, developing goodwill.

Fourth Ray "Harmony through Conflict"

Water – Venus

Ray of struggle and conflict, being torn. Decision-making crises, experiences of polarity, fighting with both ends. Often conflict where there is none, confused struggles, longing for harmony, collaboration with a part and not with the whole. Pathological sensitivity, constant crises.

Transformation

Harmony and unity. Awakening of the intuition. The fourth ray of intuition brings everything into harmony with the whole. Beauty, justice, rationality, wisdom, generosity, devotion, quick understanding and perception.

Fifth Ray   "Concrete Knowledge/Science"

Air – Mercury

The ray of knowledge and research. The urge to know, curiosity, sharp intellect. Analysis into the smallest detail, accuracy, common sense, detail is more important than the whole, formalistic sense of justice with no mercy for or understanding of weaknesses. Prejudices, no compassion, crass materialism with a distorted view of the truth, denial of the divine. Mental detachment, self-will, pride, censoriousness.

Transformation

Recognising the transience of matter. Liberation from attachment to matter. Development of a delusion-free sense of reality and a sense of reverence for life. Working for the life-sustaining laws, drawing final conclusions and taking the consequences. Studying the science of the soul.

Sixth Ray   "Devotion and Idealism"

Fire – Mars

The ray of idealists. Devotion, love, tenderness, loyalty and adoration. Will do anything for loved ones. Excessive emotions and fanaticism, one-sided clinging to an ideal, even if it is outdated. Misjudgement and spiritual blindness. Stubbornness that only recognises its own point of view. Mistrust of others' motives. Tendency to put oneself in the foreground.

Transformation

Love of truth, being still, being able to retreat, choosing the middle way. Development of willingness to make sacrifices, purity, patience, serenity, inner balance. Valuing the opinions of others, respecting others' goals. Idealism that has a constructive goal and is not exclusive.

Seventh Ray "Ceremonial Magic"

Earth – Jupiter

Organisation, order, building forms that are useful for all. Love of rhythm, of the cyclical, ritual process of things. Organisational ability, good planning and control. Will prefer to take care of a whole group of people as well as possible.

A person on the seventh ray usually has a high opinion of himself. He feels like a priest who sets the tone, like a magician who draws on supernatural powers to control others and be important. He is also able to wait until paths open up for him to reach his goal. Lack of order and chaos due to misunderstanding of plans.

Transformation

Love of planned collaboration with others – preservation of laws, rituals, rites. Revealing the nature of God, the laws of spiritual development. Helping to implement the plan, recognising oneness.

The Rays and the Masters

There is an interesting connection between the rays and the ascended masters. These are people who have achieved spiritual and physical perfection over many incarnations. They have also reached the evolutionary goal long before us. According to Alice Bailey, there are seven masters and seven ashrams that correspond to the seven rays. The soul ray of a person, which can be known definitively after the third initiation, determines which ashram they belong to. It is important to understand that these things take place on the spiritual planes of manas, buddhi and atma. They are etheric, spiritual planes. We do not need to travel anywhere to find the masters or their ashrams.

Below we provide brief descriptions of these seven masters with the corresponding rays and their spheres of activity[13].

First Ray: Master Morya

The person whose soul is upon the first ray belongs to Master Morya. He works on the development of evolution using willpower and the ability to awaken people. He brings new ideas into the world and destroys the obsolete, thus purifying the consciousness.

Second Ray: Master Kuthumi

The master of the second ray is Kuthumi. We know that Roberto Assagioli belonged to his ashram; he spiritually supported his works in the field of psychosynthesis. It deals with inner awareness, which takes place when the antakarana is constructed. We can then connect with other souls and receive the knowledge we need.

Third Ray: Master Maha Chohan

The master of the third ray is Maha Chohan, the lord of civilisation. His works are connected with human intelligence. He educates the world on how the economy should be run. Everything connected with work and the fair distribution of money and food is supported by the third ray master.

Fourth Ray: Master Serapis

The master of the fourth ray is Serapis, also often referred to as "the Egyptian". He is concerned with the arts movements in the world; with the development of music, painting, and drama. He is now giving his attention to the deva or angelic evolution, which will brings with it great revelations that are imminent in the worlds of music and painting. The fourth ray will not come fully into effect until this century.

Fifth Ray: Master Hilarion

The master of the fifth ray is Hilarion. His influence is important for the general public in our crisis-ridden times. He collaborates with those who are developing their intuition and spiritual perception. His ashram works with groups that pursue spiritual healing and scientific research.

Sixth Ray: Master Jesus

This ray embodies Master Jesus. He works through the Christian church and promotes the germination of the true spiritual life. Where possible, he tries to correct the mistaken dogmas propounded by the church and theologists. His followers are often as fanatically devoted to an ideal as the early Christian martyrs were.

Seventh Ray: Master Saint Germain

The master of the seventh ray bears the name Saint Germain (also known as Master Rakoczi). He works with the violet flame, which liberates us from old structures and karmic forces. He brings the quality of the seventh ray to all areas of human life and sponsors that which guarantees the future development of people in Europe and America. As the ambassador of the New Age, Master Saint Germain is responsible for the implementation of the divine plan on earth.

Ray Words of Power

We have already looked at the mantra of the seventh ray. Each ray has its own word of power or mantra.

1st Ray	I assert the fact.
2nd Ray	I see the greatest light.
3rd Ray	Purpose itself am I.
4th Ray	Two merge into one.
5th Ray	Three minds unite.
6th Ray	The highest light controls.
7th Ray	The highest and the lowest meet.

Figure 6.3 Ray Words of Power

First Ray: "I assert the fact"

Isn't this powerful? The first ray is the one-pointed disciple. He is the one who has the power to bring down new ideas. Whenever a new manifestation of the Plan is necessary in time and space, the first ray is active, and there are a lot of disciples on the first ray who have the task of preparing the way for the coming world. I have three first rays! Bruno has second rays. The second ray and the first ray have to work together in the New Age. You can read about this in the books.

Second Ray: "I see the greatest light"

I think your head goes up when you think on this seed thought. You look far ahead when you look for that greatest light and you have the second ray in you. If your emotional body or your mental body is second ray, then this seed thought can be very uplifting.

Third Ray: "Purpose itself am I"

When you meditate on these words it's fantastic to link up with the highest purpose in yourself. The highest purpose also means your highest motivation, that you have only this purpose – this is something, I tell you, and it is about liquidation of all that does not belong to this one purpose. It also has to do with the one-pointed Sun, with the one who sees the goal and reaches it. The third ray also has the power of the first ray in it, for it is a masculine ray.

Fourth Ray: "Two merge in One"

If ever you feel cut in two pieces, or are separated from something, "Two merge in One" is a consolation e.g. when you are suffering about love, when you are feeling alone. With "Two merge in One" then you do not need anybody anymore because you will become one in yourself. This is the best thing about the fourth ray, when it reaches harmony.

Fifth Ray: *"Three minds unite"*

You know the skittering mind of the fifth ray sometimes, when they gather so much knowledge. It's a kind of Faustian process going on in them. They learn and learn and learn, and in the end know nothing. And then three minds unite, coming together. This is what I wanted to tell you today, the whole linking up of all the ancient wisdom, which is true, and so clear and so real in the end, then this doubting, questioning and critical mind of the fifth ray will become calm.

Three minds unite – then he can sit down and he knows now. They must no longer struggle for the truth, the little ones, they have got the big one – unification again. It's always healing and liberating to know, to link up with these rays, and to understand what they mean for the whole evolution and development, but the fifth ray doesn't relax.

Sixth Ray: **"The highest light controls"**

Now you understand the Piscean Age. This mystical attitude towards the transpersonal god, this kind of longing for heaven, or whatever they wanted to reach for – "The highest light controls". They aim for their ideals, and this means devotion and opening up to higher influences, and then they will be liberated through this. The highest light controls, and when the highest light controls them, then they are satisfied, and they stay still.

Seventh Ray: **"The highest and the lowest meet"**

I have already covered the seventh ray and its mantra at the beginning of this chapter, so will not go further into it here.

In my own experience, these mantras always bring you a kind of stillness. Quietness is the word. The battle ends, in a way. You have come home. You are accepted as you are. You accept yourself as you are, and this is a kind of a power which is healing.

So again, coming back to our chart, the circle in the centre is the healing energy of your own soul, the self-healing power. When you put them up with all the rays, and the coming in of all these vibes, or even reiki's if you want to call it that – then everything is all right. Now you can sit down and say "I've done everything that was needed. Now I can wait." And then the invocation comes, and then God himself, or Sanat Kumara, or the Master, or whatever you have called for comes, softening your sorrows and worries, all this earthly stuff. This is the transformation of the personality ray into soul ray, and this happens when it comes together.

I hope I have given you a little bit of insight into this very difficult theme.

Shamballa, the Plan, and the Hierarchy

Shamballa is a golden town on the etheric level in the Gobi Desert in Tibet. In Shamballa, the will of God is known. The planetary logos lives there, and Buddha and the Christ live there also. In Shamballa there is the first ray, and the first ray is the dynamic whirl of evolutionary movement. When there comes a time at which the whole of humanity becomes stuck and there is no longer evolutionary movement, then the first ray is directed towards humanity and brings disturbances, perhaps destruction, wars, etc., according to the Plan of God which is known in Shamballa.

In the evolutionary process of humanity, because of its destructive power, the first ray impetus is usually transformed and transmuted by the Hierarchy. The spiritual hierarchy of our planet is the keeper of the second ray; it transforms the Will of God into something that can be given to humanity through disciples.

All people who have reached a certain initiation are able to bring the Plan down to humanity. They reach the stage of transformation of their own motivation where they want only to live to serve the Plan. The only motivation remaining after all the initiations is to make a creative contribution to the illusion. So the whole thing is coming down and going into humanity through us, through you. And everyone of you who has an idea, a vision of this process of the illusionary plan, the divine plan, brings it down into better forms for a lot of people. You are all asked for contribution, for co-operation with the Plan. All of you.

Cosmic Evolution

One cosmic month is 25,000 years, and one day is 72 years. One hundred and sixty years is the cosmic month according to the larger cycles of evolution.

You know that we are part of the evolution of the whole, nobody can step out of the evolutionary processes. You have to go with it, it is our goal, our purpose, our meaning in life to be part of the whole evolutionary process. When you want to step off you will fall down, you will be hit. You may be punished in a way by yourself, because when you separate yourself from the whole then you will be a separate one.

Interestingly, in Sanskrit Saturn means "the separate one". Saturn means the devil, or the separate one, the one who was kicked out of the whole process.

But you yourself can come home, you can change your consciousness, you can have the realisation that you can not step out of the evolutionary process, you can only participate. When you change and transform your consciousness into participation with the Plan then nothing can happen to you anymore, nothing. No punishment, no sorrow, no pain can really destroy you. The fear of being eliminated at the end is the ego. When you die whatever fears you have within you will be gone. At the moment when you are participating with the Plan you are on the right side. When I am on the right side then I am safe, in a way.

You yourself can come home, you can change your consciousness

---

Living the Soul's Purpose

When you know your soul ray – maybe you don't know it now but maybe you have a kind of a feeling for it – then you can find out what kind of task you have in life.

If you have the second ray, then you have to spread around love and wisdom, it's as simple as that.

When you have the third ray as soul ray then you have to pursue your purpose from morning to evening, without rest. The restlessness must be for working for the Plan and your activity and the energy will come and will flow all the time.

This is the interesting thing, when you reach the soul level energy flows all the time. You remain young, but eternal youth is something which you may have read about as the Holy Grail. This is a wonderful story about coming home, drinking from this eternal life-stuff, from the Grail. Then you will have eternal youth, because you are on the soul level and the soul lives for a long time, 2 million years or something, I don't know. It doesn't matter because the soul lives in eternity. She is always there and when we live our personal life in this incarnation we go home to our soul in a way, but only when you have consciousness of it.

If you do not have the consciousness and do not build up the Rainbow Bridge, the antakarana, then you have no idea about your soul. She is sleeping, you have first to awaken her and then you know that when death comes you will be going home. That's all, and then you come again. So I prepare myself already for the next incarnation and I am writing the book now because I want to read it when I come back!

When you reach the soul level energy flows all the time

Sacred Planets

There is also some strange stuff in *Esoteric Astrology* about sacred planets, as in Figure 6.4. I am still not clear what it means!

Ray	Sacred planets	Non-sacred planets
Ray 1	Vulcan	Pluto
Ray 2	Jupiter	Sun
Ray 3	Saturn	Earth
Ray 4	Venus[14]	Moon
Ray 5	Mercury[14]	
Ray 6	Neptune	Mars
Ray 7	Uranus	

Figure 6.4 Sacred Planets

I remember reading about sacred planets in *The Secret Doctrine*[15]. It was so confusing. Bruno and I spoke about it a long time ago and the only thing I can make out is that the sacred planets have gone through an evolutionary state, maybe where they reached a higher life form than the Earth is now, together with Pluto, the Sun, Moon and Mars. Maybe in one million years we will also become a sacred planet.

So what? You know what I mean, it's irrelevant in a way for me. You know when you think you are not on a sacred planet and you feel sorrow, you feel a little bit let down in a way because you think a sacred planet is something which has already reached a very high state.

In my experience this levels business, the initiations business such as "I am one of the third initiations, you are only one of the first", or the kind of attitude of being a sacred planet or not, gives you a wrong attitude. I don't want to cultivate this wrong attitude in you, therefore forget about it!

Audience: *I think the difference between what we call the sacred planets and the non-sacred ones is that the non-sacred planetary logoi have not taken a particular initiation and that would go for our own Sun which again is not sacred. It's that the Solar Logos has still got to go through another initiation before we become sacred.*

Louise Huber: OK, so it's their business. I just say it's not good to compare ourselves with one who has reached a greater state of evolution than we. Forget it!

In Figures 2.3 and 6.1[16] you can see seven levels. Adi is the divine plane, Anupadaka is the monadic one, Nirvana (Atma) is the spiritual one, Buddhi is the love one, the mental (Manas) is the intelligence one and the astral (Kama) is the feeling one, and the bottom is the physical level where we have the chakras.

You know we have the seven chakras on the etheric level, on the spine, and they have also to do with the Seven Rays[17]. When you deal with healing, when you deal with chakras or meditation or working on the chakras or whatever, you must know that the rays are also involved.

The Monad

I'll say a few words about the monad because I think it is important. In Figure 6.1[16] you can see the monad, the higher child on the level of Anupadaka. This is a very interesting thing, the higher child is the monad and the monad is higher than the soul. It is the highest spiritual self in a way.

You can see the personal level with the threefold personality, and between the monad and the personality is the soul. The soul links up the personality with the monad. It is the task of the soul over a long period to link up with the monadic energy and the monad exists only on the first three rays. There are no fourth ray monads, only first, second and third ray monads, and these are a vision.

Alice Bailey says that only after the third initiation will you know something about your monadic ray. However, I have made meditations on monadic power with many people in my group, and I was surprised that people immediately got some link up with their monadic power, not only with the soul. Usually the rainbow bridge was built up with the soul, the triangle atma, buddhi, manas.

Monadic consciousness is seemingly coming down more and more into people. Maybe you also have an idea about the monadic power in you; it's the divine spark, the divine primer. It's a very high quality and some people can grasp this level through meditation, music, or nature experience. When I was telling you about sensual things related to the soul, the monadic energy is probably coming down at the same moment too, because there is no gap between the monad and the soul. You can see the triad atma - buddhi - manas of the soul on its own level, linked to the higher triad of the monadic cosmic etheric, and this is maybe something which is already together.

Only at the antahkarana is there a gap between our physical brain and the soul. When you reach the first smell of your soul, in a way, the first impression of it, then probably the monadic power will immediately be sensed too. This is what I experienced from the feedback people have given when I meditate with them on monadic energy.

The higher child is a colour and these are red, blue and yellow. These are the basic colours in colour psychology. When these appear visually in meditation, then immediately they have a good, healing feeling. When you reach this monadic power, immediately you will get rid of a headache or pain, or fear, or whatever. It is really true, I tell you. To reach the monadic power, you come into a link with the planetary logos.

This is a secret, according to Alice Bailey, because she says the monadic energy, the triangle of the monad of every human being, is the same for the planetary logos. It is the eye of the planetary logos, it is for him as the clairvoyant eye, the third eye, is for us. You can meditate about this. The monads of all people living on the earth are the eye of the planetary logos – the monadic primary link with the whole of humanity, in a way.

Without monadic energy there will not be a link, even the reverse, we cannot reach the planetary logos, and his will of illusion in Shamballa, unless we have reached the monadic power. Again this invocation and evocation in which he comes half way.

It is really worthwhile to meditate on your monad, it's the divine spark in your inner being. It is even more central than the soul in my experience. When you reach this, again you are safe, you are in the right place. You will be initiated and you will get a vision of the Plan and a vision of what you have to do. You will be guided by the inner self and you know that the monadic energy is something very strong. When you are guided by this nothing can happen to you, nothing. It is indestructible – it's you.

The monadic meditation is given opposite.

Closing Thoughts

In *Esoteric Healing*[18] Alice Bailey says that in the twenty first century a lot of initiates will be going around healing with the rays. They have the knowledge about the rays, and can use this kind of energy when the glands, the chakras, are not working properly. When you get sick in some part of your body then the chakra nearby is not working properly, and so they give the ray vibes or whatever to them so they will be getting alive again and will heal themselves. The healer of the future will work with the rays.

You are the younger ones. I am preparing for the next incarnation but you still can do it here, and also work for healing possibilities with the rays. If you work in a hospital it is hard to remain on your ray consciousness. I can imagine that the ray consciousness is not awakened now in a lot of people, so it is still not manifested very strongly in the world. You can not just put the person onto the computer and the rays are there. It is still in the process of manifesting down.

Monadic Meditation

We sit in comfort in the chair and relax our physical body. Also, the breathing is a preparation for meditation. You breathe in and out and we let go all tensions. We get very calm, and we feel into our head. The front of the head gets also relaxed and the face gets friendly, and we concentrate in the centre of our brain....

We see a light shining in our brain, a point of light which gets brighter and then we shift our consciousness above our head, and we see the rainbow bridge appearing, coloured, vital. And on the other side we reach the spiritual triangle and we can visualise a beautiful lightening circle of power and energy which comes from the higher triad, from the soul. You can have a white colour, or a yellow one, blue or red and it is taking on my physical appearance in it. And then we shift our focus of consciousness even higher, higher. Then we see the monadic triangle with a blue corner, red and yellow. The yellow is shining down, mixing with all the other colours and again coming down, including my whole personality....

I feel safe, I feel secure, I feel accepted and in full union with the whole. I am a point of light within a greater light. I'm a ray of loving energy within the love divine. I am a sacrificial part within the Will of God. And thus I stand....

Then we breathe in, come back from the meditation first into the head, we turn the head left and turn it right. And then we circle the shoulders back and forth and we stretch our hands, circling the hands, opening the eyes and then we go into our body and legs and feet, and there we are again.

On the other hand I found out that in daily life, only when there is an urgent situation will you use your personality ray, and all the other rays are integrated. So probably the rays are only available when there is a good brain, a good moderation, and a good attitude or intelligence.

You have to offer something yourself to get a link with the rays all the time – to push the button and there is the energy flow. But we have to prepare ourselves for this. This must be important enough for you to prepare yourself for this kind of brain, of awareness, of love and service for others. So you will all become a channel.

We have to work quietly, without ego-stuff and only when you are working in silence with the rays and with healing and with the attitude of love and service, then it is really true.

When there is somebody telling you that "I am the one" then always doubt it. That's also something I have wanted to say to you.

7

The Law of the Triangles in the Signs

Louise Huber

The Law of the Triangles in the Signs

- Aries, Leo, Capricorn: Ray 1 •
- Libra: Ray 3 •
- Transformation Crisis •
- Cancer: Rays 3,7 •
- Aquarius: Ray 5 •
- Sagittarius: Rays 4,5,6 •
- Scorpio and Taurus : Ray 4 •
- Pisces and Virgo: Rays 2, 6 •
- Gemini: Ray 2 •

Colour and the Rays

Rays and Personality Types

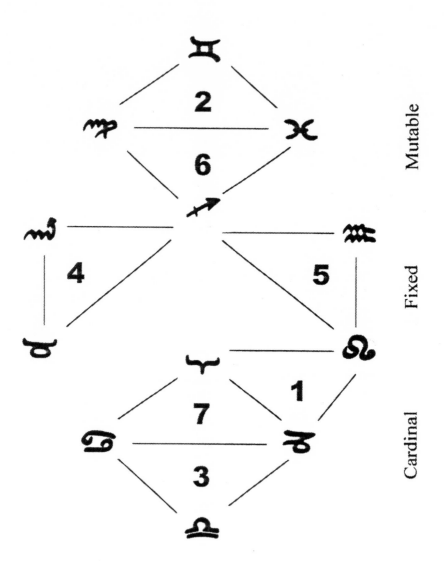

Figure 7.1 The Triangles in the Signs

The Law of the Triangles in the Signs

I was confused for some time about the Alice Bailey's Law of the Triangles in the Signs[1]. Years ago my son Michael created the diagram in Figure 7.1, showing the cosmic triangles and the seven ray energies, which helped to clear up my thoughts on this.

On the mutable cross, the second ray flows through Gemini, Virgo and Pisces, and the sixth ray through Pisces, Virgo and Sagittarius.

Linking mutable and fixed crosses, Sagittarius is linked with the fifth ray with Aquarius and Leo, and the fourth ray with Scorpio and Taurus.

On the cardinal cross, the seventh ray flows through Cancer, Aries and Capricorn, and the third ray through Capricorn, Libra and Cancer.

Linking fixed and cardinal crosses, the first ray flows through Leo, Aries and Capricorn.

Now you have to figure out why they are combined with these rays. That's not easy, I tell you, I have tried it!

Aries, Leo, Capricorn: Ray 1

As the prototype of the impulse cross, the cardinal cross, Aries clearly relates directly to the first ray. Aries is the first sign. In Aries spring arrives, leaves appear on trees, flowers come out and new cycles start. I can easily relate this first ray with Aries as it corresponds with these beginnings, powerful impulses and initiation of things, like breaking though the shell of an egg or emerging from the womb when you are born. Aries has this first ray power.

Leo has it too, another fire sign. In Aries the ego is born into the world; in the second fire sign Leo, the ego has to exercise how far he can go with his ego stuff. Maybe he also needs the first ray to take him over barriers and fear and to help him to take risks. To show your inner self sometimes needs this kind of risk, where the first ray has to be used, so that you can open up your heart and show yourself as you are, raising the mask from your face.

Leo sometimes has to do this because he very easily identifies with masks, forms, roles and functionings, and hides himself behind them. With the first ray he can open up, and say "Here I am, and I'm like that... and that's it, buster!" – the Leo-like ego.

We also have the first ray in Capricorn, the highest sign, the sign of individuation. Individuation also needs this kind of power and courage, and the will to show who you are, and how you are. In Capricorn the individuation process has to come to an end; in this sign you have to climb to the peak of the mountain, and on the peak you are alone, and say: "Here I am, and I've reached this peak by using my own power".

This also needs first ray power to come so far and not give up before reaching the goal. The first ray can give you this kind of power to reach the peak, the goal or the ambition. Capricorn has to do with power – it's something very similar to the first ray.

But Capricorn also has the third ray. I can imagine that without the third ray, Capricorn would not be so successful. The third ray is Active Intelligence, and to reach the peak of the mountain you have to prepare yourself in an intelligent way. If a foolish person takes the chair lift up into the mountains wearing no shoes, these are silly people! But Capricorn takes the right shoes and wears the right things; he's prepared himself and goes step by step up the mountain to the peak. This needs the practical intelligence of the third ray.

Libra: Ray 3

Libra is all in the third ray, so Libra people are highly intelligent, but they show it very diplomatically, subtly, elegantly. This is an air sign, and they are very skilled at making contact with others, bringing them into action or reaction. Libra has the ability to make a sound and the other will answer. It's this kind of echo, and he knows this law of the echo, and uses it very intelligently. He knows exactly that when he says "ooo-oo", they will reply "ooo-oo". It must be the same sound – what I want from others must be just exactly that which I want from myself too.

Libra has this kind of partnership knowledge about relationships, about love, and about how to get others to do things for me. In the end, Libra is very intelligent when he transforms.

Transformation Crisis

Every sign has its own three-step evolution or development, described in *Reflections and Meditations on the Signs of the Zodiac*[2]. The three steps are also very important for the signs and the Law of the Triangles in the Signs.

It's important to know that in each sign there is a transformation crisis mechanism at work. It is very simply put. The exoteric ruler works on the physical plane. With Aries the martian power is a kind of drive – libido, masculine stuff, sexual etc. The Aries person goes out with this martian power without intelligence, just getting excitement, and achieving goals.

Then he is rejected by Libra people, by the "You", and through rejection the cardinal cross comes into a crisis. It's the kind of Napoleonic power drive where you have to meet your Waterloo – rejection. No love. No applause. People say: "Get out of here, we don't want you".

This is the best crisis he can go through because he has to integrate Libra – the other side of the coin. And Libra means that you are liked and you do things nicely and sensitively etc. He has to absorb this, identify with this and bring it into his own being.

The esoteric ruler of the sign[3] will be working on the consciousness – this is Mercury. Transformation goes from the exoteric ruler, Mars, over to Libra to the esoteric ruler on the mental consciousness level. The power of words, or the seed thought of each sign[4] then comes alive. For Aries this is "I come forth, and from the plane of mind, I rule". With Mercury as the esoteric ruler of Aries, then these people are very intelligent, because they have absorbed Libra.

These three steps are very important in each sign – for your own Sun sign, your AC sign, your Moon sign, or for wherever you are now by Age Point. Wherever you are in your own chart, and whatever you are dealing with, you can look towards these words of power.

Cancer: Rays 3,7

In Cancer we have the third and the seventh ray. We think Cancer is a water sign, a feeling sign, ruled by the Moon, which is always trying to get love, encouragement, nourishment and whatever it wants to feel well – and here is the seventh and the third ray! The third is Active Intelligence and the seventh is where the Highest and the Lowest meet.

This seems strange, in my opinion. To get these together the seventh ray must also have to do with this Cancer theme of coming home. Cancer is the sign of the family, of belonging to the collective and so on. The theme of lowest and the highest meeting is a coming together and linking up, and coming home and feeling safe.

The third ray in Cancer makes them very skilled at home making, reflected in the seed thought of Cancer: "I build a lighted house and therein dwell". For building a house, you also need practical intelligence to build in all the things you need, so that you feel well there, there is plenty of light, the occupants feel well too, so this is also a kind of third ray energy. They are running around the house, cleaning up, or whatever, or moving the furniture! The third ray is always moving, moving, doing things again and making them better. Third ray people are very concerned with making things better and better! They want to improve it. This is Cancer.

Aquarius: Ray 5

Aquarius has only the fifth ray. You know this sophisticated attitude with Aquarius! There's a little bit here of the scientific people who know everything and look down on other people! Saturn is the traditional ruler of Aquarius; Uranus came later. Aquarius has to integrate Leo.

It is Aquarius who has built up this elitist consciousness: "We are the only ones who know all about things". This is a kind of pride on the mental level. Do you know such Aquarius people? They know everything and give you lots of advice and say you have to do this and that, like a kind of educator. Others down on the cosmic plane in Leo, the crowd in the fifth house, will not listen to them. They will not listen to these moralistic people who are always inhibiting their enjoyment.

Then Aquarius has to climb down from his ivory tower and become normal again, and when he is climbing down he needs the experience of love. He must fall in love. When he falls in love then he lands in bed, and this again is the lowest and the highest meeting, and with the fifth ray he becomes concrete. In the eleventh house, with the Aquarius mind, sometimes it is only a vision, a picture, an ideal, a principle or whatever – you cannot grasp it. The fifth ray makes it concrete, helps bring it down to earth, to bring it really into the fifth house.

Audience: *There is an expression "He loves humanity but has a hard time with human beings"!*

Louise Huber: Yes, that is a good expression – he needs to behave normally, eh? He also has to become concrete.

Sagittarius: Rays 4,5,6

Now we have a very interesting sign, Sagittarius, with three rays, the fourth, fifth and sixth. It's difficult for Sagittarius to combine all these three rays. This is the last fire sign, and has to do with the individuation process on the mental level. This is knowing about himself and also about the opportunity to liberate himself from the indoctrinations of the collective mind and principles. He has to find his own principles, his own knowledge, his own *weltanshauung*[5] .

Sagittarius is very able to bring everything together, to synthesise. This is a goal of Sagittarius. Therefore he has three rays. With the sixth ray "the highest light controls", he's open to transpersonal levels, and most of the time looks for higher goals – he reaches the goal and then looks for another, as in the seed thought[6].

With the fourth ray "Two merge in One", there is a merging, unifying power – which is conflicting! Most of the time conflict comes along without you needing to do anything, but the harmony, merging, becoming one in ideas is a proper goal for Sagittarius – so that it is harmonious, rounded. Jupiter is the ruler, and Jupiter is the sensual stuff of knowledge, not just knowledge which gives you some philosophical picture, it must become sensual, artistic, like a picture or something to be smelled. This is the knowledge which Sagittarius gives.

Well, Bruno is a Sagittarius and he brings the astrological concepts really into your hearts, into your feelings, into your picturing minds, into this organic knowledge, as he always says. Maybe he can do it with the fourth ray, but he also has the fifth ray, the critical scientific ray. So it's not always artistic, it can be scientific. When you hear Bruno talk, and you see all the three combinations of these rays in how he presents his talk, you see he's much more precise than me. He's fifth ray too, very scientifically oriented. You can feel it, and see why these rays go through Sagittarius!

Sagittarius is something of a central point in Figure 7.1. In my mind (a seventh ray mind) I jump straight to the Galactic Centre, the middle point of our galaxy, the Milky Way. And where is the Galactic Centre – 26° of Sagittarius. Aha! Maybe there is a link! An analogical link again – we smell something about Sagittarius, he really has the possibility of bringing together the truth so that it will become organic and meaningful. It helps a lot of people to grow into the same state of consciousness too.

Sagittarius is the great teacher or educator of the Zodiac. The world's teacher is Sagittarius, and the little teacher is the one downstairs – Gemini.

And the whole Thinking Axis is now coming into our minds – it needs to change the consciousness, to enlarge it, to bring in the whole truth, not only one part of it. These are the rays coming together in Sagittarius, bringing all together – wonderful!

Scorpio and Taurus : Ray 4

Then we have Scorpio and Taurus, both with only the fourth ray. So we can sit in a nice train, the fourth ray train. There's nothing disturbing me, there's just the fourth ray! You know, there's a kind of oneness here too, like a train on its track.

You can understand this – Taurus is sometimes very stubborn, narrow-minded – there's this kind of viewpoint and there's nothing else. The fourth ray is harmony through conflict.

Taurus seeks pleasure, beauty and a nice life and everything to eat that you want, and a nice chair, a nice car and all this stuff to make things very comfortable. This could be fourth ray harmony, and you sit there and have your nice comfort – and then somebody knocks on the door, comes into my possessions and wants to take something away from me. You always have the feeling when somebody comes into this place and disturbs this oneness that he wants something from you. There is always this paranoia behind it: "What do you want from me?" Are they here to tell me something?

In communicating you are always very eager not to be disturbed, not to be involved in any conflict, you go for harmony and comfort and for all these nice things. But what sign is on the other side – Scorpio

– danger! Scorpio with the sting in the tail can do something to you, so you are always in the defensive attitude of Taurus, because nobody is allowed to disturb your harmony.

But on the other hand the fourth ray is conflict, and that is also Scorpio. Scorpio disturbs order. He enjoys disturbing you, the Scorpion is masochistic in a way.

So the fourth ray is always creating uncertainty, whereas certainty or security is of the highest concern to the Taurus person. If there is uncertainty or danger, he defends from morn 'til night, his harmony, his own rights, his own possessions, his own comforts. Life is always coming and knocking on his door and he wants to kick out the people who are intruding on his comfort – and then he gets into conflict with them.

Harmony through conflict is life in a different way from what you see in May, when the sun is in Taurus. It is so beautiful outside with the sun shining, the flowers are coming out and you smell their aroma and this is a good feeling. But in November when the leaves are falling from the trees and the fog is rising, life goes down and there is no joy anymore, and you get a little depressive because this is the circle of life.

Taurus and Scorpio have to deal with this. Taurus, with Venus as ruler, has to integrate Scorpio, has to know that death and life cannot be avoided. It is a law of life to be alive today and to be dead tomorrow. Death is Scorpio, life is Taurus.

The esoteric ruler of Taurus is Vulcan, which is to do with the first ray. Alice Bailey writes very interesting stuff about Taurus – when Taurus is transformed the fourth ray comes through it, and humanity is on the fourth ray. Taurus can prepare men's minds for the advent of the New Age, and so he is the Cosmic Bull who is forging with the hammer so that the new time can come. This is the task of the transformed bull, Taurus. Perhaps you have read that the blacksmith Vulcan, or Hephaestus, worked with the anvil. I love this expression, the Cosmic Bull, because I feel like that. I prepare the ground for the coming age, you know this kind of working hard and turning over the soil and putting new stuff into it. This is also Taurus life – you know the green fingers of the Taurean, when they put some seeds into the earth something grows out of it.

Pisces and Virgo: Rays 2, 6

In the upper triangle of Figure 7.1 we have Pisces, Virgo and Gemini. Pisces is sixth and second ray. I think this makes sense, second ray love and wisdom for Pisces, who can easily combine these with the sixth ray "the highest light controls". You can consider that the Age of Pisces has to do with the sixth ray. Pisces is the representation of the sixth ray.

It represents this quality of devotion and of transcendance into other realms and whatever they have in mind, fantasy, poetry or whatever.

This is the Existence Axis. You have to struggle for existence, you have to work hard at your management etc. Also on the spiritual level you have to think about something very high, I mean the religious attitude towards the transcendental world where you become part of it, this kind of Piscean enlargement of consciousness.

Pisces and Virgo are both second and sixth ray, devotion and helping and ideals and idealism and being there for others, loving all people, loving all nature and creation.

Gemini: Ray 2

At the top of Figure 7.1, Gemini stands alone, with just the second ray. Now Gemini is a little bit high up? In an elevated position it seems more valued now, with Sagittarius in the middle. I told you that the Solar Logos is on the second ray and at the end of the illusion the second ray will win the battle; this is Gemini.

Love and wisdom, and Gemini can really discriminate between good and bad. It has this ability to look at both sides of the truth, and acknowledge that the other side is also truth. Therefore it is a principle of relativity, like Einstein brought relativity theory into the world. He was a Pisces and second ray dominated. So Gemini has this pure love and wisdom in it.

But most of the time we see the Mercury Gemini person who talks and talks and brings lots of knowledge to people without evaluation. Whether it is the truth or not does not matter, in journalism, press, media, television. All our media world of communication and advertising is all Gemini. Where's the love and the wisdom there? Maybe the wisdom is in it because they know how to sell their stuff!

Audience: *Just one other point about Gemini is that it's isolated up there, second ray etc, but on the other hand it's the furthest distance from the galactic centre.*

Louise Huber: That's the other side of it, it's the axis. As a Gemini you know that the exoteric ruler, Mercury, brings into the world all this knowledge without selection or evaluation. It is a kind of inflation of values and we know all about this because in our times a lot of things are offered which are not at all meaningful for people, notably when they sell stuff which does not function, or tell people something which is not true.

Then, when they have to integrate Sagittarius, they come to a crisis. The crisis of Gemini is the Faustian experience, where Faust had collected all the knowledge of all universities, of all cultures, but at the moment when he fell in love with Margareta, his knowledge was of no help at all to his inner crisis and he felt down. He sat down and said,

"Here I sit as a poor man and I am as clever as I have ever been. All my knowledge has not given me any help in this situation."

Then Sagittarius comes in, because the crisis is always in the polarisation of opposites. It is always in the opposite sign, which in the case of Gemini involves thinking about the higher meaning in life, higher truth. Sagittarius then gives him this possibility of enlarging his consciousness, to look for the truth and nothing but the truth. With its relativity, this brings him out of the inflation business downstairs. He is lost in relativity and so he looks for the absolute values of life, for the right philosophy, for religion, for meaning. Whatever he needs for life will come into his consciousness.

The esoteric ruler of Gemini is Venus, the most highly selective of the planets. Venus only takes in what is best for the body, the best for me, the nicest, beauty, etc. Then Gemini can discriminate on the consciousness level. It discriminates tremendously because Gemini will become the mediator of the ageless wisdom. Alice Bailey and Djwal Kuhl (the Tibetan) were Geminis, and Gemini can bring you the ageless wisdom as a mediator.

Venus is the selector, and the truth is the right thing and they can educate you. They are able to give you the truth so that you can take it. This a very high ability when Venus and Mercury work together, they have the right way to present it to you. In the psychological field they always say a good counsellor has to take others as they are. They have this kind of ability to give you just the truth you need now. This Gemini is the teacher, the little teacher, and Sagittarius is the big one.

When they come together with the second ray up there, they are really wise men. Wisdom is a beautiful thing when there is a wise woman or a wise man around you. You can trust them because they speak the truth, and say things right. This is the ability of a good mediator like Alice Bailey or Djwhal Khul.

Colour and the Rays

Figure 7.2 is a rather complicated drawing about the rays[7], with which I want to give you an insight into the colours and the rays.

The associated colours are red = first ray, blue = second, green = third, yellow = fourth, brown = fifth, pinkish = sixth ray, violet = seventh ray. This is what I told you about Master Rakoczi who is bringing in the violet flame as a healing flame and a healing colour. I am not quite sure what the fifth and sixth colours are but Alice Bailey gives a lot of information about the colours and the deva kingdom[8], which is also coming together with the soul kingdom to humanity. All colour healing, aromatherapy and related therapies come from the deva illusion – the parallel illusion to humanity.

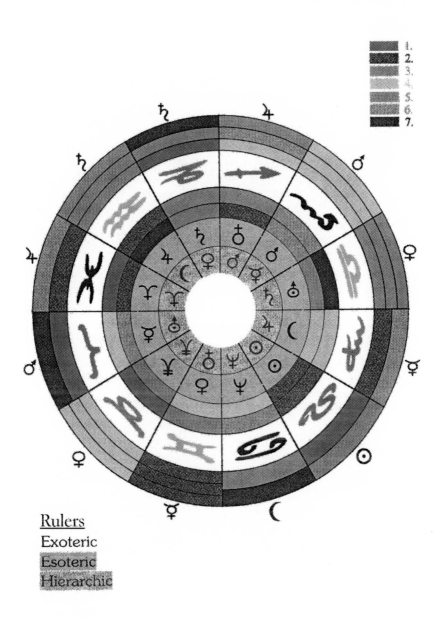

Figure 7.2 Planetary Rulers and the Seven Rays

Figure 7.2 shows the exoteric rulers of the signs in the outer circle, the esoteric rulers in the intermediate circle and the hierarchical rulers in the inner circle. I do not propose to say more about hierarchical rulers, as it will only confuse you.

The shading in the outer circles also shows the rays associated with the signs, as we have already seen.

Note that the colours of the rays are not presented consistently in the various Alice Bailey texts[9]. I think it depends on levels. If you recall that the basis of the rays is light, and light comes down and is reflecting in certain substance, on certain levels the appearance of the colour is in accordance with the substance in the level, so maybe when the substance is full of dirt the colours become muddied? But the basis is light, and when there is a clean reflection on certain levels then the colours will become pure.

In our world we have so much dirt in our astral and etheric worlds, so much rubbish, glamour or whatever. So when the light of the rays goes through all these levels before they reach me, it gets a lot of discolouring stuff in it. The colour is not so pure. For example, when the sky is clear and pure blue you can contact a different energy, I don't know if you have felt this yourself. You can breathe and the colour blue means a lot. But when there is a dirty grey and fog, it is different.

Audience: What are the inner rings in Figure 7.2. I understand that the three outer rings relate to the rays, but what do the two inner rings mean?

Louise Huber: These are the under-rays – forget it! There are sub-rays, and some schools are very skilled in using them. Douglas Baker, for instance, has written books and then the sub-rays mean so much that at the end you don't know anything anymore. Therefore, I think it's not so important, it's just an addition.

Rays and Personality Types

Figure 7.3 relates the seven rays to seven personality types, and to the corresponding signs.

The type of the first ray of will and power is the leader, the keyword is self-confidence and the trigon of signs is Aries, Leo and Capricorn.

The type of the second ray of love and wisdom is the teacher and the keyword is the will to good – goodwill.

The type of the third ray of active intelligence is the thinker. The keyword is looking for the truth.

For type of the fourth ray of harmony through conflict is the artist and the keyword is the dissemination of culture.

Ray	Type	Keyword	Signs
1	Leader	Self confidence	♑ ♈ ♌
2	Teacher	Good will	♊ ♍ ♓
3	Thinker	Truth seeker	♎ ♑ ♋
4	Artist	Culturist	♉ ♐ ♏
5	Scientist	Analysis	♐ ♌ ♒
6	Devotion	Reformer	♍ ♓ ♐
7	Ritualist	Materialist	♑ ♋ ♈

Figure 7.3 Rays and Personality Types

The type of the fifth ray of concrete knowledge is the scientist and the keyword is the analyst.

The type of the sixth ray of idealism and devotion is the devotional type, and the keyword is the reformer. Sixth ray people are reformers, and some are fanatics. Sometimes in earlier days the reformers had to be fanatics, otherwise they could not have gone through with it, such as Luther, Calvin and even Robin Hood.

The type of the seventh ray of ceremonial order is the ritualist, and that is also very interesting – what does this mean? This is a kind of acting, not as in a theatre but as in a church reading and the ritual in that. Now we have to think that the ritualist has to come down again into a life of ritual living. You get out of bed and brush your teeth. This is ritual too and at my age now this ritual is helpful for getting the body going. You know this is good stuff, this is magic also. Ceremonial magic is the seventh ray.

This ritual life is something very special, I think, and maybe in future people will live more consciously in this way. The dying process is also a ritual, or will become a ritual again. The seventh ray is the end of the tail of the ouroboric snake. It has to do with the ending – the last ray.

The keyword is the materialist. They are only looking for materialistic pleasure, money and possessions and yet here it is the keyword. Probably we have to change our snobbish attitude of sixth ray life towards the materialist. Maybe we have to become materialistic, when we integrate Saturn, which is to do with matter and this materialistic attitude. And we have transformed the attitude towards Saturn in this century. For 2,000 years we had to scourge the physical body, they said that Saturn was the malefic. No, I want you to think about materialistic in a different way. It is a good thing to be materialistic. It's fantastic to take care of your physical living, to have it nice, to make it sound. You have to love your Saturn, your body, this is a materialistic attitude. We have to dissociate Saturn from his bad image.

Audience: *Another aspect occurs to me. The new scientists are beginning to say that matter is not just inert, that it is full of life and this will bring a new attitude.*

Louise Huber: This is a fifth ray aspect to it. Matter and spirit are the same. Now we have to become materialistic when we have seven rays in our set-up. You know, you have to love matter again because we refused matter all through the years of the last Piscean age.

Audience: *The idea of bringing the highest and lowest together has to come through the thought form creation of the etheric level, and that is the material that must be used with the seventh ray. Now prior to this time that was considered magic, wasn't it, but now we are looking for a new word because magic has superstitious meanings.*

Louise Huber: Like the one with the cat on the shoulder? Magic. But we shall cultivate a materialistic attitude. We have to bring all our spiritual visions into matter. This is the seventh ray, materialistic. Now we give you permission to become a materialist, isn't it great?

8

The Spiritual Planets and Spiritual Growth

Bruno Huber

Relevance of Past Esoteric Schools

The Spiritual Planets

• Paranormal Functions •
• Time and Cosmic Order •
• Material Values •
• Uncultivated Spiritual Planets •
• Uranus •
• Neptune •
• Pluto •
• Motivation and Function •
• Questions •

Relevance of Past Esoteric Schools

We have been dealing with the personality and with the soul, and of course the natural tendency is that we see here the personality and there the soul and nothing in between. Now, I think for progressive people of today, and for people of tomorrow, it will be very important that there is none of that stuff anymore that speaks of the soul as something way up there that you have no chance to really reach.

I have been through esoteric circles of the past-age type – Theosophy, Arcane School etc. There is always this pronouncement that the soul is something very difficult to reach and, only under the guidance of the master through a whole life long of meditation and experimentation and serving, may you have the chance to get a certain hint of it. I think that is a bit outmoded.

We live in a modern world where the average people already have quite a good education in schools. Our minds are trained, and that's different from people a hundred years ago. Then, those minds had still to be educated, schooling wasn't so developed. It wasn't natural to be intelligent, one could say. People were much more emotional, even only a hundred years ago. So, of course, esoteric groupings like theosophy, for instance, had to adapt to that state of mind.

But nowadays with the schooling we have, there is a different situation. Especially in the second half of this century, we have the development of computers for instance, the internet and stuff like this, not to mention radio, television, telephone, etc. Communication has become an easy thing. Meanwhile, through computers and the internet it becomes global and we get a lot of information into our brains, and we work it through, this way, that way, according to possibilities. Anyway, our brain is pretty well equipped to deal with that mass of information. As a matter of fact, one starts speaking of the "age of information". So there is a time ahead of us that is seemingly based on global communication and therefore our brain has to understand a hell of a lot of information, sort it out and make a picture of it.

This is quite a mental stress but we are to a certain degree equipped for it, and therefore the old methods of esoteric schooling have worn out. If you have read the Tibetan's books, you might have found that he says himself that the model of the Hierarchy with masters who had ashrams – and you were part of an ashram under the control of the master and had to follow the master's advice – this model is out. He said this at the end of his writings in the mid 1940s[1].

Humanity has grown faster than expected by the Hierarchy. This is an important remark. It has been partly suppressed and the information hasn't been given out, the books have been changed. Not to speak it out too loud because otherwise students might run away and go on their own, because the consequence of that is that each single person has to go his own way.

In the future there will be no such thing anymore as being initiated. This is an old term. It has not been true for decades, whereas it was true for millennia. There was a master, there was his ashram, or whatever you called it, that proved that he had under his control these students. These pupils were obliged to conform to the rules that the master gave out. Only this absolute obligation guaranteed the process of teaching, meditating and finally reaching an initiation. That was the idea. That's out – out of service, simply.

Self-initiation

Nowadays self-initiation is in. Each person may undertake to strive forward in trying to grow in consciousness, and then this person will follow the laws of nature that are true not only for the material world but also for the emotional world, for the mental world, for the higher levels of spirit. There are always laws of nature that say "that's possible" and "that's not possible".

There are no people that tell you that you should not do that. You'll find out what doesn't work, and then you'll learn what's the right way to go, and then you go through stages of initiation. You may call it initiation or not, it's not important, but your consciousness will grow. We grow as a result of striving, very often in sudden jumps.

The Tibetan's books

What we find in the Tibetan's books with Alice Bailey, or if we look into theosophy through Blavatsky, you will find the same thing. *The Secret Doctrine²* is a bit more difficult and pretty disorderly – it's very difficult to read, to find out which bits belong with which bits. Blavatsky had a very disorderly mind.

Seemingly the Tibetan said to Alice Bailey that he wanted to put things right. It wasn't anything new, he said, that was presented in Alice Bailey's writings, it was just a bit more organised so you could look through it much better. It is still difficult, as you have probably realised.

The Spiritual Planets

We have already looked at the personality in Figure 2.3 Amphora. We have found out the rays, and we have dealt with the soul. That is, we have dealt with the causal body actually. What we are up to now is: how do we get from down here to up there?

We need the spiritual planets, as we call them, Uranus, Neptune, Pluto, because they are the tools that bridge from one area to the other. They bridge the consciousness – they are tools of consciousness.

They are not physical organs, whereas one could say that the seven classical planets are physical organs in a way. At least the classical planets can be pinpointed in the personality with no difficulty on the psychological level, although with some difficulty and some different opinions about their association with physical bodily organs. There is no unified idea in astrology. But anyway the seven planets (Sun, Moon, and the five up to Saturn) are organs, functional tools one could say, of the personality.

How can we discriminate between these seven and the three spiritual or "new" planets? What is the simple discrimination – physically? Not being able to see them with the naked eye. We can see the seven but we cannot see the three, not with our eyes, we need telescopes.

Of course there is a borderline case, one could say, and that's Uranus. The normal human eye has a perception of magnitude 1 to 6. 6 is the faintest star we can see. And Uranus has a magnitude of 6.5 so some people with very sharp eyes can see Uranus. I did when I was younger. So it's a borderline, some people see it, some people don't. Of course, you don't see it if you don't know where to look, because it is so faint that you mix it up with thousands of other faint stars. You have to know exactly where to look down to the minute of arc.

I already pointed out the position of Uranus, Neptune and Pluto in Figure 2.3 Amphora on page 19. These planets are aiming upward, and Uranus is where the top is in Assagioli's egg shape, it breaks through that egg shape. Egg-piercer – that was the name. That fits with the fact that some people can see it, some people cannot.

Most people cannot, because they are not equipped, they don't even know where to look. Anyway, this shows already that for Uranus there is not only a good sharp eye needed but also knowledge and understanding, the possibility of orienting yourself in the sky to find it, to know where it is to be found. Uranus is a mental planet.

Now to come back to the three of them, Uranus, Neptune and Pluto, to classify them and name them a bit better, to differentiate from the seven classical, visible planets. We are equipped by nature, in our bodily condition, to see seven planets, that is five planets plus Sun and Moon. That's our equipment to live, not only a normal but even a good, happy, successful, rich life, whatever you want. But it's not good enough for growing into bigger dimensions of consciousness. That's what we need the spiritual planets for.

Now, "spiritual planets" is a term which we very often use, but it's doubtful whether these planets are spiritual with a lot of people, because they can produce all kinds of very funny, dangerous, awful, hurtful things. So what's spiritual about those hurtful things? A good question!

Now there is one important thing to say. To us, to our physical equipment, eyes especially, and brain, these so-called spiritual planets are spiritual, they are not material. Of course they are material bodies in the sky, we know that by now. Satellites have been out there, taking photographs, Neptune, Saturn, Uranus. Pluto is in the offing now, next year I guess. So, of course they are physical bodies, but to us they are imperceptible. We cannot perceive them physically. They are therefore immaterial – that would be one word – or spiritual, if you prefer that term.

Now to make them into spiritual equipment it of course needs some self-training or cultivation. Without that they may be simple antennae for the things that happen in your surroundings. If you don't cultivate these qualities you may use some of them at least to a certain degree in your daily life, for your family life, for your professional career etc – with some success, but also surely with some of the opposite of success, with some flops, some hurting, even catastrophic situations. It depends upon how strongly you go.

The difference is they are like antennae, but the antennae can hang down on the ground and pick up what's down there. If you don't look after them and cultivate them they droop down there. They pick up what's on the ground, which is our physical existence in this world and all our surroundings, our family, our business, etc.

Now, if you learn to cultivate them these antennae will slowly come up and become sensitive to higher vibrations, but that's your doing. It doesn't just happen, you have to do it. **You** have to cultivate these capacities or these tools. It's better not to consider them to be physical organs, rather to consider them to be tools of consciousness. That's a very important term. Tools of consciousness, therefore immaterial.

Though the material bodies of these planets exist up there they are not perceivable by our eye. From here they are immaterial and it's better to treat them like that for the sake of getting full control of them, because you can cultivate these qualities only with your consciousness.

You have to cultivate
these capacities or tools of consciousness.

Paranormal Functions

No material thing you can do, no routine, no training of any sort, can ever guarantee cultivation of these planets. That's why I said at the beginning "esoteric" doesn't depend upon whether you eat meat or not. Eating meat, or not eating meat, doesn't guarantee anything spiritual. Or other people may have telepathic capacities. Everybody has, as a matter of fact. If you think of a person, and five minutes later a phone call comes from that person, you have a telepathic contact. Or you think of the person and two days letter a letter comes in from that person. When the person wrote the letter you had a telepathic contact. Quite a normal thing, telepathy is nothing abnormal.

Of course, the teaching in our schools doesn't tell us such, therefore it seems funny, strange. It isn't – it belongs to the personality. But it's an uncontrolled capacity and the fact that you have telepathic hunches and even control over this capacity doesn't mean that you are a spiritual person, that you have cultivated Uranus, because it's Uranus that makes you telepathic.

These are just phenomena that come from those tools, these "para" functions, telepathy or whatever, there are many sorts of paranormal functions. They are actually functions that belong to these consciousness tools. That's important.

If you have hunches every so often, or very often, this is still a function that comes from Uranus, Neptune or Pluto, but you don't have it in hand, it just comes. Cultivating that specific function, like telepathy with Uranus, doesn't guarantee that you gather spiritual insight, that you come nearer your soul consciousness, because these organs are not located down here in the physical world. They are existing planets way out there which we cannot perceive and therefore they seem to us to be immaterial, but they are there.

We can perceive these planets with our etheric body, this is built-in by nature. Also, people before the seventeenth century knew nothing of these new planets.

The ancient Greeks, for instance, found out fabulous things by way of insights which they had but couldn't name. They called it intuition, vision, whatever, gave it all kinds of names. They knew of paranormal functions, they even worked with them, but they didn't know it was these planets because they didn't know the planets. They couldn't perceive them. They didn't have telescopes, but they had the capacities, as we have. I think that's important.

You know, we all have these paranormal capacities, they are absolutely normal so you needn't be proud if you have any such. The only difference from other people who seem not to have them is that you know about and accept it and the other people say "this is strange, this is crazy". Their fault, you could say, their problem that they don't realise what it is. This is a state of completely unconscious perception. They perceive something, it sort of falls into their consciousness, they don't know why and it's very doubtful, so they mostly push it away. They don't think they have anything but normal instincts and drives, and not such funny stuff like telepathy.

The next stage is that you realise "Aha, I do have this thing and it is paranormal but I would like to call it not para-, just normal!" – because all people have these qualities in their make-up, only some believe it and others don't, that's the difference. If you believe in them, accept them as a function, then they come more often and you learn in the course of time to handle them, though very often you never succeed in controlling them in the sense of commanding them, "Now I want it".

You can see that in the sensitive people who undergo tests with scientists. More than 50% fail in these trials. That's a question of consciousness under control with your will, but you cannot control them properly. You can control them to a certain degree but the best control is if there is real need for them from your surroundings. Real need, not demand.

You know, if a journalist comes up to you and says, "now prove it, show me something", it won't function. We fail and the journalist says, "I said it was junk, forget it", and writes it in the paper. But that's not the right attitude. Willing is not the function to use because it doesn't work.

You always need a situation that demands this function, and this situation should not be my situation but our situation. Do you get what I mean with this? These functions are transpersonal, that is, they are there to lead us away from our own little ego with a little world around it, to a concern with the surrounding world – on whichever level, it's not important – to understand through these functions how we are inter-related and evolving with all people in this world, with humanity as a whole. This is what we can learn from having such capacities. Not more, but that's important.

These functions are transpersonal, that is, they are there to lead us away from our own little ego.

The real cultivation then, of course goes further, upwards on an in-depth discovery, of the soul, of the being that I am without existing – existing in this world that is. They are tools of consciousness. They are transpersonal, this is a strict natural law to them.

If you misuse these capacities for your personal sake you get a hard beating. In one or way or another, sooner or later, sometimes later. But anyway, it will come. There is no way of misusing them for personal reasons, for personal satisfaction. If you want to go on an ego trip with a transpersonal capacity of any sort you'll flop at some point and you will be trampled on.

History is full of such experiences. All those sensitives, hypnotics, etc., people who have eaten swords and stuff like this, or that fellow from Israel, Uri Geller, who bent forks. Who talks of Uri Geller today? Some know him still, but he had a complete flop. When put under test it didn't work, so he's nobody anymore. He was on everyone's tongue and in all the papers and the television, but then...?

Or another case in my youth, when I was 16 or 17 there was a fellow in the biggest cinema theatre in Zurich. Every evening he got up on the stage and would not only eat swords but push them through his heart and his lungs and pull them out, no blood, nothing. One day he was dead, not on the stage – in the hospital, because he had infected himself with an unclean sword – gone!

Destiny knows many means to correct such misuse and it is always hard to take. It's a transpersonal function, Uranus, Neptune and Pluto. It is there for recognising the interwoven quality of my being with the rest of humanity, with the rest of nature if you want. These instruments are good for perceiving those things, to perceive more than your recognising mind can ever pick up, formulate and write down.

Time and Cosmic Order

You know about the vitality not only of a plant but also of a rock, a piece of rock, you can perceive it. That's different from what you read about rocks, isn't it? Read a geological book – very interesting, but dead matter. Seemingly it's dead matter, only the clock goes differently with dead matter. It's much slower, takes a hundred thousand years to show changes while we change in 10 years. That's all the difference. What's time in eternity?

Also, that experience of going beyond the time limitations of our day-to-day thinking, all those times we have to keep, when we hurry and rush and get all worked up and sick etc. Time dimensions are immense and little things of our daily consciousness play practically no part. They are just functional to some idea that leads our life, and our life is short. As I keep saying, we are cosmic flies, one-day flies. They live one day, one cosmic day. 72 years – it's a cosmic day. Twenty-eight thousand years is a cosmic year, so we are cosmic flies with an average of 72 years.

Material Values

One more word is needed on the importance of material values. We may tend, because we are spiritually oriented, to neglect the value of the material. To put it down, to say " huh, I've nothing to do with that – I'm beyond that". It's very nice to feel that "I'm beyond the material".

The material world belongs to the cosmos, and it's not dead, and it's not stupid. If you look at nature, how it forms the surface of this planet earth. With what consistent powers it works, puts up mountains, shoves around continents. Crazy! Gigantic!

This life, this planet, this body, this round body is not dead. It's 6,000 degrees hot in its centre, and it's fluid, and we are living on a 50 mile-thick crust of a body that measures 12,000 kilometres across. Everything moves and we wonder "why does it move?" Earthquakes, volcanoes, and stuff like this. If that is not life – it is – on a big scale.

We are little one-day flies who are just afraid of these happenings because we don't understand them. So don't now judge and maltreat the material. It's real in the sense that it is an expression of cosmic laws and cosmic order and we can study the material world, for instance physics.

I find, for instance, if I come to a clear formulation of physical laws of nature I can straightforwardly apply them to the psychological, they are true there too. With bits of reformulation, of course, and changing some words, but of the same meaning.

Cosmic laws are an expression of life. They order and control life and make it possible for life to grow, and that's true for all levels. So don't float away, feeling above all those things. You may lose control of the best of your parts.

Uncultivated Spiritual Planets

Again, Uranus, Neptune and Pluto are transpersonal and I would like to expand a bit on the two possible sides of an uncultivated spiritual planet and a cultivated one. As a matter of fact for the uncultivated qualities of these spiritual planets, you just read any old astrological book. Not by the Hubers – others. Because it's strictly assembled it's mostly negative stuff, or in some books pure hallelujah stuff, but of this world so the old dichotomy of material and spiritual and nothing in between prevails. It has all to do with cultivation or non-cultivation.

Uranus

Non-cultivated Uranus, for instance, makes you liable for all the structures human society has developed because Uranus is a structural function. It is a mental tool for higher order, for bigger size one could say, with a certain clear thrust so it has kinship with Mercury. But Mercury has no thrust - it just considers this and that and names it and puts it all in the same drawer. Naming is important, not valuing – we cannot value things.

Uranus is thrusting forward to find new explanations but he uses mental equipment and is trying to discover, searching to discover natural law. And he then is creating structures that are, if possible, in line with the natural law, so we can put away the dangers of being hurt by natural laws which we don't know, and their outcomes, their functioning.

So with Uranus we have in the past centuries built up our civilisation, our technology etc. Uranus is if you drive your car and find lines there on the ground and traffic lights and police standing there – that's Uranus. It's structures that society has built up in order to make traffic for millions of people possible, to rule and control traffic. But your car is also an outcome of Uranus. It has been developed to be able to transport you at your utmost ease. To make transport possible, to move you miles and miles away. You can take your meal here and your coffee 50 miles away, it's no problem. You hop into your car, drive away and you take coffee there. No problem today. Think of 200 years ago, 50 miles away was a day's travel. A day's travel, and not by foot. By post carriage... it was not very pleasant and comfortable!

So Uranus is building up technology in different ways in order to secure life, but based on research of how nature functions and what the natural laws are – the rules of the physical world. That's what science is doing, or should be doing at least. Sometimes it doesn't do it, but anyway... What science finds out as natural laws, the laws of nature, technology then makes into apparatus and system. That's all Uranus.

Now if you know well how to work with the computer, that's fine. You'll have little loss of data. But if you have no knowledge or little knowledge and you try, you lose a lot of data. It doesn't work, it collapses, you have to restart it and all the data that you produced before vanished. It's one of those experiences – it's a Uranian experience, par excellence.

Try out something produced by men, but which you don't know yet, an apparatus, some system produced by human craftsmanship but before that by human minds. If you try you'll have a process of trial and error and that's Uranian. You'll find out what they have done there and you'll find out what it is good for.

I remember when I first picked up the first little pocket calculator that came on the market. I said to myself, this is not for me anymore, I'll keep it for the next life. That was 20 years ago, more, 25 or so. Then one day I couldn't resist it anymore and bought myself one – just a tiny thing with a little booklet to it. I read that booklet, tried it all out and within a month I had taken it so far that I could do things with that little apparatus that the booklet didn't say.

That set me off on a trail and I started going into that. Now I sit in the middle of a network of six computers in the house and I'm the chief of it and know all about them. I put in graphics and words and stuff, mix it up and produce a newspaper with it etc., all out of this apparatus. Fabulous! It's fun really, a big joy, if you control it.

But I have to find out step by step because you can't read all these manuals they give you. You never understand what they mean so you have to try it out. It's the best way. This is Uranian. Find out. Accept the risk of failure, because the failure tells you how it's not.

But for many people any risk is too dangerous and therefore, "No, Uranus, forget it!" And what does Uranus do then? It makes you liable for the all mistakes that can ever be made in a system which human beings have created. In any system, apparatus, structures, like regulations, highway code, signals and all that stuff, or machinery or social structures.

Take capitalism and communism – social structures. Fixed ideas about how society must function – Uranian. Uranus can function on different levels, but they mustn't be material in the direct sense. Social structures are not a material thing, though the material thing lies in your life, if you are part of it. Structures control something or meet dangers, that's the idea, but they are also limitations. The more these structures are in accordance with natural law, the less they will limit you because natural law is very wide. Human-made laws of structuring are normally pretty narrow because our own minds are narrow.

So if you had a traffic accident, there is something wrong with your Uranus handling. You don't have full control of that Uranus. It sort of gives you an itch to go about the road in a certain way which is not exactly the right way, in order not to endanger yourself, but not regarding others. You hear of road accidents where those who are not at fault are the worst off. The person who did it perhaps came out alive, while the others are dead. It's pretty tough!

So there is some need for you to try to understand Uranus better. To understand that as long as I am liable to just blindly follow the structures of this world that human beings have set up, have constructed, I am in for trouble, more or less.

If I use Uranus to find out, if I make Uranus a searcher, a researcher even, then I am on my way to control Uranus and to use it as a spiritual tool. Searching or researching is the way of Uranus. "Find out why!" Again the question "why?", you remember. "Find out why" functions this way and how could I formulate a law of nature about this? So that I can get control of it. To get control is the utmost drive of Uranus. The function is researching, to find out. There is always a risk to it – any researcher runs risks. Some come out with a triumphant result, others come out with no result and some never come out again.

To get control is the utmost drive of Uranus.

Neptune

Neptune is a bit more difficult because to most people, especially astrologers, it is so diffuse, so nebulous. There is something about that nebulous stuff but it's mostly smoke in their brains.

Also Neptune has these two sides. Neptune is able to perceive two things in relationship and is able to enjoy to the utmost whatever he experiences. This capacity is to identify with whatever he encounters, be it beings or things. He sort of penetrates through it, understands the nature, and quality, and quality of being.

Where, for instance, does that famous over-used word "intuition" come from? This is the capacity of identification. I don't mean over-identification, that's a bad psychological word. I mean identification, the capacity to go into the other without losing myself. It's not losing myself in the other. Very important!

Neptune can do that, but the negative or passive Neptune consistently loses itself, because that is not this self-controlled being that produces the identification, it just happens. And of course Neptune is largely misused to escape the hardship of this world – see how drugs function, see how we have huge audiences for television. The escape into a world that is not real. Neptune can produce gigantic cinemas – human cinemas. They may be on the screen there in front of you, they may be inside your head, for instance if you dream your mind-cinema is on.

There is no end to the fantasy of Neptune, one could say. If you want to get away, if you are on an escape from the hardship, from the toughness of this life, from the fighting, from the having to stand strong, like "I won!" etc, then Neptune is fabulous. Whatever your speciality is, or your tool. Some need tools, like television or drugs or alcohol etc. Fine! That's the individual choice. It has to do with the rest of your personality, how that is built.

But Neptune is on the one hand perceiving these addictions of humanity or of society. Addictions like drugs or alcohol are part of society. They are the so called counter-establishment. There is a whole world that lives on them, like show business, the film business, etc. Not to speak of alcohol producers who live on them, they are counter-establishment.

The establishment comprises the orderly people that only do good things. And the counter-establishment is that which nourishes your weaknesses, your tendency to escape and delivers picture material for you. Informal drugs, or other eatable or drinkable substances, or in the form of theatre be it on the television or on the stage, or in film. Not reality, but a dream in a way. It's understandable that it's difficult to find out what it is exactly and therefore Neptune is called nebulous. It's in a big fog, everything is in a big fog, it's too undifferentiated.

The positive functioning of Neptune perceives love as something real, something that you experience and is not dependent on how the person in front of you reacts to it. You perceive the person and you love the person, and you love a beautiful person and a crippled person in the same way. Not the same way in quality because it is a different quality from person to person, but the intensity of experience is the same which you can only call Love. Because you understand why this person is built that way and you find it OK, you find it fine, you find it good and it may be that the person doesn't really realise himself how he is built, but you realise and you can tell.

It would be a task of astrologers reading charts for people, for instance. Telling them how they are built because they are puzzled with themselves. Most people are puzzled with themselves. They see some parts of themselves somewhat in shape but other parts are funny, strange, or bad, or shameful. So they don't really look at them. They keep them out of the normal frame so they remain diffuse. A pure cultivated Neptune can perceive all that and also these shadowy or dark or nebulous parts in the personality, and can understand just from experiencing it why it is so and how it is functioning, and immediately know what one can see and do about it.

Understanding is the first thing and I think a really good title for the functioning of Neptune is to love unconditionally. That second word is very important. Real love of the Neptune order knows no conditions. That is, I never demand that a person should love me this way or that way, it's a transpersonal function. It's there for perceiving you and me. Perceiving you by becoming you without losing myself. That is, while I am being the other person I still have my own location where I am. But I am not an onlooker, I am living within.

As I said at the beginning, it's a bit difficult to explain in words. But a good word, as I said, is unconditional love. Love that doesn't put conditions, doesn't put demands on the You.

A really good title for the functioning of Neptune is to love unconditionally

In this way you can perceive the life and its quality in all subjects and objects. You can understand the simplest things like a spectacle or a glass. You perceive the life of it. Some people see things, some smell things, others hear things. It doesn't matter, that's individual, there's no rule to that. Mostly it's that sensory organ which is the best developed in the person that delivers the pictures, that sends all your pictures of the different senses - hearing pictures, smelling pictures etc.

Of course, if you start telling people about what you see or hear or smell then the person listening to you might say "Eh? Well, nothing to do with what I see!" It's difficult to talk about that – it's not there for talking about, it's there for living and that's different. There's no propaganda, and it needs no feedback from others like "You're doing well", not really, because when I experience I'm convinced it's there, it's functioning. I don't need any feedback, any saying "you are good" because I feel how good it is, how it functions, how it works. That's real! That is confirmation enough. So that's Neptune,

Pluto

Of course the most difficult is Pluto. I have not mentioned yet, but it's clear from Figure 2.3 that Uranus corresponds with the third ray, Neptune with the second, and Pluto with the first.

But the first ray is always a bit difficult to understand for the rest of humanity, that is for the other six rays. Because he is not asking "should I or should I not?" or "Do you like it this way?" or such things...

It wills and does. Willing is already doing. There is something very immediate about the first ray. That's why it shouldn't work all the time because it would the kill the rest of the world if it were there all the time.

It normally comes to people in pushes when the situation needs it. We have the rest of the rays of the personality that do work. What is Pluto?

Relationship with Uranus and Neptune

First I have to make a relationship with the other two. All three are in the last extent ideals. That is, I have an image of perfection which is mostly very diffuse but I know how it should be. Not down to the details, but I know how it should be.

The aim of these three planets is different. Uranus is aimed at the world. It is in constant search for the perfect world. That is, in Uranus we have the idea of the paradise or the Kingdom of God or Sharafia, or whatever the names are.

And we have had a number of social concepts, like for instance, communism, that were a trial for producing a perfect social system, a kind of paradise on Earth. It didn't hold up so well, it seems that it wasn't quite so perfect, otherwise it would have gone further. Of course, humans make such paradises and according to the capacity, the depth of consciousness, of the person doing so, that paradise will be a more or less narrow vision of an ideal world.

Neptune is the vision of perfect love. What Christ produced as a message somehow explains what he was after. There are figures, mostly saints, that can show that somehow, like St Francis. He could understand the birds and talk to the grasses. That somehow shows where this ideal world lies, in an absolutely harmonious world that only follows natural laws and doesn't ever exclude anything. I think is a saying of St Francis that exclusion is the first and worst of all sins. Exclusion. Think of yourself, how many times you exclude, people, conditions, etc. It's a hard job to get rid of that, a real hard job.

Exclusion makes for barriers, for borders, and you can see this in the attempt of Europe to become one Europe, how there is this attitude and where it hinges. This nation wants this kind of flag and that nation wants this kind of round lights and you know, this sort of stuff. Idiotic! Exclusions! Well, Europe will come, they say. We'll see! Anyway, I'm not a politician such as I hear on television, so I find it very funny.

Ideal Human Being

Pluto has a vision too, an ideal of the human being – the individual. What is an individual at its highest? Again this vision has different sizes according to the brain producing it. It can be anything from a teacher with a seven- or eight-year old child who thinks he is a demigod, to one big shot somewhere in sport. But on the other hand, dear God personally and everything in between, gurus and politicians and artists, stars, etc, all can function as perfect models which I want to become, in Pluto.

> **Pluto has a vision, an ideal of the human being. What is an individual at its highest?**

For instance, I've watched this in the German speaking area very closely for decades now, people in the building business – houses, etc. There is again and again this phenomenon that one chap comes up like a rocket and he builds and builds and owns and owns, a big shot. Millions, millions. He builds only big stuff. Suddenly he collapses, and there is nothing left but air and a lot of debts. It happened again and again. I have observed that many of these cases had Pluto up in the tenth house, and a Sun buried away somewhere low down on a low point or intercepted, or without aspects.

In other words, they used an image of the big shot owning a whole city or something because they had an inferiority complex of sorts to compensate. It is a frequently used trick amongst plutonian people. They go for the big stuff, they are big shots. "Nobody is better than me, I'm the King!" The absolute top shot, the star, etc. And they may collapse at some point, completely. This very often happens.

This is of course strong ego stuff and, as with the other two, it is forbidden by the law of nature to use Pluto for an ego trip. For instance, a big shot may own half of Frankfurt, built with foreign money, not his own money, borrowed money, but anyway he has built it. He's not God, he's not even God-like! He's a greedy fella with an inferiority complex! That's a pretty damn thing - ugh! And he does a lot of damage to others. Some go crazy in the ultimate process of breakdown, and not a few, quite a lot of them, either immediately or later. Some politicians go the same way!

So that's a mistaken idealism of the perfection of the human being. It's a too worldly and too egotistic picture. Therefore plutonians of the wrong kind, the uncultivated plutonian type, have big shows on one hand and do a lot of destruction on the other. Be it by trying to get as big as they want to, be it by collapsing afterwards and leaving a lot of people with no money in their pocket because they have given it to him. But nothing is left for such things. Poor people, because that big shot wants to reorganise a whole quarter and kicks out all the people that live there. That lived there for forty years, but he kicks them out with foul tricks, and even, as you probably know, with more than foul tricks, for instance murder and stuff like this. In order to get that claim to build his big gigantic fantastic phenomenon that gives a lot of trouble to a lot of people.

We are coming to very difficult situations, probably through this being pushed out and so on. So Pluto is more difficult than the others because it can unleash quite strong energy in the personality. And I say unleash.

If you have this sort of corrosive picture of "I must become this", then this picture activates in you all the energies available down to the last bit in order to push through, because you need an enormous power to push through, to push others away, to push your way through all the walls etc. – to get to where you are. This may in the first place lead to exhaustion and very often to collapse, also in a material sense as we can see very nicely from recent history.

There is a big mistake Pluto can make as long as it is uncultivated. It projects the image for the other world "I must become a big shot in this world and I must build there this and that and that". Or "I must rule America", or whatever. They project that image onto the world. They work not on themselves but on the world. They do something to the world and mostly very forcefully.

With Pluto it should be forbidden by the law of nature. It is forbidden to work outwardly. Pluto is for me, not for others. Pluto has no right to demand anything of others. For instance, "You must become like me. Look at me, how perfect I am" – guru sort of stuff. That's projecting. The work goes inward, I have to work on myself.

A Pluto that's understood and cultivated is for a long time not realised by the surroundings, while an uncultivated Pluto is prematurely known by the world. Most of these people somehow become known, in different degrees, in the very early years of their life.

Motivation and Function

Now, one further compilation between the three. In Figure 6.2 on page 117, the table with the planets in three columns and three layers, we have the new planets on the uppermost level.

There we have Uranus on the female line and Pluto on the male line. This would mean, of course, that Uranus is female and Pluto is male, which is true and not true. It's true and not true at the same time. Because with good argument you could put these two the other way round. But you would have to reformulate them because the order is on the basis of their motivation. What do they want?

Uranus wants greater security of life. That's why he builds the systems. That's the same motivation as Saturn and Venus have on their levels – security, an orderly controlled, dependable, harmonious life etc.

Pluto wants growth of the individual, wants to grow to ever more perfection. That's why it needs a picture of perfection as target to aim for.

That's the level of motivation but the level of function of these two planets is vice versa. Because the main function would be activity, wouldn't it? Pluto is not active, he's passive. But Uranus is active, hyperactive very often. Uranus can work through the night, two days and a third afterwards, still through the night, 24 hours around until he has found what he is looking for. He can be hyperactive, see, look, hectic activity. Or look at the waves in the air from the radio and television stations and telephone, satellite etc, in all directions all through your brain. Happily enough you don't perceive it. Hyperactivity is very frequent with Uranus and that would be male.

So that's a discrimination again – with the spiritual planets the usage of male/female is not really the same. And if you want to discriminate between active and passive for instance, that would be one thing, or extroversion/introversion or other such polarities then you would have to discriminate between the level of motivation of the planets and the level of action or functioning because they are vice versa.

So the actually passively motivated Uranus that only seeks greater security – that's a passive demand – gets awfully active to reach it. It behaves maybe in a basically female way. And Pluto who wants growth which is a male growth, which is an activity, a growing, he becomes still.

I use the word contemplation for the activities of Pluto. That is no activity, contemplate means sitting still and watching or seeing or perceiving. It's not a doing, it's a being.

I always say to educate your Pluto for a first trial go into a museum, look for a very beautiful picture that you love at first sight. Sit in front of it and start looking at that picture, trying to not see the details and not see the surrounding wall and the people going around but just the picture itself. At wide screen – the whole picture with one sight. Do that for as long as you can. If you then get up and go away it's your picture, you needn't buy it. Fantastic trick – no? You have stolen the picture but they still have it, and you have paid nothing! Because this kind of perception is what Pluto can do.

One could say stare at that picture of perfection and that makes you change without doing. You become that picture. Give it some time because you have to stick to it, to this contemplation. To see that picture of perfection and before that, in the trial, to get control of the plutonian quality and functioning, you have to understand piece by piece what parts of that picture, of that ideal picture of the perfect human being, have been pushed on you by education, by schooling, by books, etc, and which are parts that come from your innermost being. That's a long process of discrimination and it's pretty heavy psychological work on one's self. That takes time, clearly.

So, this discrimination is very important, motivation is seemingly contradictory to action or function with the spiritual planets.

With Neptune you can make no such differentiation. It's not in the nature of Neptune to have sex or be active or passive or there's no terms you can use there. This is another state of being, but a state of being of "being in contact".

Pluto knows nothing of contact – it is absolutely single. Neptune is me and us, everyone, but still I am me. I have a location in that "us". So activity, passivity are not words to be used there, this is senseless, but with Uranus and Pluto it's that way. They are two-faced, one could say.

Activity and motivation are seemingly contradictory so you could set them in your scheme there for a change, the other way round, if you want, it's your free choice, but you have to know why you do it. That's important. If for you the motivation is more important then leave it the way it is. If the functioning is more important then this may be good to cultivate for a while, then change, it – that's fine.

Questions

Audience: *[Question on interpretation of spiritual planets]*

Bruno Huber: If you look at the signs you will very often find little variation in the position of the spiritual planets between charts because these planets move very slowly. So for seven years Uranus is in the same sign, Neptune around twelve years and Pluto for 12 to 32 years (recently he only needed 12 years through Scorpio but in Taurus he needs 32 years).

There is not so much to get from the signs that is personal but what is very important is where in the house system each of these planets is positioned. I have sometimes found charts where all the spiritual planets are, for instance, on one side, say on the left side, right side, up or down and the rest are on the other side. This very often happens. Or you'll find the spiritual planets in strong positions and the rest are somewhere else. Or you'll find a spiritual planet near a cusp or even near a main angular cusp, and there are different evaluations that I think are important.

There are certain rules one should watch when you look at the spiritual planets. Basically, spiritual planets induce more often the tendency to look deeper, to go for the spiritual value, if they are nearing the low point in a house. In the lower areas of the curve, it needn't be the low point but in the lower, in the weaker part of the house, that is the part before the low point and the part afterwards, the lower part of the intensity curve.

Because if a spiritual planet is near a cusp it has been formed by the environment to a certain degree. That is, some of the ideals you have there may come from your surroundings, not from you, and may therefore not necessarily be your ideal but an implanted ideal, to put it in strong terms, superimposed by the educating surroundings. It was their ideal and they said that's what you have to reach for and then it of course depends very much on the quality of that environment and it's judging of values, what is important in life etc. So if in addition to this you have been equipped with a certain more or less clearly formulated ideal, near a cusp and you have been pushed to try to fulfil that. So there is a certain, how could I say, a certain "must" with these. I must do this – a certain coercion, in a way, that you should fulfil what's in that ideal.

And this may be misleading. It may lead you to outward results instead of inner results, as the energies in the vicinity of the cusps push outwards – that's a basic rule. Whereas at low point areas they push inwards or draw inwards, whichever way you put it. So it's normally easier to find a spiritual way with spiritual planets near a low point than with them on or near cusps. You come earlier to the idea that you could look on the inside instead of the outside.

Audience: *How about a spiritual planet which is on the low point in an intercepted sign?*

Bruno Huber: Well that doesn't change much, I mean it's a low point planet. In an intercepted sign there is this additional thing to be considered, the feeling of it being left out. Otherwise it would be only low point, that is, not very well-equipped, a diffused picture or a nebulous picture of the ideal. Low point – that is it hasn't been formed very strongly by the surroundings. This is basically true for all planets that are in the vicinity of a low point, they haven't been strongly formed, they haven't been told how to go about things in this capacity.

Therefore they are hanging loose somehow, you don't know exactly how to act with that planet. Your reaction may be not to use it at all, or to shy away whenever this planet's quality is demanded from the situation. If it's at a low point in an intercepted sign then this is the addition. It's basically important to watch this. The most tricky ones are those on the main cusps, that is in the vicinity of AC, DC, MC or IC. They are the most difficult, like I am riding the horse of a different person.

Audience: *What orb should you use on that?*

Bruno Huber: Well I would go forwards at least halfway to the balance point, and about halfway from the low point before the cusp, but you can't really exactly tell.

Audience: *Does it make a difference if it's in the same sign as the sign on the angles, if the planet is in the same sign?*

Bruno Huber: That always makes a difference, yes. Because the angle wants to put out the energy of the other sign instead of that which the planet is in. This is to be considered as well, of course. But, if it's near, say you have 28 degrees of a sign, say Gemini on the MC, and on 5 degrees in Cancer, you have Neptune, for instance, then you have a bit of a difficult situation. It's only 7 degrees from the MC and it would like to be on the MC but it is not, there is this border line in-between. So it's not easy to go to the MC and to be fully equipped to work there so there is a disappointment that may lead to overcompensation, rather similar to a planet in the shadow of an axis.

Generally these planets near the cusp lead you through a good part of your life in the terms that you have received from the education you had. The ideal has been formed largely by your surroundings, whether it was certain people, or the whole surroundings, or parts of them, or whatever, you have been pushed into a certain vision and you try to fulfil that. If it's a main cusp, because it is a cardinal cusp now, pretty strong or pushy or forceful or whatever, and you may have a certain big success with it but still it seems a rather dangerous undertaking because it may lead you away from your own path of development.

This is more true for Neptune and Pluto than for Uranus because Neptune may give you wonderful pictures of a holy world where all people are angels, and if you meet the world with a lot of non-angels then you want to make them all angels. By sheer force if necessary! Like the Christians of the tenth and eleventh centuries going to the near east to get Jerusalem in the name of love of Christ.

This sort of thing can happen and with Pluto you may develop a certain feeling of superiority, if not a complex, to supersede anything around you, to be the biggest or something very special. This is very often the case, probably more in the horizontal, AC or DC, that you find yourself to be out of this world and not understood by this world and therefore you must turn the world around, be a missionary to teach the world how they really should be. This can be a nuisance to your surroundings as well, and can mislead. It's also often a bit of guru kick or trip that goes with it, so be careful with these.

In my chart, I have Neptune on a major cusp on the DC, 4-5 degrees above. Up to the age of about sixty I followed a rule, a formulation of love that came from my mother. I have a trine from Saturn in the eleventh house in Capricorn to that Neptune which shows it clearly comes from the mother. My mother said "You must always be good to people. If you do good to people they will be good as well." She made me take that profession, and made me work around the clock in doing so. Until I got a heart attack.

At the age of sixty one I had a heart attack – because I had done too much, because I couldn't say "No, now it's enough, stop!" When people came and asked questions, demanded something, wanted help, etc. I would work around the clock. Nobody can do that really. So until the age of sixty I didn't realise that I had this fixation, then suddenly I could clearly denominate it, could see it. It came from the mother, she worked and lived that way.

She was a hairdresser, had a little business, and worked with people like that. Somebody could come at 9.30 in the evening and my mother would say "Oh, you have a headache, come in", and the person would go away without a headache. Fine, great. But, one day a policeman stood there and said "You're working at the wrong time – no good." She was told this way, I was told by a harder way. I did it much longer. Can you see what I mean, as an instance?

It's tricky with Neptune. It's even more tricky with Pluto because the feeling of greatness overshadows even more your rational thinking, your proportional thinking.

Audience: What do you do when you have this pair of planets at the main angles?

Bruno Huber: Come to realise what the egotism is in it, in what degree you serve your ego with it. That is the real problem. You know, in what I mentioned as my own case I had what we call a "helping syndrome". This term is used in psychology. I wanted to help everybody. It depends on the planet, which of the three it is, but anyway it is a helping syndrome that helps my ego to be good, strong, OK, or whatever.

But that's not good enough. That's why one day the heart said "Stop it, that's enough now." Since then I have learnt to say no, when my energies have come to a limit. I'm still learning!

So you have to find out to what degree, or how much energy goes into that function that serves your ego. If you take that out it will be OK. But that ego has a certain ease in being involved with the planet. With a main cusp position it has the greatest ease. On another cusp it's not so important mostly, but on the main cusps it has to do with the personality consciousness as we saw with the personality ray, when we took the main cusps. Those are important for the ego to have its shape in the world. Therefore if a spiritual planet is on a main cusp it is used and also misused in order to give the personality shape.

Audience: *Presumably there are positive aspects to having it like this as well?*

Bruno Huber: The positive aspects are the worldly success. And this may be an important experience for a period of life. You may grow in stature as a personality through this. I would say, for instance, with my own example I would not like to miss the complete story of that, because I wouldn't have become what I am now. It also brought me a lot of wisdom about human beings because I cared so much about people. So that's an advantage, and I became somebody in the world. I'm known worldwide now, which I didn't drive at consciously but it so happened, which gives my personality again a stature in front of people. That's also an advantage.

It's also a disadvantage for me because then the demands come stronger so that I have to learn to put limits to those demands. But it makes you feel a mission in yourself and with conscious use of the spiritual planets a mission will form in your life to be important in some way – your own mission. If you have such a mission then it's good to have a certain radiation that you are being seen and watched and heard so that you can work and have effect and push forward things demanded by your mission.

If you have no reaction, if you are not seen and heard, you sit in a corner. You sit in a corner and talk to yourself. That's of little effect. The point is, I would not really put it so much in terms of good and bad but rather discriminate what kind of effect and what the drawbacks may be, and what the advantages are, and what you pay for them.

The one thing with the spiritual planets is that they are transpersonal. If you misuse them for your ego business to a certain degree above the limit that the law of nature allows you – I mean you can draw a certain nourishment for your ego if you do things that are spiritual in their idea, that's natural – but if it goes above that, if it becomes strong, compulsive, then it's no good any more because it eats up spiritual energies for a selfish purpose and that's no good. It makes you less effective in the spiritual sense.

Audience: What you said about Pluto was quite correct because it does work in an underground sort of state. I have Pluto bang on my descendant so, yes, I can understand what you say.

Bruno Huber: Well, you see, they can be very strong, they can be leading qualities in your life but as long as your ego needs that something is wrong and one day you will pay for that. There's nobody saying to you "you're bad". The law of nature will tell you "There's an end, now stop it!"

Audience: If they're used impersonally doesn't it give you a tremendous impulse for the betterment of humanity, so actually it's learning to manage that in the sense that you let it use you because things that better humanity are really large are they not? They are impersonal kinds of things like the invention of soap, vaccinations – they aren't personal inventions that really better humanity so you really have to let these large energies just flow through you.

Bruno Huber: They are transpersonal deeds – right. That's what the spiritual planets are there for. That in the beginning you will put your own ego business with it is quite natural in younger years. The longer it goes on, the more critical it becomes. You should sort of put that behind you and find that it's a bit too much – take it a bit softer.

Audience: Just commenting on that, I think it's a question of Pluto knows no mediocrity. For example, when we just mentioned about the inventor of soap and inoculations, how many people have been killed as a result of the initial inoculations in the sense that it was well meaning but the dose would be too drastic therefore you could have killed, unintentionally, quite a large amount of humanity. So you say that Pluto is impersonal but it can have its reflection on the person who has initiated the situation whether they've liked it or not.

Bruno Huber: Sure, that's right. Such transpersonal deeds that are good for humanity very often have a certain initial price, but before that many people were sick and died from it who didn't have the things that they then had. But a few of them had to suffer death for it. So, the esoteric view is always a long-distance view in time. Of course, one could say one should have gone about it more carefully but probably the ego also played a part at the wrong moment and overdid it. That's possible. It's difficult to judge from the outside.

Audience: [Question on Conjunction with Spiritual Planets]

Bruno Huber: There are three related questions of general interest. What if you have one of the spiritual planets in conjunction with the node, with the ego planets, or with other spiritual planets?

Let's take first the Node. If the North Node is in conjunction with one of the spiritual planets, or near it (it needn't necessarily be in conjunction as if it's in the same sign you have already to a certain degree to attach the same importance to it) that capacity should be used to go forward to create something that is spiritually motivated, and that is good for others or for all. And that's the way you grow best yourself.

If a spiritual planet is in conjunction with an ego planet (Sun, Moon, Saturn), the effect is more or less the same as what I said about the main cusp position. Though the effect at a cusp may be stronger, the impulse of a Sun, Moon or Saturn ego may tend more to take over. But this is easier to see than with the cuspal position because the cuspal position shows you were as a child sort of permeated with this ideal at an age where you were not able to discriminate.

With Sun, Moon or Saturn in conjunction you have, in a way, brought it with you that you want to do it this way and therefore it's easier to detect. It mostly becomes evident earlier with a main cusp position but otherwise the effect may be very similar.

Audience: *Would you think other people pick up on that?*

Bruno Huber: Yes, it's also that people tell you more that you are probably not completely right, while with cuspal positions, main cusp positions, they will not necessarily tell you. Very often they don't. That is, with say a Sun-Pluto conjunction to take a drastic combination, people keep coming back to you and telling you that you are too strong or too forceful or too self-centred or big-shottish.

Audience: *I have Pluto conjunct Mars.*

Bruno Huber: Well Mars is not an ego planet, it is a motor. That can make it sort of compulsive in the sense of 'there is a motor that drives you on that can't stop so easily'. But it's not an ego thing as such.

Audience: *What happens if you have two of the spiritual planets in the same house, but in different signs.*

Bruno Huber: Yes, that applies for a lot of people, for instance, born in the 1960s because they were in the same sign at that time. In the mid-sixties Uranus and Pluto were in conjunction, 1964-5-6. That means that the two extremes meet and I would say that time has a special meaning for history.

I mean, that Uranus is the mother image and Pluto the father image. It contains ideas about the roles of the sexes. These have been put to nought. They have no distance any more from each other, no aspect where they can act together or against each other in different ways. If they have a distance from each other, they can see each other so they are differentiated. Distance makes for differentiation.

Conjunction is no differentiation. That's why all conjunct planets are one planet in the perception and experience of the person who has them. So those two images, father and mother images, were put to nought, having no differentiation any more. It's from that generation on that unisex came about. Nowadays with youngsters, from afar you can often hardly discriminate if it's a male or a female.

That's only an outward sign but there was a change of mentality. The youngsters born from there on don't believe any more in the old patterns of male and female, father and mother and all that stuff, this role business is out of business. A new one will have to be built and it will take time because it's a historical development of quite a big size.

So history will talk about this time of the sixties for sure, not only because of the Beatles. There was the sex revolution, there was the universities starting revolution in 1968 etc. There was a hell of a lot, there was flower power and all that. So it was an important time. It has to do with that.

Audience: *What about the nineties with the Uranus Neptune conjunction as well at the beginning of the decade.*

Bruno Huber: Yes, but that's different, because Neptune has nothing to do with sex, it has to do with love.

The astrologers will be set to nought because some astrologers identify themselves with Neptune and others with Uranus. The intuitive ones are the Neptunian ones and the very tricksy ones that know all the techniques and calculate like hell are the Uranian ones.

So there's always been this fight on for centuries. They will come to nought, that is they have to come together to find a new mode, as an instance from the astrological world. Technophilia contra love, put to nought, what do we make out of that package?

That's also of a big order, no question about it. What slow planets, the new planets, do to each other when they come together, either in conjunction or opposition, is always of historical importance. No way out of that! Look at those major transits, conjunctions and oppositions of the new planets. They may play a part in your chart because they hinge on aspect-wise with some positions in your chart.

Audience: You talked about low point intercepted planets, what about balance point intercepted planets?

Bruno Huber: Well it's much the same because on balance points it's already far enough from the cusp not to formulate the illusion it could jump back to the cusp. If it's only a few degrees away from the cusp, but intercepted, then it tries to sort of portray itself. "I'm on the cusp!" It keeps telling itself "I'm a cuspal". But on the balance point it's too far away. You can't trick yourself like that. It's just like a low point feeling.

Audience: What about shadow planets intercepted? I've a shadow Neptune, it's only three degrees before the cusp but still intercepted.

Bruno Huber: Three degrees. It depends how big the house is, but three degrees seems pretty near.

Audience: It's just in Scorpio but the cusp is just in Sagittarius.

Bruno Huber: Well, you have to check it out, whether it's like that or not, as I said. You have to find out yourself whether those compulsive over-compensatory things probably play a part. I would have to see the chart exactly and say – well I would judge it's more like this or more like that.

9

Questions

Bruno and Louise Huber

Questions

Astrological Psychology

Questions

Audience: I believe that Alice Bailey said the kind of rays that would be used for healing in this day and age. Is it just by visualisation or is there another way that you can use them? How do you use them in healing?

Bruno Huber: Well I think colour always, you can only pick up by visualisation of operating colour. Of course you can sense colour on all the other essential levels but it's not so logical. Colour is a function of light and light is a question of seeing. Of course, light can also be felt otherwise, but it's the best way to handle it because then you operate with your mind if you see it so, it's a question of visualisation in the first place. I mean, for instance, the patient may not see that colour but he may feel it somehow. So that's up to him, up to his equipment.

Louise Huber: To bring it down more to the material level you also have dresses from which you choose colours for today – yellow or blue.

Audience: That's what I was wondering, whether you could actually use physical things, use coloured light, chromotherapy or prisms or something like that...

Louise Huber: You use colour also with material means, also coloured light. Many people know that a room with green walls has a healing effect, or something like this. This is also healing.

Bruno Huber: Sure, but still it's a question of seeing. A visual impact. That's of course true that colour as such, whether I see it or not, if it's there, say in form of light, will have an effect. But for the operator, the healer, I would say that visualisation is the tool.

Audience: This is a question about rays and signs. We are given the rays of the different planets and signs. When it comes to rulerships there seems to be a contradictory factor appearing. If one thinks of Taurus, the exoteric ruler is Venus which fits very well with the fourth Ray and it's a purely fourth Ray sign, and yet the esoteric and hierarchical ruler Vulcan is essentially first Ray. The same happens with Pisces. You think of Pisces as a sixth and a second Ray sign and yet the esoteric and hierarchical ruler is Pluto, again first Ray. The only sign that seems to fit everything is Leo which has the Sun as its ruler of all three factors, hierarchical, exoteric and esoteric, and it does have a certain amount of second ray nature about it. Could you try to reconcile the contradictions here?

Bruno Huber: The confusion? Well that's not easy. It's a big question, because it depends on the level from which you look at things. On different levels you always get different schemes of ray, colour and all that stuff. So to put that all together in an orderly way would take a book, or more.

What you read from the Tibetan in Alice Bailey's books is seen from a rather high level. It is not always at just one level, so there are different perspectives at different levels. While the level we present here is from the personality level, but including the levels up to the whole of the soul, so this is a workable scheme. If you try with the other Bailey books you get all mixed up again and again, and you can be rather ineffective. That's the problem.

That's why I worked so hard to find where these rays fit with astrology. Astrology is built for the human being, to lead the human being to initiation. So to get up there with your consciousness you have a proper way in the way we presented it, because it's manoeuvrable by your mind, including feeling and everything that belongs to the personality. But anyway that's where you can clearly see an order and therefore clear ways to go.

So I would say I cannot go further at this point because it would take a book to explain all those other levels and the ways it looks from there. If you find contradiction this is seeming contradiction because it's seen from a different level than the one we were talking about here. So it's not a real contradiction, it's a different view.

It's like you go out and look at this building from this side and then you look from that side and it looks all different – and you're probably not sure whether it's the same building if you haven't made the way yourself. Then you go up into a helicopter and it looks different again, and you can't even realise it's the same place.

Audience: I was interested when you were saying that the transpersonal planets were in the etheric body. I can't make the connection with why they should be in the etheric body, not any of the outer bodies.

Bruno Huber: Simply for the reason that we have easy access to them. To the soul, they don't have that easy access, not even to the causal body because it's on mental and higher levels. But to the etheric body, because it belongs to the general physical realm we have easy access, just by clearing out our physically conditioned thoughts about physical things we can already tune in to those etheric planets.

Also, it's logical. We can see the planets up to Saturn and we cannot see the new ones. But they are there physically, so for us they are near but not visible, you see. So the visible thing is everything that is seeable by the eye which we have from nature, and the other is 'next door', so to speak. We can reach out for it by consciousness and then we get it, so again dense physical existence and etheric existence are not two things, they are one but we can't see the etheric.

We can perceive it by expanding our consciousness into that realm, like for instance having a parapsychological capacity developed, or suddenly having hunches jumping up etc. That's already reaching beyond sheer physically dense existence, beyond body-ness. So it's for easy access nature has put it that way, otherwise it would be more difficult if they were up, say, on the soul level.

Audience: You spoke about self-initiation, as opposed to the old-style initiation. Can you comment on how this ties in with what the Tibetan says about group initiation into a particular ashram of service for the New Age?

Bruno Huber: The last news the Tibetan gave out, shortly before Alice Bailey died, said that the hierarchy, which the Tibetan is part of, was in its present and past state dissolved.

The Masters are supposed to reincarnate into humanity. That's one thing. So the old rule of group initiation, in the sense of being integrated into an ashram, is not true anymore. There will be group initiations in future, not because they belong to an ashram, but because they are on the same beam, I don't say ray – beam, feelingwise, etc. They have the same or similar picture of how things go, find themselves in a similar state of development, and find it together and can go through a group initiation. Also, there is the big thing of humanity going through a group initiation in these times. This, of course, takes centuries.

Audience: What I was actually wondering was, I believe it's probably in Discipleship in the New Age, where they talk about the probationer coming closer to an ashram, one of the first things that happens is that the security structures are blown apart. I was wondering if this was reflected in charts?

Bruno Huber: That's hard to say. One could say officially the ashrams are dissolved, because the hierarchy dissolved. But of course these ashrams will go on for quite a while but under different rules, that is they are not controlled by the master any more. The master will be present if needed but they work their way out themselves. And some of the ashrams will go away and others may come in, so it's a fluid movement that will change in the course of time.

To see that in the chart would mean that you have to check out if you feel 'I belong' to that quality group, it's a question of quality, and then you would have to check, in a way, like doing click horoscopes with the others of the ashram. See where the points of relation are. More, I couldn't say. This is to be investigated because this business is only starting.

Louise Huber: I will say something about group initiation. We found out in our groups, when we have two-week seminars, then something like group initiation happens to the participants. I feel this also here in this group, when you get into the knowledge of the rays with your whole inner awareness, then you would be changed in a way through a kind of initiation which has happened at that moment, and you grasp it, and you get it.

Bruno Huber: It is a form of group initiation, surely.

Audience: Let me ask you, in the five levels of the chart, the inner circle, aspects, planets, etc. do the rays meet somewhere there?

Bruno Huber: No, that would be mixing up things. You have planes of substance and energy that are of a different rate. That's the storeys in the five levels we have in the chart, isn't it?

The highest storey is the soul itself, not visible in the chart, then the aspect structure etc, down to the houses. These are similar to the planes of energy and substance used in esoteric views, they are the area where the human being exists and can reach for. It's the same, it's just a simple exposition in terms of the chart, so it's planes of substance and energy and any ray can work in any of the planes.

It depends what you have there. So you cannot say the plane has a ray. Of course, there would be seven such planes of substance and energy, esoterically seen. We have dealt with five of them. Remember the two uppermost levels of figure 2.3, I haven't even been talking about Adi and Anupadaka. They are so divine we cannot grasp them, and nothing of that is shown in the chart. What is shown is the soul level, so we have five storeys. In the chart we have five levels or planes of substance and energy in the esoteric view, leaving out the top two, which would then make seven. And, of course, these you could put into ray qualities but this doesn't help you along in any way. It's more principles again, manifested in form and in substance and energy.

Audience: Have you any reflection on the kind of experience people are recounting from dream levels or other kind of levels about the connection with UFOs and other dimensions. Do you accept UFOs as reality?

Bruno Huber: It is not exactly my business to judge and evaluate this because it is a very difficult area, and there are a lot of projections, and a lot of projections of people who have no notion of spirituality. So we have a lot of puzzling material coming across from all kinds of media and people.

In principle I see no problem that these things may exist. Then it would be a question for us to find out from where they come, from what level, so to speak, or from what area in the cosmos.

I have strong doubts about whether the many and varied stories do contain a lot of truth, because they're so different and have such different qualities depending from where they come, so that it is difficult to make pure reason from that. And that's what we need – pure reason. So I wouldn't give a value judgement on that.

I'm open and I'm interested that other entities from different planes or different worlds may contact us. OK, fine. I think I would be prepared to face up to it, but I would demand from those entities where they come from, and what they are and what they want. With all that is delivered to us from the world around we have no chance to ask that and that's not good enough for me. I don't see the point.

The world is much bigger, the cosmos is bigger, and these hierarchical orders of planes are bigger, than we can ever perceive, so everything is possible – that we are being contacted from other levels or other worlds. I don't see a point of doubt there as such, but I would like to have proof, and proof that clearly declares where it comes from and what it is and what it wants of us.

Audience: Is it not just as possible that these are actually things that have been manifested out of the collective unconscious?

Bruno Huber: Now that is part of the game. That's why such a lot of different information comes. There are a lot of projections – projections of wishful thinking, of drive nature, fears, wish for power, collective unconscious stuff in the mass, pictures that come from there that are partly of great age, so that to sort it out is practically impossible. You would have to check every person that gives out information about that stuff. Check the person psychologically – where is what coming from in that person. There's a hell of a business!

Audience: In a previous seminar, we were given a sheet of ten points to consider when we look at charts and one of them referred to looking at the ruler of the ascendant. We don't usually use rulers, so I wondered if you could expand on that.

Louise Huber: It was not the ruler of the ascendant but it was the same thing I was explaining yesterday – that the sign on the AC is the beginning of your life, and you have to develop the most spiritual quality of the sign. You can use the esoteric seed thought of the sign to get out of it the quality you have to develop.

This is what it is, and the Node is the first step. It is with these ten rules that you take the first step with the North Node, which leads to this quality.

Bruno Huber: We have nothing to do with that normal 'ruler' business in astrology. Forget it!

Louise Huber: Use the rulers in so far as we say the exoteric ruler of a sign works on the physical, materialistic and drive level, and the esoteric planet works on the consciousness level.

The crises start when you experience the opposition from the sign on the other side of the axis. The crisis comes in and then you can develop the esoteric ruler. This is what I said yesterday about the three steps of development. With the crisis mechanism in a sign axis the opposite sign is always creating crises which awaken your consciousness.

You need this conflict, opposition, polarisation, otherwise you will not grow into the level of consciousness controlled by the esoteric ruler. And the Moon Node shows you the first step you have to take.

Bruno Huber: I think it's important to recall again and again that a sign is made of three qualities – a cross, a temperament and a ruling planet. I don't like the word 'ruling'. It doesn't rule – it takes part in it and is at home there. It brings it's own quality into the quality of the sign.

The sign is not a single quality, is not a principle. It's composed of three principles, the cross, the temperament and the planet that's at home there. So you can't go and take the sign for one of these because it's always the totality of these three qualities that work together to make the quality of the sign.

So this ruler business as used in astrology largely to make all kind of tricky things is a lopsided view of signs. It's one of the helpless movements people make who don't get the stuff right, who don't make the right discriminations. Discrimination of levels, for instance, is completely forgotten about in the astrology of today, so they need these helping tricks to get something out of the chart. So never be put up to such a thing as to take the ruler of the ascendant sign, that would be way off.

Audience: I wonder if you are placing any special significance on the solar eclipse next summer, in August.

Bruno Huber: I'm going to write an article about it in *Astrolog*[1]. One thing to say is that every year we normally have an average of four eclipses, two moon and two sun. It can be three moon and one sun, it can be five in total, but that's the average.

Now old rules say that, and are mostly used in the way that, a solar or lunar eclipse can have a period of working out for half the year or more. If you make a little calculation there's not enough time in the year them all to work out. Four times half a year makes two years. So you would be very busy to work all those eclipses out. Funnily enough, this year there was only one solar eclipse and no lunar eclipse. Next year will be two solar eclipses and one lunar eclipse, I'm not sure.

The point is, nobody ever talks about where eclipses hit on the earth. Why should that not be considered? Eclipses have a band of shadow, for instance a solar eclipse has a band of something like 110 kilometres across and they make a track for 2 or 3 thousand kilometres or more across the planet, and the rest of the world doesn't see the eclipse. So most people don't see it – just those in that band.

Next year's eclipse in August will hit you here. It will hit the south of Germany but not us in Switzerland because we are out of the shadow. Now a question which I think should be considered is that eclipses should be considered where they are, where they are perceivable. I'm sure they won't have any effect where they don't hit. This can be checked out by looking into recent history and comparing it with the eclipses. You mostly have some effects, often very doubtful, but some effects you can detect within those areas where the shadows go, but not outside. So that whole business about the eclipses is very diffuse. Of course, that one in August goes right across Europe. It goes across Austria, Hungary and touches the Black Sea and ends over in Pakistan somewhere. I think that should be investigated.

To make such a noise because it's hitting us in Europe is a good reason for those that might be touched by it, not for the rest of the world. But it probably makes such a big noise because it's the last one in this millennium and those astrologers who want something to predict "Ooohh" things. They need something so they take one of those eclipses, one that hits Europe! But nobody, funnily enough, talks about Europe being hit by it, they take it for the whole of the world. American astrologers make the same noise.

Audience: *It doesn't touch America.*

Bruno Huber: Not by far. It begins somewhere out in the Atlantic, south of Greenland. I think there is huge fumbling about eclipses and there are very diffused rules used, different rules used by different astrologers. There's no way of really knowing about them.

No research has ever been done, as far as I know, and I think one of the foremost things is that Ptolemy could not talk about it because he didn't know about the phenomenon. But it should be investigated – where they hit, how they hit and what the real rules are. So I say if you don't observe it, forget it.

I mean, if it hits you you'll experience it because it's something like two and a half minutes black, lights going out in the day, it's around midday so you will perceive it. That's fine, make your own sense of it, but don't push it to the next millennium. To make the millennium go in according to this eclipse is stupid.

Audience: *What do you feel about the big conjunction of planets in May 2000?*

Bruno Huber: Well, we just had a big conjunction of planets in Leo, five of them. So why make a noise? I mean, this is a stellium, it happens all the time. It's very dangerous to pick a particular one out. Every few years you have such stelliums. We just had one, which dissolved a week ago. There were three planets left, before that we had five and not long before the Node was in it. So, did you observe anything very special? No?

You know, many astrologers have the need to be seen, to be heard, and the easiest way is to predict something. They pick on points and elements, the ephemeris, where you have clusters, for instance, or a combination of sharp red aspects, or something. That's a great love of astrologers since Ptolemy and before, but it's not necessarily good astrology, because it's there for making people fear things and this is pretty cheap business, isn't it? So, we have nothing to do with that.

Louise Huber: Are you aware that we have really clearly cut out the predictions business in our astrology? It is written in our codex and we tell it all the time. We have nothing to do with prediction and all this charlatanry. We are professional astrological psychologists.

Audience: I was puzzled by you saying that the personality ray depends on the crosses. Now the crosses at the equator are 90 degrees away from each other, so people there have the same cross. The higher north you get the more difficult it becomes and the crosses become very uneven; therefore the personality ray of people at the equator would be very different from those at the higher latitudes.

Bruno Huber: Well, if you observe people living there, I mean not the people that have moved from the north or somewhere else into that area, but the people who live there naturally all the time, the races living there are much more of an even population. That is, single individuals don't show so much differentiation as individuals hereabouts. Here you are so different. Look at each other, how different you look, how differently you behave, how different your outlooks are, etc.

Even on the equator you can still have two different if it's near the border, because small differentiations are still there. Up to five degrees or so. So it can happen, and those then are the few individuals who stick out in those surroundings. They mostly link up with the rest of the world, with the modern civilised world nowadays. Earlier they became a chief or something because they were expressed individualities, while the others were of a big lump of very similar individuals. This is a factual truth to be observed. Doesn't this explain things?

Audience: These people born at low latitudes must be on rays one, two, three while the others are also on minor rays.

Bruno Huber: It's true. Yes they have major rays, which again means the possibility of less differentiation, because the major rays are bigger lumps, reaching over a greater area of life than the minor rays. The latter are more specialised because they tell you how to go about things, so I think that's all natural.

I think it's very important in astrology always to look back to nature, to reality, to people. Don't move in your astrological world alone and make arguments from there, it's no good. You have to link it up to reality.

Like those people going about and saying "Oh this house system is no good because up north, above 66 degrees it doesn't work" and then

It's very important in astrology always to look back to nature, to reality, to people.

they take equal houses, because they work up there. But equal houses is a construct, it has nothing to do with reality. They don't accept that life up there in that northern latitude is so simple and straightforward, limited by nature, that you have hardly a space to move.

Nature doesn't let you, so if you do charts with the Koch house system you may have a house that is 175 degrees big and the rest of the five houses on that half are five degrees altogether. But that's showing a reality of life up there. Life is reduced to very few functions, and that's it. So always go back to reality, check with reality. The chart is not a thing up there in itself. It is derived from nature, so it must be true.

But with questions like this, if you are in doubt about something because your logic says so, then you have to go back to nature and say how is it to live down there, how are the people there – and then you get the answer.

Audience: We mentioned Vulcan which is technically between Mercury and the Sun and therefore placing it on a chart, it would have to have a smaller degree of elongation than Mercury. So Vulcan, in everybody's chart, must of necessity be almost conjunct the Sun.

Bruno Huber: Vulcan would have to be by sheer astronomical calculation, if it existed, within eight degrees of the Sun. Which means in constant conjunction with the Sun. Of course there's no astronomical evidence for a planet there and the logic of what we know about planets around suns in the cosmos from reality is that a physical planet wouldn't exist there very long. It would be drawn into the sun and vanish in the course of time. So it can only be a spiritual thing, rather, a symbol that you place there.

Never has any evidence of a physical object inside Mercury's orbit been found, and you know we've had solar modules going very near the Sun and they should have detected it. No way, nothing found. So far, it must be a spiritual component and in a normal chart it is a symbol. A symbol of an energy which is meant to be standing behind a certain sign. No physical object.

Audience: This is a very controversial question, the planetoid Chiron. We talk about the rainbow bridge between the planets of Saturn at the limit and the transpersonal ones. But on the other hand the link between the Saturn as the limit to those outer planets appears to be Chiron.

Bruno Huber: Chiron is probably a sort of half-dead comet, very weak in the expansion of gases at its tail, which is quite normal for comets. It's a captured body that came in from outside and happened to be stopped there between Saturn and Uranus. It nearly touches the two orbits.

But it is a small body – at most the size of 300 km across, probably smaller. It is not a stable body and does not have a stable orbit. At the present time we can check an orbit that seems to be somewhat stable, but within some two or three dozen revolutions it will probably already be out of its present orbit and have gone into Saturn or Uranus, or be pushed somewhere out of the solar system.

So it's not a stable thing, and of course it doesn't belong to the order of planets because of its size. The smallest planet is Pluto, which is still 2,300 km across so that's a different order. Thousands of kilometres across is the order of planets. But hundreds is a satellite or a big comet or an asteroid or something like that, up to 1,000 km across.

So it can't be put together with the planets by way of argument. It's a different order. If we start to include that smaller order, then we have to take into account at least fifteen asteroids that have the same size within the solar system. Otherwise it's incongruent just to pick out one. Some go so far as to take four more – Ceres, Pallas, Vesta and Juno. But still that's only four plus Chiron, five out of fifteen that have the size of that order. So that's incongruent.

Either you do it completely, or you don't do it. But to pick out one? Some don't take Vesta and the Vesta group, but take only Chiron, and now they have Pholus with it as well – a body of similar shape and size. This is sheer betrayal of people, in my opinion. It's a choice by force, so to speak. "I pick this one and this is the big one. This is also a planet now."

You can't do that; it's not proper. It's also not very scientific. In terms of natural laws it's not orderly. So either you use all the bodies of that class between say 100 km and 1,000 km across, a class of bodies of which there are at least fifteen. And you should use them all and put them in a second order, not on the same plane as you put the planets. They therefore don't have the quality of a principle, they are additions.

I've done research into other asteroids and have found that yes you can say something about them, but if you correctly do a chart reading without them, what you can find with that asteroid is already there. It can be that it is a bit more specified, but specification also leads to over-emphasis, and then you get it out of proportion. That's why I warn that it's better not to use those asteroids. Or do proper research into it and then take all of them, not those you like, forgetting the rest. So I'm against using it, and that's it.

Lousie Huber: I want to add something. It has been a reality for years that some astrologers have projected onto Chiron those questions or fields of research to which they otherwise have no answer. They project onto Chiron questions like, this is the rainbow bridge between Saturn and Uranus and therefore it's a healer and therefore it will bring in the transpersonal planets, and other things you find in the books about Chiron.

But there must be a reason why people are looking for a Chiron to put all these questions onto. This is a kind of a help, a kind of 'as if' method to overcome the gap in consciousness. In my opinion it also has it's value.

Bruno Huber: Well, it's a bridge to the bridges! Or, I would say it's a crutch.

Louise Huber: Yes, he's the scientific mind. From the astronomical point of view it's really a small thing, but from the spiritual point of view in my experience with people who use Chiron as bridging and so on, it has its value.

Bruno Huber: It's the same people who do not properly define Uranus, Neptune and Pluto. They're not properly going at these planets and as you saw yesterday they are the bridges to the spiritual dimension. So those who are not able to formulate them name these bridges, they need a bridge to these bridges. But that's a spiritual crutch.

Audience: What is the meaning of Lilith, and does it fit into the scheme?

Bruno Huber: Lilith is pure wishful thinking, I think. There seem to be waves of interest for objects such a Lilith that are not the normal equipment. I have ephemerides for Lilith from three different waves. If you compare them, they have absolutely nothing in common. They even let Lilith move at very different speeds.

Now, the most recent explanation is supposed to be the apsis points of the Moon's orbit. Does this tell you anything? Apsis points are the points where it's square to the node line. It's the point of greatest distance to the body it circles around, that is the Earth, and the nearest point. The most modern ephemeris takes these points and says that's Lilith, the black moon.

It's a pure fiction. The nodal line is something real because it produces phenomena, eclipses. If Sun and Moon are on or near that line at the time of the full moon, you have an eclipse, either of Sun or Moon. This is very obvious. This is a physical phenomenon.

The apsis produces nothing whatever in the sky. Nothing, ever. So it's funny to take it as an important thing. You can construct any number of such points that are astronomical, mathematical points. No problem. I could just produce a number of ephemerides of that sort from the different planets, they have apses too. Hey, that's a wonderful business, we have so many elements to talk about...

It's no good. Lilith is an invention, a fiction. It's nothing astronomically or astrologically real. But of course it's largely used by females because they like the idea of having their 'own' planet. It's those women going a bit too far on the extreme left or right or, I don't know where they stand politically, but those that are against men. They are "going to show them", and it is largely they who use it and push it out. Read those books about Lilith, they are feministic – Women's Lib. You get this sort of tone. Nothing against women and their emancipation on my part, you know. But this busines is overdone. They get a bit shadowy, as shadowy as Lilith, so they are on a sideline. They have gone out of astrology really and are doing their business with Lilith.

Audience: Can I just clarify what you are saying, that it is actually another one of these projections and has no spiritual reality, unlike Vulcan which has a spiritual reality.

Bruno Huber: Yes, that's right. Lilith also comes up in esoteric writings but it's always coming out of the dark and producing something dark.

Real esotericism never talks about darkness, it talks about light. Darkness is just the absence of light. It's not something by itself and therefore you cannot give it a body. It's important, a question of definition. So Lilith doesn't exist, by definition.

And if the Moon is on its apsis lines it's not dark, it's in its strongest position. Old astrology called that area of the apsis points the "belly of the Moon", where it is in its full power. When it is in the upper apsis, which is used as the Lilith point, probably it's in its time when it's the highest in the sky.

You know that the Moon goes up and down? This is considered by farmers, and still used. In the old ages they used it very strongly, upper and lower moon. In the positive apsis point it's high up so it's in full power. That's what they call the "belly" of it, the thick belly, there's substance in it, this was the idea.

Louise Huber: Lilith is also in my opinion a kind of stick or helping 'as if' method for this period of emancipation of women where they have to develop more self-consciousness, so they project something special onto Lilith.

Bruno Huber: Yes, maybe a crutch but crutches won't make you develop, you know. They help you along while you are crippled.

Audience: How about trans-Pluto?

Bruno Huber: Trans-Pluto doesn't exist. There are trans-Pluto's of any amount. They are bodies like Chiron out there beyond Pluto, the so-called Kuyper belt. Today we have already found something like fifty such bodies in the size around 200 to 500 km across. They are pinpointed, measured and their orbits known. They just have numbers presently, but not yet names. They are asteroids in a sense and it's called the outer asteroid belt nowadays in astronomy. There may be several tens of thousands of them out there, just as in the asteroid belt between Mars and Jupiter there are more than 10,000 bodies.

A big body of the size of a planet would have been found long ago[2]. So, I think that's none of our astrological business.

Audience: Can you say anything about synchronicity in the naming of the planets Uranus, Neptune, Pluto, about how they came to be named. Was it coming from the collective unconscious? I know there's a great story about naming Pluto for example, an astronomer's name.

Bruno Huber: I've done a lot of research into the names of planets specifically, through all the ages back to the beginning. Planets have been changing names partly, partly not at all. For instance, Zeus is Greek, Jupiter is Roman, that's only a change of name.

Now the point is that the creators of the original meanings of the planets, not names but meanings, are the Sumerians and they named the planets by trying to give an idea of the quality or meaning through the name. These names were not taken very far but the meaning was transported to the Babylonians, to the Chaldeans, to the Greeks, to England etc. So the meaning goes on but the names change.

I have a collection of over a hundred such names of the planets, all in an orderly historical order and how they came about in different cultures. This is part of my glossary of astrology[3]. This gives you deep insight in the development of, and evaluation of, the planets. The meaning always has been kept by all different cultures and times but the evaluation has been different.

One instance – Saturn. In early Germanic namings you have the name "Satiar". which means saturated or rich year. Then came the late Germanic translations and it has become "Nocklykstjerna" which means something like 'bad powerful thing' – say 300 years later by the Germanic people living in the south of Sweden and north of Germany. Whereas before it was a good positive thing, at that time around 1000 AD Saturn suddenly changed to a very bad name. That's typical.

It's not the name that makes it. The meaning is still the same but the definition, evaluation, is different. It follows the morals and ethics of a culture. So that's very interesting. That's what I try to show in the glossary – it's very interesting.

Audience: Would it mean that Uranus, Neptune, Pluto have been named by astronomers.

Bruno Huber: Yes. Among astronomers it's an absolute rule that the astronomer discovering a body can also give it the name. With Uranus this seemed to work quite well.

With Neptune there was a big battle between nations because two individuals, an English and a Frenchman, discovered it at the same time with the same calculations. Both wanted to give it a name. Because they couldn't find the right one, others intruded and wanted to give it names, so there was a big battle. Finally Neptune was accepted.

With Pluto it's even worse. The discoverer of Pluto, or the one who wanted to discover it, Percival Lowell, was already dead when it was discovered and the man who discovered it on photo plates was a student of astronomy, Clyde Tombaugh, who was not accepted as the discoverer by the scientific community. So everybody felt right to give it a name. There were thousands of names given to the planet in the first run until they built up a group at the centre in Flagstaff which had to decide on one. They were given many possibilities and finally accepted Pluto, which was suggested by a 14 year old English girl.

With good argument. The girl seemingly knew Greek mythology well and argued that if you have Neptune/Poseidon then its brother was Pluto/Hades. So it would have to be Hades/Pluto. Proper argument, because it has the same rank in the Greek mythological hierarchy. Brother and brother – so it was accepted for that reason. So, hail England, a 14 year old girl gave the name to Pluto. It wasn't the Pluto of Walt Disney. That story goes around as well.

Audience: About choosing that word Pluto – it had the initials of Percival Lowell "P.L." and the "T.O." of Tombaugh. I believe that the girl Venetia Verney took it accidentally from Walt Disney's dog, Pluto, and Mickey Mouse.

Bruno Huber: But it's not, because that came afterwards. Pluto came into the game with Walt Disney in 1932 or '34 or something. Before that, it was Mickey and Minnie Mouse.

Audience: I was thinking that a lot of people in this room are going to end up being teachers of Huber astrology in the next 20 or 30 years and we've looked a lot at how there are always things like Chiron coming along. And recently there's been somebody saying, "Oh no, you should look at Ceres". And then they say, "Oh no, you should look at this, you should look at that". And yet for me that's all taking astrology away from looking at the self by trying to look outside and find something else that's exciting rather than looking at what's going on inside and seeing how to develop that. But on the other hand I don't want to see Huber astrology actually being fixed and stuck. As you say, it's an organic process and it's something that moves on. I was wondering if you had something you could put in a short sentence, like a guideline, in terms of how you see Huber astrology growing into the future but not actually moving away from its fundamental principles.

Bruno Huber: Well, I think the principles are clear, they are in the teaching and they are in the API Code, they are in the books etc. I don't think there's a danger of it really turning into nothingness.

It's a question of how you go about it and of what you probably add to it. I mean, a lot of our students tend to use other specialities of working with people like healing of sorts or other training forms, psychological forms, psychosynthesis for instance, etc. That's fine. But it may be that some methods might lead you away from this. If so, then you cannot call it Huber astrology or astrological psychology any more.

It is important to say that enunciation – that we are not psychological astrology – we are astrological psychology. The main word is psychology, so that's our frame of work. To that we can add other things, above and below, but we should not allow ourselves to distort what this astrological psychology is by other ways of thinking of these additions. Then we have to keep it apart and do the one thing for one reason and the other thing for another reason.

We have to be there in the psychological dimension of thinking and working with our astrology. We may add, for instance, medical astrology but that would need a lot of research first. Research which even I haven't done yet which I could think of doing – but being a psychologist I've had to do that first and it took the greater part of my life. So I leave it for the next life, probably.

There are many things you can do with astrology, you know. I did it with psychology and out came a psychology that really works on the basis of astrological chart reading. And that should be clear, it should remain clear.

If you add things you should try to correlate and if you have a contradiction you should keep the contradiction out of that psychology and try to find out how it could be surmounted. It may be that something is missing in our astrology, yes, it's possible. But it may be that something is missing or wrong in the other method and then you would probably have to abandon it there.

That is a way of searching for more clarity for every one of you. You cannot be protected against that hardship. You will be faced with such contradictions coming from other fields of thinking and that belongs to life, I would say. And we are not there to watch you if you do right. We would be pretty busy with the many students we have had all these years. It's your responsibility to keep that clear.

Astrological Psychology

Bruno Huber

I think that leads us anyway to the end of this seminar. I would like to go on with the thought just put with that question. There is a need for a certain purity of that kind of astrology which we do, because it is so different in many aspects from what astrology is now. You have perceived that, for sure, by yourself in your own surroundings. The main word is psychology, that is we go at the psychology of the human being because I'm convinced, also my method is convinced, of the fact that the human being is mainly psyche. Of course you have a physical body but we handle our body also from our psyche. By psyche I now mean feeling and mind.

> **There is a need for a certain purity
> of that kind of astrology which we do...
> The main word is psychology.**

Therefore psychology is the way to deal with human beings if they are in trouble, even if they are in physical trouble, because there is mostly a psychological reason for that. They select some sort of trouble out of a psychological condition in them so we have to detect these, clear them and then the trouble will go away.

That is also true for medical problems. They always have a psychological background and doctors already accept that if the person is in good humour while sick the healing is better. That's at least something already, which is an acceptance of psychosomatic function.

So this psychological approach to astrology is, in the way that we do it, absolutely new to this planet. Big words! But it's new to this planet. Look around, read books, any number of good books, good astrology books – it's new, it's different.

You know the best of astrologers, of whom we can say to our students "do read these books", like Liz Greene or Stephen Arroyo, are psychologically deep. However, from my perspective, they are astrologically back in the Middle Ages. They use the techniques of the past and it doesn't ever really fit. If you try to go from that point of view, as in those books, it doesn't really fit. They sort of twist it like this and make it fit. But it doesn't work out because it's not consistent.

The system of definition and delineation mostly used in astrology is mediaeval in its mental structure. It doesn't have the knowledge about human beings that modern thinking has and that modern psychology brings us in a very differentiated way. There is no way in the old terminology of astrology, I've tried for years and years and years to correlate modern psychological thinking with the wordings of delineations of the old patterned astrology. No way – it doesn't function because similar terms in the two fields may mean different things and similar things may have such different names that you never come to the idea "that's that". It doesn't work.

So this, for the time being, is the only astrology that really correlates the two fields into one. That's why it has this name "astrological psychology". It's one thing, it's not astrology plus psychology. I think that it's important that you keep that in mind so you will be always there standing up for this progressive modern approach to astrology. And you will have to stand up some times.

> ## This is the only astrology that really correlates the two fields into one. That's why it has this name "astrological psychology". It's one thing, it's not astrology plus psychology.

If other astrologers come up to you and say "Why are you doing this? Why is it not seven years instead of six years for the age progression and why do you have Saturn as the mother – it's no good" and stuff like this. You will have to stand up and say that that's the truth if you watch carefully. If you put Saturn to be the father or something else and you don't watch, then it may fit your argument but it's not the truth psychologically – it's not.

So, you're up to something in the world going ahead with this kind of astrology or astrological psychology. It is a certain responsibility which you have from a point of view of ethics. Because astrology is being applied to people, to human beings, and human beings can suffer if they are misled by wrong advice.

You can do damage and that's no good, or would you say it's good to do damage? I think certain realisations coming from this kind of psychology may hurt the client, but that's momentary. Then the client always has two possibilities – shrink back from this process, forget it that is, not accept it, or work it through – and we can deliver more than just a remark.

That again is different from normal astrology – they give you a remark, a statement about that planet there and that ruler over there etc. and no further psychological explanation – they just name it with some words. We can go through explanations of how things are constructed and how they came about, as every psychologist does, only we have the tool of the chart, a diagnostic tool that is very fast.

What I do in two hours, a good therapist needs one or two years to get the same clarity of picture. This is not a pompous utterance, it is sheer fact. It's practice. So don't make too much of a point in front of psychologists, they don't like that. They don't like the idea that it can be shortened down to two hours, especially not the psychiatrists, they will shoot at you!

What I do in two hours, a good therapist needs one or two years to get the same clarity of picture

But life is incredibly interesting living with this astrological psychology. It's interesting, and you will see that more and more you will attract more interesting people.

In the first instance all kinds of people may come because they hear "Aha! Tell me when my mother will die, I want to get the money!" Greed is one thing, wishful thinking is another thing. It's all been projected onto astrology and astrologers love to serve that. Many, too many, still do.

So, in the course of time you will select just by doing right, not by making propaganda in that sense, but doing right because those who have been with you go to other people and tell them. That's the best way to do it. Mouth propaganda we call it, word of mouth.

Now, one thing which I think is important. If you do something which is so important and responsible and professional, (it is professional, your astrological education is of the most professional you can get in this world), then you should also try to keep track of developments.

You should go on learning more and more about it. You learn in two ways. You learn from sheer practice from the material that comes from the clients, you get more and more live material which can fill in your understanding of charts. This is a way of automatic research and one should be a researcher, in that sense at least. That is, ready to learn more about astrological psychology each time I deal with a person. That's one thing.

The other thing, of course, is to try to catch up with the developments that have been found within our special field. New discoveries etc. They will come across to you, through writing partly, but also through further seminars you can go to. And, of course, through meeting up in little groups to discuss matters and find out.

You should do something about growing further into this fantastic new field of thinking in order to go with the times because the times are changing very fast. People are changing very fast, conditions are changing very fast, problems are changing very fast. So get with it, keep going with it – I think it's important.

You should do something about growing further
into this fantastic new field of thinking.
So get with it, keep going with it.
I think it's important.

Notes and References

1. INTRODUCTION

1. Alice A Bailey (1880-1949) was a founder of the Arcane School (below) and, working with the Tibetan Djwal Khul, wrote a series of books presenting the next phase in the continuity of the Ageless Wisdom teaching. Her life story is partially presented in *The Unfinished Autobiography*, Alice Bailey. The full series of 24 books of esoteric philosophy is available from Lucis Press, Suite 54, 3 Whitehall Court, London SW1A 2EF.

2. The Arcane School was established in 1923 to help meet an obvious and growing demand for further teaching and training in the science of the soul. The purpose of the esoteric training given by the Arcane School is to help the student grow spiritually towards acceptance of discipleship responsibility and to serve the divine plan by serving humanity - esotericism as a practical way of life. Details from Arcane School, Suite 54, 3 Whitehall Court, London SW1A 2EF.

3. Italian psychologist Roberto Assagioli was founder of the spiritually-based psychology known as *psychosynthesis*.

4. *Psychosynthesis - A Manual of Principles and Techniques*, Roberto Assagioli.

5. The Swiss Astrological Psychology Institute was founded by Bruno and Louise Huber in 1968. For current information see www.astro-api.ch.

6. The foreword to Alice Bailey's *A Treatise on the Seven Rays* indicates that this lays the foundation for the needed new psychology.

7. *A Treatise on the Seven Rays*, Alice Bailey, Volume 1 page 295.

8. See *Esoteric Healing* and *Telepathy and the Etheric Vehicle*, Alice Bailey.

2. WHAT DOES ESOTERIC MEAN?

1. For more explanation of Assagioli's Egg model, see for example *Psychosynthesis – A Manual of Principles and Techniques*, Roberto Assagioli.

2. Bruno and Louise Huber spent three years working with Roberto Assagioli in Florence. Coming out of this period was Bruno's mission to connect the worlds of astrology and psychosynthesis, which became the focus of his life work.

3. The symbol ♅ is widely used to symbolise Uranus on the continent, in preference to the English ♅. Similarly ♇ is widely used to symbolise Pluto, in preference to ♇.

4. *Faust*, J.W.Goethe

3. THE ENTITY OF THE SEVEN COSMIC RAYS

pages 29-48

1. Alice Bailey's *Treatise on the Seven Rays* comprises five volumes: *I,II Esoteric Psychology, III Esoteric Astrology, IV Esoteric Healing and V The Rays and the Initiations.* The teaching on the Seven Rays has also been gathered together in a shorter compendium *The Seven Rays of Life.* All are available from the Lucis Press.

2. "...when all the brutal stuff was happening in France" – Louise is referring to the second World War.

3. ADI - Louise is referring to the logoic plane – the highest plane. See Figure 2.3 *Amphora* or Figure 6.1 *The Constitution of Man.*

4. The kingdoms and their relationships with the rays are covered in detail in *Esoteric Psychology I*, Alice Bailey, page 215 onward.

5. Planetary logos – "The Being Who is the life of our planet, the One in Whom we live and move and have our being." – *A Treatise on White Magic*, Alice Bailey, page 531.

6. For more explanation of Shamballa see for example *Telepathy and the Etheric Vehicle,* Alice Bailey, page 183.

7. The Great Invocation is a world prayer developed by Alice Bailey and the Tibetan. It can be found in each of the Alice Bailey books. Copies of the Great Invocation on leaflets or cards are available from the Lucis Trust. The text is referring to the third verse: "From the Centre where the Will of God is known, Let purpose guide the little wills of men – The purpose which the Masters know and serve."

8. The passing out of sixth ray and the coming in of the seventh ray are touched upon in *Esoteric Psychology I*, Alice Bailey. Page 190 says that the influence of the sixth ray 'will not entirely disappear for another 21000 years'! Page 411 shows the sixth ray as 'passing rapidly out of manifestation. Began to pass out in 1625AD', and the seventh ray as 'in manifestation since 1675AD'.

9. Transition from blue to violet ray – there is mention of this for example in *Esoteric Psychology I* (Alice Bailey) page 121-2. However this particular source appears to be inconsistent in attributing colours to rays, which may of course be deliberate and provocative.

10. Agni Yoga. A series of books, e.g. *Agni Yoga* (1929), is published by the Agni Yoga Society, New York. They are available from the Lucis Press.

11. *Discipleship in the New Age I*, Alice Bailey, begins on page 3 with a discourse on the emergence of the fifth/ soul kingdom, and continues with much advice and guidance on the needs of developing disciples in helping to bring this kingdom about.

12. For details of current publications by Assagioli/ on psychosynthesis contact Psychosynthesis and Education Trust, 92-94 Tooley Street, London Bridge, London SE1 2TH, www.psychosynthesis.edu.

13. Initiation of Sanat Kumara – see *The Rays and the Initiations*, Alice Bailey, pages 550-1, 690-1.

14. For more information on the initiations see e.g. *Discipleship in the New Age I*, Alice Bailey.

4. FINDING THE RAYS IN YOUR CHART   pages 49-78

1. Bruno is referring to the relationship of the Angles with the Cardinal, Fixed and Mutable Crosses. See e.g. Figure 2.1.

2. Manas, Buddhi and Atma in Figure 2.3 are also reflected in Figure 6.1 *The Constitution of Man*. The Mental, Buddhic and Atmic permanent atoms are known as the 'spiritual triad' in Alice Bailey's terms.

3. Programmes that will print the rays in the form specified by Bruno include *MegaStar*, *Regulus*, and *AstroCora*.

5. THE EFFECT OF THE RAYS ON THE PERSONALITY
pages 79-106

1. See also *Psychosynthesis Typology*, Roberto Assagioli.

2. Kuthumi – one of the Masters of Wisdom. According to *Letters on Occult Meditation*, Alice Bailey, page 259 a Master of Wisdom is One Who has undergone the fifth initiation. That means that His consciousness has undergone such an expansion, that it now includes the fifth or spiritual kingdom. Kuthumi is said to have been an early instructor of Krishnamurti – see *The Masters and the Path*, C.W.Leadbeater 1929, Theosophical Publishing House.

3. *Discipleship in the New Age,* Volumes I and II, Alice Bailey.

4. *ibid*

5. *Moon Node Astrology*, Bruno and Louise Huber. Combines psychological understanding with the concept of reincarnation, bringing a new astrological focus on the shadow personality and the evolutionary process of the individual.

6. The Tibetan – Djwal Khul, second ray master/ adept, who worked in close contact with Alice Bailey in the development of her teachings. According to AAB's book *Initiation Human and Solar* the Tibetan also greatly influenced Helena Blavatsky's *The Secret Doctrine*.

7. This interaction was with Richard Llewellyn, with fifth ray astral and mental bodies and third ray physical. Louise is referring to the fact that Richard created the English Huber School in 1983, with course manuals which gave out the Hubers' teaching in a new form in the English language. The manuals were subsequently translated into German to support a correspondence course in that language.

8. *Telepathy and the Etheric Vehicle*, Alice Bailey.

9. The meaning of the various rays in this representation has already been given on page 77.

6. TRANSFORMATIONS   pages 107-132

1. Page 515 onward of *The Rays and the Initiations*, Alice Bailey give the words of power associated with the Rays, as part of the Science of Building the Antahkarana.

2. *The Rays and the Initiations*, Alice Bailey.

3. Avatar of Synthesis – an extra-planetary being, Who is working in cooperation with the Christ – according to *The Rays and the Initiations*, Alice Bailey, page 734-5.

4. Louise here refers to Bruno's diagram of the Amphora, see figure 2.3.

5. Invocation and evocation – see for example the 'science' of invocation and evocation replacing the role of prayer and worship as part of the new world religion – see *The Reappearance of the Christ*, Alice Bailey, pages 150-2.

6. Figure 6.1 is a representation of the diagram of the constitution of man that is repeated in many of Alice Bailey's books.

7. Antahkarana – the Antahkarana, or Rainbow Bridge, needs to be built by the disciple to bridge the gap in consciousness on the mental plane and achieve contact with the higher spiritual qualities. There is much advice on building the antahkarana in many of the Alice Bailey books e.g. *The Rays and the Initiations* or *Discipleship in the New Age II*.

8. Laws of refusal – Alice Bailey refers to the 'Law of Repulse' in *Esoteric Psychology II*, related to the active rejection of aspects of the form life that are not consistent with the demands of the soul. It "produces a discriminating contact which leads eventually to what is esoterically called 'the Way of divine refusal'".

9. Kuthumi – see chapter 5 note 2.

10. Atma – spiritual will, Buddhi – intuitive understanding, Manas – higher mind. See e.g. *Discipleship in the New Age I*, Alice Bailey, page 71.

11. *The Secret Doctrine – The Synthesis of Science, Religion and Philosophy*, Helena Petrovna Blavatsky, first published 1888. Comprises two volumes – *I Cosmogenesis* and *II Anthropogenesis*.

12. For more on atma-Pluto see e.g. *The Planets and their Psychological Meaning*, Bruno and Louise Huber, page 88.

13. There is more about the Masters and the Rays in *Initiation, Human and Solar*, Alice Bailey.

14. Figure 6.4. Venus and Mercury are switched in this table compared to the original in *Esoteric Astrology* page 513. See Bruno's earlier comments about his perception of Alice Bailey's misunderstanding of these two planets.

15. *The Secret Doctrine*, Helena Blavatsky.

16. See pages 19 and 113 for Figures 2.3 and 6.1 respectively.

17. Chakras and their relationship to the Seven Rays are covered in *Esoteric Healing*, Alice Bailey. For example, page 51 gives a tabulation of the rays against the centres, which correspond with the chakras.

18. *Esoteric Healing* – Volume 4 of Alice Bailey's 5-volume *Treatise on the Seven Rays*.

7. THE LAW OF THE TRIANGLES IN THE SIGNS
pages 133-146

1. See *Esoteric Astrology*, Alice Bailey, page 407 on.

2. *Reflections and Meditations on the Signs of the Zodiac*, Louise Huber.

3. Exoteric and esoteric rulers of the signs of the zodiac are discussed in *Esoteric Astrology*, Alice Bailey. Page 590 gives a tabulation of these for each sign. Their role in the cirisi mechanism for each sign is discussed in *Reflections and Meditations on the Signs of the Zodiac*, Louise Huber.

4. Seed thoughts of the signs – see *Reflections and Meditations on the Signs of the Zodiac*, Louise Huber.

5. *Weltanshauung* – Philosophy of life, world view.

6. Seed thought for Sagittarius – "I see the goal. I reach that goal and then I see another". See note 4 above.

7. Figure 7.2 – the original was coloured; shading illustrates the colours used.

8. *Letters on Occult Meditation*, Alice Bailey.

9. The colours of the Rays are presented differently in eg *Letters in Occult Meditation* and *A Treatise on the Seven Rays*.

8. THE SPIRITUAL PLANETS AND SPIRITUAL GROWTH
pages 147-172

1. The question of what the Tibetan meant about the future of ashrams etc is returned to in the Session 9 questions.

2. *The Secret Doctrine*, Helena Blavatsky.

9. QUESTIONS
pages 173-192

1. *Astrolog* is the magazine of API Swizerland, published bi-monthly in German.

2. Bruno was of course speaking before the discovery of 2003 UB313, an object of similar dimensions to Pluto but further out in the solar system.

3. *Astro Glossarium*, Bruno Huber. The first part of Bruno's astrological glossary is currently only available in German, and he was still working on the remainder at the time of his death.

Index

Agni Yoga, 42
Akashic Records, 6, 71
amphora/ Huber bottle, 19,23
analogical thinking, 31
antahkarana, 114, 115
API family, 2
Aquarius, 108, 137
Arcane School, 2, 114-6, 148
Aries, 135
as above so below, 31, 32, 40
aspect structure, 13, 70
Assagioli, Roberto, 2, 18, 42, 43,
  80, 81, 106, 115, 116
astrologers' oath, 2
astrological psychology, 2, 189-91
atma, 117, 118
atmic plane, 25
Avatar of Synthesis, 109

Bailey, Alice, 2, 4, 9, 19, 27, 32, 33,
  36, 38, 39, 41, 44, 47, 81, 82, 93,
  97, 106, 109, 112, 114, 116, 117,
  122, 142, 145, 149, 175, 176
Blavatsky, Helena, 19, 117
body rays, 50, 54
buddhi, 117, 118
buddhic plane, 24

Cancer, 137
Capricorn, 135
causal body, 8, 70
centre of chart, 8, 112
chakras, 7, 9, 145
Chiron, 182
colour, 142
colour key, 69
conjunction, with spiritual planets,
  169
consciousness, 15, 18, 41, 69, 110,
  114, 127
crosses, 14, 16, 35

egg, Assagioli's, 18, 23
Einstein, Albert, 62-4, 106
emotional/astral body, 8, 90, 112
emotional/astral plane, 21
emotions, 21
esoteric/esotericism, 2, 3, 12, 17,
  39
esoteric schools, 148
ethereal world, 4
etheric body, 7, 83
etheric plane, 21, 34

Faust, 131
feelings, 21
fifth kingdom, 43
fifth ray, 39, 87, 94, 97, 103, 121,
  137, 138
first ray, 35, 36, 61, 84, 91, 96, 99,
  119, 135
form key, 69
fourth ray, 38, 87, 93, 97, 102, 120,
  138, 139

Gemini, 141, 142
Great Invocation, 35

Huber, Bruno, 52-3
Huber Method, 2
Huber School, 2, 58, 94

initiation, 44, 45, 117, 149, 176
intercepted, 165
invocation and evocation, 111

Jung, Carl Gustav, 106
Jupiter, 41, 122, 139

Kuthumi, Master, 115, 122

Leo, 108, 135
Libra, 136
light, 5
Lilith, 184

major rays, 16, 38, 51
manas, 117, 118
Mars, 25, 40, 121
material values, 154
mental body, 8, 96, 112
mental plane, 22
Mercury, 47, 121
minor rays, 16, 38, 52
monad, 5, 70, 129-131
Moon, 8, 37, 54, 92, 112, 117, 120, 137
Moon's Node, 8, 65-7, 170
Morya, Master, 119

Neptune, 24-5, 37, 117, 118, 150-4, 159-60, 164, 171, 186
new age, psychology of, 4, 33

paranormal functions, 152
personality types, 144-5
personality ray, 46, 47, 57, 99, 181
physical body, 7, 84, 112
physical plane, 20
Piscean Age, 43, 98
Pisces, 140
planetary logos, 34, 44, 46
planetary rulers, 143
Pluto, 25-6, 46, 117, 118, 150-4, 160-2, 163, 166, 186
principles, 13
psychosynthesis, 2, 18, 80

Rakoczi, Master, 42, 123, 142
ray words of power, 124-5

sacred planets, 128
Sagittarius, 46, 138, 142
Sanat Kumara, 44
Saturn, 7, 23, 37, 54, 85, 86, 112, 117, 120, 126, 175
science, 6
Scorpio, 139
second ray, 37, 60, 85, 92, 96, 100, 120, 140, 141

seven lords, 32
seven planes, 20
seven rays, 4, 5, 7, 16, 30, 33, 35
seven solar systems, 33
seventh ray, 40, 52, 57, 59, 89, 95, 98, 105, 108, 122, 137
Shamballa, 35, 126
sixth ray, 40, 63, 88, 94, 98, 104, 121, 138, 140
solar logos, 33, 46
solar system, 32
soul kingdom, 42, 109
soul ray, 68-74
spiritual planets, 150, 155, 164
Sumeria, 17, 27
Sun, 8, 30, 47, 54, 96, 112, 117, 119

Taurus, 139
temperaments, 14, 16, 35
third ray, 37, 86, 92, 97, 101, 120, 136, 137
Tibetan, 47, 82, 92, 115, 148, 149, 175, 176
transformation crisis, 136
trans-Pluto, 185

Uranus, 22-4, 37, 62, 117, 118, 150-4, 155-7, 160, 163, 166, 171, 186

Venus, 47, 120, 140
violet flame, 42
Virgo, 140
Vulcan, 140, 182

Contacts and Resources

The Astrological Psychology Institute (UK)

A MODERN APPROACH to SELF-AWARENESS and PERSONAL GROWTH

Astrology has become recognised as a valuable tool for the development of self awareness and human potential. Bruno and Louise Huber researched and developed this approach over many years, combining selective astrology with Roberto Assagioli's psychosynthesis. Our courses are based on their results and inspiration.

PERSONAL GROWTH Most of our Diploma students not only learn astrology, chart interpretation and astrological counselling skills, but find that the course helps develop their own self understanding and personal and spiritual growth.

COURSES We offer Foundation Modules to those new to astrology or to the Huber Method. Our Modular Diploma Course teaches the Hubers' psychological approach to chart interpretation for working with clients. Details are in our prospectus.

EVENTS Our programme of seminars, workshops and conferences includes annual workshops that are an integral part of the Diploma in Astrological Counselling.

CONJUNCTION Our magazine *Conjunction* contains articles, news and supplementary teaching materials.

API (UK) Enquiries and Membership
P.O. Box 29, Upton, Wirral CH49 3BG, England
Tel: 00 44 (0)151 605 0039; Email: api.enquiries@btopenworld.com
Website: www.api-uk.org

API(UK) Bookshop
Books and API(UK) publications related to the Huber Method.
Linda Tinsley, API(UK) Bookshop
70 Kensington Road, Southport PR9 0RY, UK
Tel: 00 44 (0)1704 544652, Email: lucindatinsley@tiscali.co.uk

API Chart Data Service
Provides colour-printed Huber-style charts and chart data.
Richard Llewellyn, API Chart Data Service
PO Box 29, Upton, Wirral CH49 3BG, UK
Tel: 00 44 (0)151 606 8551, Email: r.llewellyn@btinternet.com

Software for Huber-style Charts
AstroCora, MegaStar, Regulus, Regulus Light Special Huber Edition.
On CD: Elly Gibbs Tel: 00 44 (0)151-605-0039
                 Email: software.api@btinternet.com
Download: Cathar Software Website: www.catharsoftware.com

Recent Publications on Astrological Psychology

A Modern Approach to Self Awareness and Personal Growth

Astrological Psychology was developed by Swiss astrologers/psychologists Bruno and Louise Huber and links with the psychosynthesis of Italian Psychiatrist Roberto Assagioli. Based on extensive research, it combines the best of traditional astrology with modern growth psychology, providing a powerful tool for self understanding and psychological and spiritual growth. These books complement the seven others available in English on the Hubers' comprehensive approach.

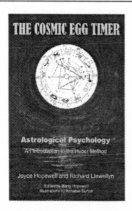

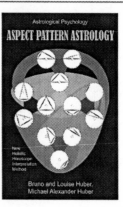

A practical introduction to Astrological Psychology	Understanding motivation through aspect patterns
by Joyce Hopewell & Richard Llewellyn *Illustrated*	by Bruno, Louise & Michael Huber *Translated by Heather Ross*
The Cosmic Egg Timer offers a new and exciting way of using astrology, and is intended for all who are interested in finding out more about astrological psychology - and themselves!	*Aspect Pattern Astrology* provides, for the first time in English, details of a key feature of this holistic method of interpreting the horoscope.
Using your own birth chart alongside this book you will gain insights into the kind of person you are, what makes you tick, and which areas of life offer you the greatest potential.	The overall pattern of the aspects reveals the structure and basic motivations of an individual's consciousness. Whether novice or experienced astrologer, aspect patterns can provide immediate significant revelations about yourself and other people.
The first overview of the Huber Method available in any language.	A basic reference work on astrological psychology.
ISBN 0-9547680-0-0	**ISBN 0-9547680-1-9**

Published by HopeWell, PO Box 118, Knutsford WA16 8TG UK

Printed in the United Kingdom
by Lightning Source UK Ltd.
125941UK00001B/259/A